NOODLE SOUP

NOODLE SOUP
RECIPES, TECHNIQUES, OBSESSION

KEN ALBALA

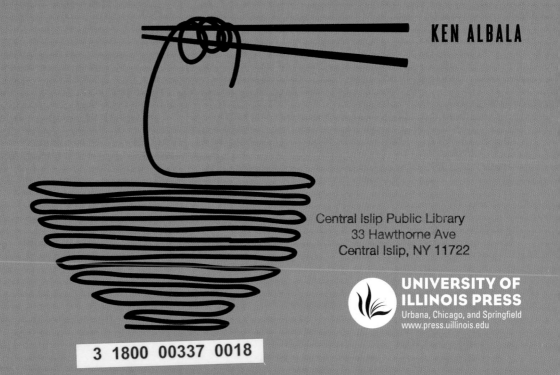

UNIVERSITY OF
ILLINOIS PRESS
Urbana, Chicago, and Springfield
www.press.uillinois.edu

Library of Congress Cataloging-in-Publication Data
Names: Albala, Ken, 1964– author.
Title: Noodle soup : recipes, techniques, obsession / Ken Albala.
Description: Urbana : University of Illinois, [2018] | Includes
    bibliographical references and index.
Identifiers: LCCN 2017047639 | ISBN 9780252083181 (pbk. :
    acid-free paper)
Subjects: LCSH: Noodle soups. | LCGFT: Cookbooks.
Classification: LCC TX757 .A428 2018 | DDC 641.81/3—dc23
LC record available at https://lccn.loc.gov/2017047639

CONTENTS

NOODLE SOUP

$\textcircled{1}$ INTRODUCTION

This book has one simple purpose: to get you in the kitchen making noodle soup. I don't mean boiling water and dumping in a packet of instant ramen, though that's where my quest began. I'm talking about really delicious soup from scratch with handmade noodles and fresh ingredients, and I intend to show you why it's worth the time to make at home. There are quick and simple recipes, absurdly complicated ones, and a few that boggle the mind. This book is partly a personal odyssey, a story of my own discovery and obsession with noodle soup, interlarded with history, social commentary, plus bizarre experiments using unusual ingredients. There is some serious philosophy on how best to eat noodle soup. Most importantly, this is a book about technique, the goal of which is to have you rummaging through ethnic grocery stores, finding yourself arm deep in dough early in the morning or tenderly caring for a simmering stockpot for hours. That is, I intend to infect you with my crazed enthusiasm.

This story begins in the summer of 2014, when I was teaching a class on distillation for a few weeks at Boston University. For accommodations, I was provided a spacious dorm apartment high above Commonwealth Avenue sporting a bright and airy kitchen. However, to my surprise, there was not a single utensil therein—not a pan, pot, plate, or knife. Being the sort of person who prefers to be in the kitchen cooking, I was not about to be undone, especially for my favorite meal—breakfast. So I meandered for a few blocks to an Asian market, where I found an inexpensive pot, a melamine bowl, a cheap knife, some chopsticks. That should suffice, but what to cook? And then I saw it, piled at the corner of a ramshackle aisle: ramen noodles, an unusual Malaysian brand. I'm not sure how I had escaped instant noodles thus far in life, but I'd never eaten them before, not even in college. Maybe with some fresh ingredients they could be interesting, a few shrimp, some vegetables, and lime.

These noodles were a revelation. Spicy, sour, chewy, above all else comforting. Ramen, where have you been all my life? I wasn't happy about eating the dried soup mix, but at least I would have a good staple for breakfast that I could manage with my makeshift utensils. As the days passed, I started getting more adventurous, slipping in some thinly sliced chicken or pork, a handful of cilantro, or a drizzle of coconut milk. The possibilities seemed endless. I was hooked.

When I got home to California, I was determined to reconstruct that first noodle soup experience from scratch. Little did I know that making broth from fresh ingredients is absolutely simple. Even a deep rich stock can be made overnight in the oven and takes no effort at all. Noodles too can easily be made from just flour and water. There are actually dozens of types of flour that can be rolled and cut by hand without any equipment. I had owned a hand-cranked noodle machine for years but was finding it far more pleasurable to roll them by out myself as a kind of meditative experience. I was on a mission to taste every possible noodle soup combination around the world. I've never looked back at the instant ramen.

Two and a half years later, I still devote maybe 15 to 30 minutes every morning to a new noodle soup, varying with the weather, the season, and my mood. Sometimes I use frozen stock made on the weekend or noodles rolled out in my spare time. When pressed for time, I might use a stock concentrate and a store-bought noodle. The fact is, nothing needs to be instant or poor quality. A rich satisfying soup made with fresh ingredients can be as simple or as complicated as you like. And of course it can be made for lunch or dinner as well. Some days I had noodle soup both for breakfast and dinner. Now I am determined to show you how it's done.

A NOTE ON SERVING SIZES

Partly because I make these noodle soups for my own breakfast, recipes throughout the book are for a single serving. Also, many people cook for themselves nowadays. Then there's the simple fact that multiplying anything by one is much easier than figuring out how to increase a recipe for four servings when you have seven people or something like that. Normally I would say, what does it matter? Make a little extra and you'll have leftovers. With stock and some ingredients sure, but noodles, alas, have but one life to offer. When left over soaking in soup they become a soggy mess and never improve overnight in the fridge. So my intent is to provide recipes for a fairly hearty serving that constitutes a whole meal. If served as a first course or a smaller meal, naturally, reduce as you see fit.

So you can get a sense of what a serving size means in this book, generally I put 4 ounces (113.398 grams) dried noodles in a soup or use dough made from 1 cup flour (946 ml), then formed into noodles, which is about the same in the soup. Sometimes I overshoot, but a ball of dough about the size of a person's fist should feed that same person. About 4 ounces meat or less is also plenty for a bowl of soup, and about the same of vegetables. I never actually weigh these, but I do believe that a bowl of noodle soup should be balanced like a good plate with carbs, vegetables, and protein in roughly equal proportion.

The quantity of broth for each recipe was a lot more tricky to gauge. When I freeze broth it's in 3-cup (24 fluid oz.) containers, which does make a fine serving. But if you're cooking the noodles right in the pot you might need 4 cups, especially if the noodles are dried, because they soak up liquid, and you end up having to add water, diluting the broth. On the other hand if you are adding cooked noodles to a bowl, 2 cups broth is often fine. In the recipes that follow I have called for 3 cups liquid as a rule. I figure that it's always better to have a little extra liquid than too little. And noodles are happier cooking in a bit more liquid than a bit less. If you have extra broth that doesn't fit in your bowl, strain and refrigerate it and use it the next day.

When exact measurements are needed, I provide them, though my instinct is really to let you decide how much you want to eat. Even the measurements are not intended to be slavishly followed. In fact, I hope you try my proportions once, then move on to your own, cook according to your own taste preferences. Oftentimes I simply describe a procedure rather than offer a full recipe. This is always either because I have provided a recipe elsewhere or because the procedure is so simple that a recipe would be ridiculous to write out. Apparently I am inordinately fond of sour flavors, so the juice of a whole lime might go into a soup, or a huge handful of cilantro. If you prefer less, by all means put in what you like. If you want more meat, go ahead. I have no qualms about your substituting anything here—in fact, I applaud it.

My intention is not of course that servings of one should be standard; by all means eat with others! For some recipes it was too difficult to reduce since the main ingredient would feed about four people. Unless otherwise specified all recipes here are for one; some are for more people, and in those cases I indicate how to save leftover ingredients.

A NOTE ON AUTHENTICITY

This word authenticity is a real conundrum for both historians and cooks. There are very good reasons people use the term. I can understand why, when people are faced with industrial bastardizations of world cuisines—ironically often their first encounter with the culture—they want to know how cooks in a foreign country do it themselves. Authenticity implies cooking with the same ingredients, same techniques, same modes of service. In other words, once you've had Taco Bell, you might want to know what they really eat in Mexico, or better yet in a particular region like Oaxaca or Michoacán. Much food writing today involves hunting down the rare, exotic, and hopefully hot new cuisine, presented as authentically as possible.

This tends to place immigrant cuisines in an unfortunate position, though. Most immigrant cuisines undergo a kind of evolution after being transplanted. At first immigrants are forced to substitute ingredients or adapt to new cooking utensils. In restaurants they may tone down the cuisine to appeal to a broader clientele. But eventually that clientele wants more of the real thing. Unusual ingredients eventually become available. And then people learn about the cooking of a distinctive group within that country or perhaps one city. Then suddenly the adapted immigrant cuisine, whether Italian American, Chinese American, or whatever, seems somehow debased or inferior to what they're still cooking back in the homeland. Of course nothing could be further from the truth: the immigrant cuisine has simply evolved, as does every cuisine over time. Ironically, sometimes a dish in the immigrant cuisine survives as a kind of time capsule of bygone practices while it has disappeared in the homeland. Spaghetti and meatballs is looked down on by modern Italians as a bizarre Italian American invention, but in fact they were making it themselves over a century ago in southern Italy.

The real problem with the idea of authenticity, apart from denigrating hybridity, is that it's a constantly moving target. Are you talking about one particular restaurant or one home cook? We all know everyone cooks a dish slightly differently. Are you talking about a specific time and place, and even if so, will it not necessarily change when you try to replicate it elsewhere? In other words, I think authenticity is impossible, both for contemporary cuisines and definitely for cooking in the past.

That's not to say we shouldn't try. Use the same ingredients and cooking methods whenever possible, even eat food in the same way when you can. But all the same, recognize that what you are doing will necessarily be different. And of course you can never replicate the context. We all have different taste buds, different memories of food, different expectations. Even if the dish were nearly exactly the same, you and I would not experience it in the same way as someone on the other side of Earth. There's nothing wrong with that—just don't make the pretense of authenticity.

On that note, I have tasted many of the dishes presented here in situ, but I have not seen the whole world. And I have no doubt that many cooks will say I'm doing it all wrong, even though I may have learned from another equally qualified cook from the same place. This is especially true of the more complex cuisines. I swear I would finally figure out what to call a particular Italian pasta only to have someone else tell me I'm completely wrong. Or I would master a dish only to learn that I was doing it backward, but I still like my version better. I was once on Irish television with a local chef who was making Irish stew when he threw raw lamb chops into boiling water. I asked, "Wait—aren't you going to brown them?" Everyone in the studio, and I'm sure every person in Ireland, gave me a look like "what could you possibly be thinking, Yank?" I still think it's better browned first.

So let me declare from the outset: I make no claim that the recipes contained here are absolutely faithful replications of those you would find in far-flung places on the planet. But I will tell you they often come pretty close and they all taste great. As you'll see, I'm perfectly clear when I've made something up. Many of the recipes here are my own personal inventions spun from pure fancy and never eaten anywhere on Earth. Others are translated directly from historic cookbooks.

AN EPISTEMOLOGY OF NOODLE SOUP

How do we know what counts as noodle soup? Should we just make an empirical catalog of every example on the planet and categorize them, or are there certain objective criteria for understanding the nature of noodleness? I am going to be careful with this question, lest someone accuse me of omitting their favorite noodle or wonder why I've included something bizarre and outlandish. Defining the parameters is not as easy as it might seem. First, if you are talking about a long thin strip, flat or rounded, made of some starchy dough, something that anyone on Earth would look at and say "nice noodle," then there is no question it belongs here. That includes rice noodles, tapioca, mung bean, and pretty much anything that holds its shape and reflects the Platonic form of noodle. I balk at the idea that a spiralized zucchini or squash is a noodle. It's a noodle-shaped vegetable that might go well in a soup, but I hesitate to call it a noodle, and in fact I take it as a grave insult to common sense and decency. There are other foods that pass as noodles because they are so close: tofu skins cut like noodles and kampyo, which are dried strips of gourd from Japan that could easily fool many people. They're not noodles, but they are good. An extruded pasta shape in the form of a spiral, a radiator, a quill pen, macaroni, or any other shape made of dough, even the tiniest pastina, I include as a noodle. In other words pasta and noodle will be considered synonymous. I would have titled this book "pasta soup," but the convention in English demands the word noodle. I won't argue if couscous is a pasta, though it is, because it's made of flour, not a crushed grain like, say, bulgur. But it doesn't go in soup anyway. What about a tapioca pearl or boba? These are made with the same ingredients as a long tapioca noodle, so why not?

I struggled with kanten, which is a kind of thick gelatinous block made from agar-agar, cut with a special press (tentsuki) to form long squared noodle-like things. Honestly, these are more like a cut jelly than a noodle. They're fun to make and come in neat colors. They're also easy to make with these neat poufy rectangles of dried agar, but a noodle?

But now we get into turbulent waters: what if you take a noodle dough, roll it flat, fill it with something else, and cut it into shapes? Does it cease to be a noodle merely by being stuffed? Does a wonton or ravioli sacrifice its noodle status and suddenly become a dumpling? We can't even begin to answer this question until we know what dumpling means. In one context it means a crumb and egg mixture or batter dumped into water or broth. That's an entirely different creature from a stuffed noodle. The confusion arises because the panoply of stuffed dim sum and the like, for lack of a better term, were dubbed dumplings in English, but of course they're not. We don't call ravioli or any other stuffed Italian pasta a dumpling, nor should we call Chinese ones dumplings generically—especially since many of them are steamed, not dumped into liquid.

At the risk of excising a massive amount of subject matter, I ask you to conjure an image of tortellini. Would you under any circumstances say "nice noodle"? It's a slipshod way of defining, but cultural norms seem the only rational means of solving this problem. If the filling is in the soup on its own and the noodle is still a noodle, then sure, but stuffed it does become something else.

Must the dumpling made from batter therefore be excluded as well? Wait a minute, a dumped batter that resembles a noodle and is treated gastronomically like a noodle—like spaetzle or even more problematic passatelli, which are long bread crumb dumplings—these come so very close to noodledom. If we go back in history, many forms of macaroni were made with bread crumbs and flour and were 100 percent bona fide noodles. So I include these on the same grounds that the tomato is considered a vegetable. Botanically we know it isn't, but we eat it in a salad, so gastronomically it's a vegetable. For the same reasons, noodle-like preparations made in unusual ways but eaten as noodles and made from similar ingredients count as noodles in my book.

2 UTENSILS

BOWLS

Before you embark on noodle soup making, I offer a philosophical discourse on the beauty of the soup bowl and its associated utensils. I truly believe that, like wine, and actually even more so, the vessel in which you serve soup will make an enormous difference in your final appreciation of the dish, not only as a matter of aesthetics but solely from the vantage point of physics. First, as with wine, there are some noodle soups that are delicate and whose aroma needs to be focused and concentrated so they waft up the nostrils directly even before you dig in. These should have a rim fairly narrow in circumference. On the other hand, a strongly flavored broth would assail you in the face if you bent over it to appreciate the aroma, so for these a wider rim makes sense. The season will also dictate the aperture of the bowl. When it's cold out, you want to use a thick-walled clay vessel, preferably of stoneware, to retain the heat. A narrow rim will help too. In summer a shallow bowl with a very wide rim makes more sense because you don't want the soup to remain piping hot

Also take note that not every bowl is intended for noodle soup, even though it may be a soup bowl. You have to fish your noodles out of the bowl, so something with a very narrow circumference will only make that difficult. Likewise, a broad rim with a high stem that can be toppled over if nudged might work fine for a pureed soup but is only asking for disaster with noodles and other ingredients in the vessel. I think of this every time I'm tempted to put a soup in a martini glass. Looks cool, but a terrible idea. The stability of the bowl is a consideration, and the wider the base the more assured you can be if you have some fiddling around to do with the contents. This is why in much of Europe they use a soup dish, not a bowl. This is a flat-bottomed dish with a very broad rim only a few inches in height. In the United States it is sometimes known as a rimmed soup bowl. It's designed so you can see all the contents and if necessary cut them with the side of your spoon. The rim catches any drips as you bring the spoon to your mouth. Think of a big dumpling or matzo ball, large pieces of carrot, and even noodles. If you're making an Eastern European noodle soup, this is the appropriate shape.

Bowls fresh off the potter's wheel still seem alive

There are other formal considerations of bowl shape, and here I employ the anthropomorphized language potters themselves use. I should perhaps mention that I've been working in clay half my life and making soup bowls is among my favorite ways to spend time. So a pot is much like a person. Its rim is referred to as a lip. Its upper body is a shoulder and lower body a hip. Whatever raises the body from the bottom is called a foot, often cut with a tool on the leather-hard clay after throwing. A handle is sometimes referred to as an arm, especially if there are two small ones situated as they would be on a human body. This is all a little more deep than linguistic convention. A pot has to work well with the human body and in our case with the noodle soup too. So a straight-edged cylinder has to be wide enough to get a utensil inside. The upper lip can't flare out so wide that it will topple or spill soup when slightly tipped. But a bowl with a wide horizontal ledge around the rim is sometimes ideal for showing off a profusion of distinct ingredients in the soup, especially when arranged carefully, as in Japanese ramen. The bowl should also feel nice in the hands, not too light or too heavy, and if you will drink directly from it, it should be comfortable to handle. Try holding it with your middle fingers on the foot and your thumbs on the rims. You should be able to pick up and sip even from a hot bowl this way.

There are also certain perfect abstract forms we find aesthetically pleasing because they resonate with shapes found in nature and even with our own bodies. A half sphere makes an exquisitely beautiful bowl because it echoes the sun and moon. And there are vessels with a long graceful neck, wide shoulders and slim waistlines that are simply pleasant to look at: think of an amphora. Or sometimes nature itself imposes a form on the clay simply because of the way it turns on the wheel. Look at a Japanese tea bowl with its small foot, straight sides and uneven rim and you will begin to appreciate *wabi sabi*, or natural imperfection. All handmade pottery reflects this to some degree, especially since the modern art pottery movement was so heavily influenced in the early twentieth century by theorists like Soetsu Yanagi (*The Unknown Craftsman*) and the great potter Shoji Hamada. The industrial aesthetic that had long pervaded Western ceramics since the time of Wedgewood still influences most tables where we expect every pot to be standard, uniform, and even, and come in perfectly matching sets. The handmade pot is very different; it proudly displays its uniqueness, its quirks, and of course the mark of the maker's hand. Much like humans.

CHAPTER 2

10

Indulge me for a moment while I take the human analogy further, here borrowed from one of my favorite poets, Omar Khayyám. His *Rubáiyát* contains a section where the speaker is wandering through Potter's Row and notes the ancestral dust on every turning wheel, the clay made from the hands of kings and beggars' feet. One jug was a doleful lover and its arm once entwined another's neck. We are reminded that every drop of wine spilled from the bowl serves to quench the souls of those below. This is not just a metaphor; it's literal truth. Clay does contain the molecules of our ancestors. When you hold a pot, you may very well be holding a bit of someone recycled. The idea isn't meant to gross you out but just remind you that we have a connection to inanimate objects that goes way beyond their market value in a capitalist economy. A bowl can and should have deep meaning, should be treated with respect and even buried when broken, so some future archaeologist will have a field day digging up your backyard.

The color of the bowl also makes a big difference. If you want to see through a clear soup, make sure it's a white bowl, either porcelain or made with a white slip. Some colors reflect the contents well, especially green—my favorite color. The color known as oxblood also makes for a stunningly beautiful glaze—think of a dark Ming vase. As far as patterns are concerned, of course match the bowl to the culture. A dark brown temmoku glaze goes with Japanese food, red and white porcelain with Chinese, majolica with the Mediterranean. Mexican earthenware goes with the appropriate soup. Delftware with cobalt blue painting just seems to go with northern European soups. I tend to prefer darker colors and subtle glaze effects in winter and bright patterns in summer.

A new firing nestled in St. Theresa, my beloved kiln

Can you enjoy soup out of a machine-made bowl? Of course. But some of the aesthetic experience will be missing. If cost is really a consideration, find a potter with affordable wares, buy secondhand, or seek out nice pots that look craftsy. On the other hand, you can't always be serious. I have a whole stack of inexpensive melamine majolica bowls that look so much like the real thing, people can't even tell the difference in a picture. I also have sets of small plastic Asian bowls. Soup cools down too quickly in them, but if you're serving a crowd, they sure come in handy. Save your contemplative bowls for yourself and those close to you.

Once in a while a glass bowl is appropriate, especially for cold soups you want to see through. But normally glass heats up too quickly and even risks breaking if you pour in very hot soup. I've never heard of hot soup in a metal bowl, though I'm sure someone does it somewhere.

Wood makes a great soup bowl, but keep in mind its thermal effects are exactly opposite to clay. It does not get so hot from the contents and doesn't hold in the heat either. Having said that, holding and eating from wood is incomparably pleasant; it was once a living creature. I have a large bowl made by a food anthropologist friend (Richard Wilk) that is ingeniously turned. He left a little ledge three-fourths down on the outer surface that perfectly matches the span of the human hand, so you can hold the bowl with your fingers on the ledge and thumbs on the rim. The pattern of the wood is exquisite. I also have a small shallow bowl I got from a company in Ireland that tells you exactly what tree it came from and where, and you can go online and see if picture of the tree before it fell. That's respect. You have to care for your wooden bowls, make sure they're dry when you put them away, and don't do anything silly like rub garlic in them—that's only for salad bowls.

Lacquerware can also be delightful. It's the very lightweight black or red bowls in which miso soup is served. I love that another smaller bowl is placed on top and serves as a lid to keep the contents warm. Pottery bowls also sometimes come with similar matching lids.

Lastly there are other natural materials out of which you can make bowls yourself with just a few tools. A bottle-neck gourd dried, cut into a bowl shape, and the end sanded smooth is a lot of fun. Even better and much sturdier is a coconut shell sanded smooth and rubbed with mineral oil so it's shiny. In the Middle Ages, these were rare and exotic and mounted with silver or carved with elaborate scenes. I adore bamboo and have been trying to figure out a way to make a bowl out of it, either upright or halved on its side. For the moment, chopsticks made from my own bamboo will have to suffice.

Below: Chopsticks cut fresh from the author's yard
Opposite: Revive leftovers with fresh vegetables, noodles, and more stock

CHOPSTICKS

These too are crucial in constructing the entire noodle soup aesthetic. I am generally against any chopstick with a garish or noisy pattern, as it distracts from the soup itself. The length, diameter, material, and even the tip are all serious considerations. To start, a Chinese chopstick is usually squared on the part you hold and rounded on the part that touches the food, it only tapers slightly, and the tips are blunt. If you need an all-purpose chopstick, these will always work. Bamboo is cheap, replenishable as a natural resource, and I think beautiful too. A Japanese chopstick is usually a little shorter, tapers more dramatically, and is more pointy on the tip. Not that you should ever have to stab food to pick it up—in fact, that's considered quite rude—but a pointed end is the conventional design, presumably for precision in grabbing small distinct items. They are also often made of truly beautiful wood and can be an absolute delight to hold. Korean chopsticks are often stainless steel, flat, and as elsewhere in Asia are used with a long metal spoon. Obviously you can match the set with the cuisine where it's used.

But I admit to having a few favorite sets I use all the time regardless of cuisine. Eating an Italian or German noodle soup with chopsticks does seem a little absurd, but I contend that it's the superior utensil for the job. Unless you're talking about a very small noodle in broth, in which case a spoon alone with do, then the loveliest chopsticks you can find should work well with every recipe in this book. In many cultures, a knife and fork should never come anywhere near a noodle soup—they're considered barbaric. And if you've ever tried to eat a noodle of any kind with them, you'll understand why I recommend chopsticks.

Chopsticks come not only in a wide variety of colors and sizes but in materials, as well. Surprisingly, titanium with a buff finish is really light, holds onto the noodle well, and comes in a handy carrying case. Porcelain chopsticks are useless for noodle soup. They're slippery in your hands, and food slips out of the end as well. So keep in mind, especially for noodle dishes, that you don't want a perfectly slick, polished chopstick. Plastic doesn't work well for this very reason. Wood is perfect for the exact opposite reason: it holds a slippery noodle. There are also shiny lacquered chopsticks that are very beautiful but not ideal for tackling noodles.

The chopstick should be a size that fits in your hand nicely and a diameter that helps you get a firm grip as you lift noodles or other ingredients from the bowl. I like a really thick diameter, and a pair I found in Japan with five sides rather than four is ingenious. You can also find chopsticks made from recycled materials that are extraordinarily thin and pleasant to use. They even make portable metal chopsticks, one half of which fits inside the other; they have wooden tips. I think they're made for sushi but are fun on the road or with a small bowl of noodle soup. Ivan Orkin's ramen shop in Manhattan offers chopsticks with tiny toothlike nubbins on the ends. A noodle will never slip out of these, though if you drag the end of the chopstick through your teeth it can be a little unnerving. In the end, choose the chopsticks you like best, but keep in mind some work better with noodle soup.

As with bowls, the color of the chopstick makes a difference, not that it needs to match the bowl, but lighter colors like bamboo go with lighter soups. Dark cherry, maple, and heavier woods match the aesthetics of a stoneware bowl nicely as well as a heavier soup.

SPOONS

Unless you are making a Japanese soup and will sip directly from the bowl, a spoon is requisite for every recipe in this book. Right-handed people hold the spoon in the left hand and chopsticks in the right, using them in tandem, with arms akimbo. Although you can just grab a capacious tablespoon, an extra-long handle makes it easier to plunge the depths of your bowl for the last drop. Spoons can be works of art in their own right. You can find wooden spoons to match your chopsticks, or go for long ceramic spoons with small round ends, which are nice to use with a big bowl of phở or laksa.

There is also the short Chinese soup spoon. Its shape derives solely from the fact that it was originally made of clay and had to be fired standing on its own, which is why it is flat on the bottom. Nowadays you see these spoons made of lacquer or plastic, and the Japanese ones often have a little notch in the handle so they'll rest facing downward in a bowl of soup without sliding in. That's ingenuity. This kind of spoon works well with a small bowl of soup, but not so well with a large meal-sized bowl, because you have to put your whole hand in the bowl and maneuver the spoon horizontally to prevent spilling the contents. So save these for smaller or shallow bowls.

ETIQUETTE

In certain cultures it is considered impolite *not* to slurp your noodles noisily. This is not a random rule of willful malfeasance but a careful consideration of the physical properties of the noodles themselves. Since they are served very hot, the diner indeed wants them hot going into the mouth but not so hot as to burn. Since across most of Asia knives are not part of the table service, cutting noodles is not an option. Slurping

Choose the perfect spoon length for your bowl

maximizes the aesthetic experience, cools the noodle and aerates it, much as wine is similarly aerated by swirling and slurping. Moreover, there is no effective way to get the whole noodle in your mouth without some slurp. Having said that, slurping requires a judicious application of suction or the noodles will be directed by the over-enthusiastic eater straight into the lungs—not a pretty situation. I've done it.

Then there is the matter of exactly how many noodles to grab with your chopsticks. You will certainly see people grab a huge wad, tilt their heads sideways, and stuff the whole mess in with a few shoveling gestures. While not exactly rude, this obviates the pleasure of savoring individual strands, feeling their slipperiness pass over the lips. So consider your mouth slightly pursed, and if you can fit maybe three or four strands of noodles in there comfortably, that's probably the amount you should consider grabbing with your chopsticks—not for any reason of politesse, but really so you can taste them fully, well soaked with broth. For this reason I suggest using a spoon in tandem with the sticks to convey an appropriate quantity of soup and other ingredients into your mouth at the same time as the noodles. Grabbing individual noodles would be the height of folly, unless of course they are mammoth wads of dough that will fill your whole mouth. This is a rule that applies to all food of course: you want no more than a gobbet of food in your mouth that will allow comfortable chewing, aeration, a thorough mingling with lubricating saliva, and most importantly the facilitation for aromas to enter olfactory canals at the rear of your gullet. We smell and taste food together, not only through our noses, but via sensory organs in our heads. An overly stuffed mouth prevents that crucial reception of flavor and aroma.

There are other purely technical considerations with eating noodle soup, and I tender this advice based solely on my hard-won personal experience. Others may have arrived at very different solutions to these conundrums. First, my heavy writing schedule and sitting in front of a computer most of the day has rendered my eyes virtually useless at close range without the aid of spectacles. This means that to see what is in my bowl I need to be wearing my glasses, which inevitably steam up as my face hovers over the hot bowl. Waiting for the bowl to cool is not an option, though neither is eating in a fog. My solution, albeit imperfect, is to look closely at a distance, then push my glasses back on top of my head as I dive in for the kill, and then tip them back once the noodles are safely ensconced in my mouth. The dexterity required for this absurd maneuver may be too much for you if you are farsighted, in which case I suggest looking first, then removing your glasses, only putting them back on once the steam has subsided.

Of greater concern for gentlemen is the issue of facial hair. I suppose this applies to many foods, but none more so than the wagging wet noodle that lashes against your chin in the act of slurpage. In the interest of efficiency, given my devotion to noodles, I gave up and shaved. And I am ready to advise stringently that a goatee and noodle soup do not make good table fellows. If you eat alone, a napkin can remedy any chance dribbling, but this is not something you want to do constantly while in company. And heaven forfend you find traces of soup in your beard later in the day.

Now what, you ask, if you are eating a European noodle soup, without the aid of chopsticks and in a place where slurping is frowned upon entirely? Here, my friends, you must resort to the ingenious device known as the soup spoon. This is not a diminutive spoon with a round rather than elliptical bowl on the end. A proper soup spoon has a large deep well that tapers on the end, precisely so it can be directed accurately into your mouth with the contents intact like a train entering a tunnel full steam ahead. The little round spoons are meant for clear broth sipped from the side of the spoon daintily. Unless you have miniscule sipping noodles like pastina, I recommend a big spoon with that is narrower on the end to aid aerodynamics.

Having said that, I am also very fond of spoons that were common five centuries ago. They were tear shaped, wider at the point that goes into your mouth, and because of the nature of silversmithing in that age, the bowl of the spoon was connected directly to a rounded rod with a finial on the end rather than to a swooping flat-hammered handle like we see nowadays. You have to open your mouth wider to use a medieval spoon, but there is something aesthetically pleasing about this, especially if the spoon is loaded with noodles and other ingredients. It seems to heighten the resonance of biting in your head, creating a larger sound box, as it were. If you happen to find a reproduction of one, they are quite nice to use with soup.

There are considerations about service. A soup with long noodles really must be doled out in the kitchen and brought to the table in separate bowls. It's simply too sloppy to try to portion out in front of guests, and you might end up splashing hot soup all over them. This is especially true if you are carefully composing your

bowls. In the interest of keeping the soup warm, lidded bowls are very effective and add a measure of surprise. The same of course can be achieved by a waiter with a large tureen and the flourishing *révéler* as the lid is removed at the table and the aromas waft upward to stimulate the appetite. Although they have gone quite out of fashion, a soup tureen can be a lovely thing, especially if the soup is your main meal and you expect people to want a second bowl. The only caution is that you must be able to ladle out the contents without it sloshing all over the place, which is again why long noodles really don't work with a tureen. You could theoretically have a long set of chopsticks or tongs to remove noodles and a ladle for the rest, and if you decide to go to such lengths I certainly won't deride your efforts.

As for the practice of sipping out of the bowl? Do it and don't ask if it's poor manners. If you can't get the last bit of soup out of the bottom of your bowl, better it should go to waste to uphold some bygone point of foppery? I particularly like the idea of pouring a glug of wine into your bowl, swishing it around and drinking that, to get every last drop of goodness.

3

NOODLE SOUP HISTORY

PREHISTORY

In this chapter I don my formal historian's hat and provide detailed references (at the end of the book) for those who might like to explore my primary sources. As far as possible I attempt to tell this story from the perspective of noodle soup rather than noodles per se, which have received a good deal of scholarly treatment, though some of that can bear a little revision. Searching for the earliest noodle soup or even pinpointing a place where they might have been invented is futile, not only because no evidence exists that could affirm such a guess, but also because extensive archaeological remains simply don't survive.

Nonetheless, the oldest noodles ever found were at the Bronze Age site in the northwest of what is now China, in the Qinghai province at a site called Lajia, which is associated with the Quijia culture.[1] The noodles are four thousand years old and are made from foxtail millet (*Setaria italica*) and broom millet (*Panicum miliaceum*). They were discovered early in the new millennium and reported in the respected scientific journal *Nature*. The wispy yellow filaments were found in an overturned bowl that preserved them from a natural disaster, probably an earthquake and flash flood. There's no way of telling for certain if they were in soup or not, but the animal bones found nearby suggest they probably were. The archaeologists did speculate that they were served in meat broth. Although pictures were taken the moment the noodles were discovered, they quickly disintegrated, so chemical analysis was basically made on a pile of prehistoric millet dust.

Controversy has surrounded this discovery mostly because the original report said the noodles were pulled and stretched like modern lamian (think noodle dough worked like taffy). Anyone who's made a noodle—including the teams of experimental archaeologists who gamely tried with dough made from all-millet flour—knows that stretching is impossible without the glutens in wheat dough, and though theoretically wheat could have been used in these ancient noodles, it didn't become common in China until the Tang dynasty (AD 618-907). The scientists revised this gaffe and correctly suggested that the noodles were extruded—you can indeed make extruded noodles from 100 percent millet.[2] A simple wooden cylinder with holes in the bottom and the ball of dough forced through directly into hot water (something like a modern ricer) would give you a noodle very much like those found at Lajia. Not that millet noodles taste that good, but that's beside the point.

In all likelihood, people in this area had been eating millet noodles well before 2,000 BC; it was the staple before rice. I would go so far as to speculate that there were wheat noodles independently discovered in the Middle East long before any archaeological evidence as well. The simple fact is that if you grind grains—and we know this occurred long before domestication using wild, gathered primitive wheat—you will eventually figure out a few efficient ways of cooking them. Adding water and heating them on a flat surface gives you a flat bread or a kind of pancake. If you have a vessel, like a ceramic pot, to cook in, then simply adding water and cooking the flour yields gruel. Add water and forming into pasta shapes that are boiled either in water or broth, and you have noodle soup. We know prehistoric peoples cooked bones in pots in order to extract the marrow, since there are fat residues on the rims of prehistoric pots everywhere.[3] It is only one step further to imagine throwing pasta shapes into the pot for noodle soup.

ASIA

With written records we are much firmer ground. In Han dynasty China, one Shu Xi composed an *Ode to Bing* around AD 281. It recounts not only the various pasta shapes—dog's tongues and piglet's ears, dagger laces, cupping glasses, and candles—but the tactile quality of the sticky dough, rolled out fine and thin, and even eating them with ivory chopsticks.[4] All these shapes can easily be imagined, some probably not unlike spaghetti, orecchietti, and long ziti. They were made of wheat, though the word *bing* was used to cover all manner of wheat-based products, including steamed buns and flatbreads as well as noodles in broth (*tangbing*). The poet Hong Junju described the artistry of a chef in action: "He kneaded the dough to the right consistency. Then he would drop it into the water, In long strings, White like Autumn silk. In a half a bowl of soup, We would gulp them all down at once."[5] There is ample historical evidence that all sorts of *bing* products were enjoyed at the Han court. Eventually the word *bing* comes to mean only flat breads and the word *mian* then refers to noodles by the tenth century.

The earliest written recipes are older though and are found in the agricultural text *Qimin yaoshu*, composed by Jia Sixie about AD 540. The text most likely contains material from two older, now-lost texts as well.[6] Jia described various different types of noodle, but one in particular involved soaking the dough, which achieved the effect of making the noodles slippery. "Shape the dough into pieces the size of a thumb: about 6 cm in length. Soak them in a dish of cold water. Then press each piece against the side of the dish until the dough is very thin and drop it into rapidly boiling water. When the pieces float, they are done—glistening white, delectable, slippery, truly extraordinary."[7] Apparently what happens with this procedure is that the gluten chains are able to develop, while some of the wheat starch seeps out into the water, making the noodle slippery, something appreciated to this day. Such noodles presented to the emperor were called Hua *bing*.

Jia also described various other noodle shapes, some that resemble discs from the game Go that were precooked and dried, as well as cut noodle shapes. One intriguing noodle is made with broth instead of water. The effect is no different from drying the noodles and then cooking them in broth, but as a technique it does work.

Jia also describes a fascinating procedure for making extruded starch noodles and even explains how to fashion an extruding contraption using a section of cow's horn. The horn has holes or small slits cut into it and is affixed to a silk bag holding the dough. The dough is squeezed from the bag so that long noodles are extruded directly into boiling water. These were made from millet starch (*fen*) and thus called *fenbing*.[8] These may very well be exactly what those millet noodles two and a half millennia earlier were like.

The proliferation of wheat products, including noodles, in medieval China is the result of several factors. They spread south as the capital was moved in the Southern Song dynasty (AD 1127-1279), and high prices prompted the government to exempt wheat from taxes, which encouraged farmers to plant it.[9] Linguistically, the word *mian* for noodles comes to dominate, and many new techniques were invented in this period as well. Further innovations and foreign influences were introduced under Mongol rule (Yuan dynasty, 1297-1368) in the following years, deriving from the Muslim world, and as far as Persia and Turkey, which were at the far end of the massive Mongol Empire. This is also when pulled noodles made their way westward.

A fourteenth-century text by Ni Tsan rather succinctly describes the process of noodle making:

Cooking Noodles

If one wants to eat the noodles at noon, at dawn use salted water to make up a (wheat flour) dough. Knead thirty or twenty [*sic*] times. Cover and let stand. In a short while, repeat. Do this with the dough four times. Sprinkle fine starch powder on a board, roll the dough out and cut up. To cook: Bring water to a boil, stir, and put in the noodles. When the water boils again, cover the fire. Turn up the fire again, let boil, then take out and put in broth.[10]

A medical treatise *Yin-shan Cheng-yao* (Proper and essential things for the emperor's food) written by Hu Szu-hui in the fourteenth century and translated into English as *A Soup for the Qan* mentions many of the new noodles, and the word *qamh* may very well refer to a durum wheat flour suitable for making dried noodles. Others are made of barley, and the use of foreign words implies a whole range of new noodles moving west to east. Here's a small taste of the text.

Barley Samsa Noodles

They supplement the center, and increase ch'i. They strengthen spleen and stomach. Mutton (leg; bone and cut up), tsaoko cardamoms (five), chickpeas (half a sheng; remove the skins). Boil ingredients together into a soup. Strain [broth. Set aside meat]. Make [samsa] noodles from a combination of 3 chin of barley flour, 1 chin of bean paste. [Fill with] mutton and fry. Adjust flavors with a fine qima, 2 ho of juice of sprouting ginger, coriander leaves, salt, and vinegar.[11]

The diffusion of noodle technology throughout the Pacific also intensified in the Song dynasty when Chinese traders increasingly carried goods by sea and sought exotic imports. When Marco Polo arrived, he remarked how cosmopolitan Chinese society was, and also that they use wheat to make vermicelli. More or less he was saying that they have noodles much like ours. By the fifteenth century, Zheng He had traversed the Indian Ocean to Africa. The noodles found throughout the Pacific are often descendants of Chinese versions and often still bear names revealing this ancestry.

Japan of course had its own noodle history too. The older noodle forms are soba made of buckwheat; udon, which are thick and chewy; and sōmen, very thin noodles. Soba comes in many different varieties: today there are four main types. Ni-hachi uses 1 part wheat flour to 4 parts buckwheat. Sarashina is lighter and translucent; Sarashina Ki-ippon are considered the best of this type and contain no wheat at all, but rather the buckwheat starch, bound with hot water and cooked for only a few seconds lest they fall apart. There is also Inaka soba, which is firm and dark brown, and lastly Dattan soba, which is reputed to have medicinal qualities.

Sōmen were probably first made of rice flour, but by the Kamakura period (1185-1333) were more commonly made of wheat. Today rice flour noodles are fairly unknown in Japan. The Hyogo Prefecture became associated with these noodles, and customarily they were eaten every July 7 at the Tanabata festival to ward off sickness. Ramen, despite its current popularity and even status as a national dish of Japan, were actually the last to arrive, around the 1880s with migrant workers from Guangdong, China, arriving in Yokohama. After the turn of the century it became a food for laborers, known as Chuka soba or Shina soba, meaning that they came from China. We pick up with the story of modern noodles in chapter 8.

THE WEST

The ancient Greeks and Romans had a few products that, if they weren't noodles as we would recognize them, are certainly the ancestors both literally and etymologically. We immediately recognize the word *laganon* in Greek, *laganum* in Latin, plural *laganae* as a relative of lasagna. These were a kind of flat sheet of dough that was eaten with oil and could be fried or cooked in chicken broth. I can't imagine what that latter form would be other than a noodle soup, unless it's a kind of cracker soaked in the broth. Whichever it was, the poet Horace considered it a simple food and insisted that it's what he wanted to eat rather than socialize with the rich. "Inde domum me, ad porri et ciceris refero laganique catinum," or loosely translated, "I'm going home to my pot of leeks, chickpeas, and noodles." The very fact that it's cooked together in a pot suggests to me a noodle soup, but there is no doubt that the word had many other generic uses for other wheat products, much like the word *bing* in China, though here it is definitely something flat. But there is also no doubt that it was soft, and presumably noodle-like, because the medical writer Celsus said that people with a broken jaw should eat liquid foods and then laganum.[12] Alas, there is simply no way to be sure if these were actually sheets of boiled dough that we would think of as a noodle.

With *itria* we come a little closer. These were shapes made of wheat that were first boiled and then added to a sweet dish. They were used in sacrifices made to the gods, and ironically the Aramaic word *itriya* is used in the Talmud, which was composed in Jerusalem in the fifth century AD, where it is described in greater detail in a discussion of proper sacrificial foods. Apparently boiled dough was fine for supper but not sacrifice. Brief glimpses in medical writings also suggest that these were long string shapes. And there is no doubt that's exactly what they were in the medieval Muslim world.

By the time we get to Baghdad in the thirteenth century, there are also undeniable noodle soup recipes. This comes from an author known as the scribe of Baghdad (Muhammad b. al-Hasan b. Muhammad b. al-Karim) Should you like to try this, understandably, you're not likely to find sheep tail fat, so olive oil should work, along with lamb shoulder for the meat. The author unfortunately doesn't describe how to make the noodles, but certainly go for some shape you can grab a handful of, which could either be a small shape or a bunch of dried spaghettilike noodles.

Itriya

The way to make it is to cut up fat meat medium, melt tail fat, remove its cracklings, throw the meat in the fat and stew it in it. Then throw on a little salt and a stick of cinnamon, then throw on enough warm water to cover it. Cut up two onions and throw them (in), before throwing the water (on), with peeled chickpeas, stalks of chard and two handfuls of cleaned washed rice. Then, when the meat is done, throw in finely pounded dry coriander, pepper, and mastic. When it comes to a full boil, add a handful and a half of *itriya* noodles to the pot. Then, when the pot is done, sprinkle finely ground cinnamon on its surface, and wipe its sides with a clean cloth, and leave it to grow quiet on the fire, and take it up.[13]

The other noodle the author uses is described in greater detail and these, called rashta, definitely are flat noodles in the shape of thongs four finger widths long. The dish is made very simply with meat in a pot, covered with water, a cinnamon stick, a handful of chickpeas and half a handful of lentils (I really like how this guy measures). That's boiled for a while. Then toss in your freshly rolled-out and cut noodles. It's not very complicated but quite delicious. There is still an Iranian dish called Reshteh (see chapter 6).

Meanwhile in medieval Europe, the name *itriya* seems to have been simplified to simply *tria*, which were long bits of dough resembling string. Perhaps by false association, the term trili or trills was also used. In the physician Benedict of Norcia's fifteenth-century dietary, he mentions that trills are threads or laces made from dough, adding that they're difficult to digest so are best cooked with fatty meat.[14]

Tria is not the word that stuck in common parlance though—for this another strange borrowing took place. *Makaria* was a kind of barley soup in classical Greece. Somehow the barley was replaced with a noodle and the word *macaroni* was born. In the Middle Ages and Renaissance, this was a generic term for all kinds of pasta, whether long strips, hollow tubes similar to those we now call macaroni, and even boiled lumps or "knuckles" of dough, aka gnocchi. As for the spelling, *maccheroni* is also perfectly legitimate.

There is a recipe for *tria ianuensis* (lit. tria from Genoa) in the fourteenth-century *Liber de coquina*. Since there is no instruction to drain the noodles, it seems they are boiled in the water with the fried onions, making this a proper noodle soup, with spices like cinnamon and saffron, along with a little meat if you feel like it.

> Ad triam ianusenssem, suffrige cipolas cum oleo et mite in aqua bullienti, decoque, et super pone species, et colora et assapora sicut vis. Cum istis pones caseum grattatum vel incisum. Et da quandocumque placet com caponibus et cum ovis vel quibuscumque carnibus.[15]

> For Genovese noodles, fry onions in oil and place in boiling water, boil down, and place over them spices and coloring and flavorings as you like. With this add cheese grated or sliced. And whenever it pleases you, add chicken and with eggs or whatever meat.

There are other pasta recipes in *Liber de coquina* as well, this one is almost exactly the same as the modern corzetti, also made around Genoa, which are stamped rounds of pasta, named originally for the crosses they once bore. There are also similar square shapes elsewhere in the book, called *lasanis*.

> Eodem modo fiunt croseti, et de eadem pasta, nisi quod sint formati rotundi et oblungi ad quantitatem unius pollicis; et cum digito sunt con-

cauati. Est tamen sciendum quod, tam in lasanis quam in crosetis, debet poni magna quantitas casei grattati.[16]

———————

> The same way you make crosets, and from the same pasta, except that they [*lasanis*] are formed round and oblong and the size of a thumb; and with your finger they are concave. And you should know that just as with lasagna, you ought to add a great quantity of grated cheese.

Another pasta form in place at this time is ravioli. The name is curious since it means "little radish," which suggests that rather than two squares pressed around the filling, they were probably filled and then the edges were all drawn together and pinched closed at the top, so the bottom would be round and the top like radish leaves. The cookbook author known as Anonimo Veneziano penned several recipes for these, one including herbs and cheese. Another form is called *licaproprii*, which means something like "lick yourself," which makes sense since they are round ravioli the size of an apple, filled with cheese, and sprinkled with sugar.[17]

By the time we get to the Renaissance, the culture of noodle soup is going full steam. In the very first printed cookbook, *De honesta voluptate* (ca. 1470) by Platina, we find a whole range of macaroni dishes. The recipes were actually taken from a cookbook written by his friend, Martino of Como, which were stuffed into this larger work that included natural history and medical advice. In gussying up the original Italian into neoclassical Latin, Platina made some odd choices that even more strangely were then translated back into Italian, French, and a few other languages. I try to reconstruct Martino's original intentions using a variety of texts, because sometimes Platina clarifies Martino's terse instructions for the general reader. For example, in the recipe for Roman macaroni, Martino says to roll out a dough "et avoltola intorno ad un bastone," which has been translated as "wrap it around a stick."[18] But Platina's Latin adds "involvitoque ei ligno tereti quidem et oblongo quo uti in tali ministerio pistores solent," meaning roll it onto an oblong rounded wooden pin, of the kind bakers use in their business.[19] Martino then says to remove the stick, presumably leaving the dough still rolled up, and slice it into pieces the width of your finger. Martino seems to be making dough like Italian professional pasta ladies do it with a really long narrow pin, around which the dough is rolled and stretched, and then, with the pin removed but the dough still rolled up, it's cut into long flat noodles. These are cooked in broth or during Lent in water with butter and salt. Cheese, butter, and sweet spices are added at the end.

Let's turn to the recipe for vermicelli. The first direction for dealing with the flour in Martino's Italian is *distempera*, which Platina translates to *subigito*—to pound or knead. That's not actually what Martino meant though. In medieval cooking, to distemper means to add liquid to loosen the texture, so he's referring to the point where you add water to the flour, or a combination of egg whites and rose water, which was much more fashionable at the time. Here the dough is worked into long threads by hand and then broken into pieces so they look like little worms. These are then dried in the sun and should last two or three years. Even more remarkably, when they are finally cooked in good fatty meat broth or chicken broth, it's for a whole hour. At a vigorous boil, of course they would disintegrate, which would make the whole worm shaping superfluous. I don't believe he wanted us to cook until they turn to mush, but rather to cook gently so they are thoroughly soft.

There is no doubt that Renaissance diners preferred their noodles soft. In fact, given the medical advice of the day, pasta was suspect precisely because it was difficult to digest and might cause clogs through the body, which could lead to innumerable illnesses. It's no wonder they cooked noodles for an hour. Actually Martino's following comments support this idea. When it's a fasting day, he advises to cook noodles in almond milk with sugar or with goat's milk, but being sure to boil first in a little water or else they won't be sufficiently cooked through. He also adds that this is a good idea for lasagna and tritte (apparently another corruption of *itria*), or as he calls them *fermentine*, which comes from the word for wheat.

Moving into the sixteenth century, we get some remarkably tasty noodle soups, though very different from anything we might think of as Italian. Christoforo di Messisbugo was the majordomo in the first half of the sixteenth century for the d'Este family, dukes of Ferrara. He not only organized all the banquets for the entire household but managed its budget as well. The banquets he threw were recorded in his book of this name, published in 1549. His Neapolitan macaroni recipe sounds very strange to our sensibilities, but I cooked it for a group of people at the New York Academy of Medicine in a demonstration and everyone loved it. This should feed three or four people for dinner or a tasting for about twenty. I've reduced his measurements by one-eighth for a smaller batch, and I think it works, keeping in mind his pound was 12 ounces. The dough will be very easy to roll out because of the crumbs—no glutens will develop.

MACCHERONI NAPOLETANA

2½ cups white flour
½ cup bread crumbs moistened with rose water
3½ teaspoons sugar
½ egg
6 cups fatty chicken broth

Simply roll out your dough using the first four ingredients, cut into strips, and cook directly in the broth. A mixed broth of several meats works nicely. Messisbugo suggests serving it with duck or chicken, which is a great idea, or with butter sprinkled with cinnamon and sugar, which is also nice, even on top of the noodle soup. If you serve this with roasted duck, the sugar goes surprisingly well and is very typical of the Renaissance flavor preferences.

To avoid your getting the impression that the Italians were the only ones making noodle soups, here's a recipe from a manuscript of fifteenth-century Vienna that interestingly uses milk as the soup base.

Zotatz Gmues

Nim schon semeln mel, zeuch ein taig ab mit weissen von ayern und hab ein siedunde milch in einer phann. Nym den taig und zeuch in klain dar in, dy weil sy seudet dy milch. Sol varhin gesultzen sein. Ein smaltz tue auch doran. Schaw das es gewürmlet beleib. Versaltz es nit. Gib es hin.

Shaggy Spoon Dish

Take good white flour and make a dough with egg white. Have boiling milk ready in a pan and pull the dough into little pieces, throwing them in as the milk boils. It is to be salted beforehand. Also add fat. See that it stays worm shaped. Do not oversalt it. Serve it.

(Dorotheenkloster MS150)[20]

We must also not forget that Spain had its own noodle traditions, ultimately linked back to the Arab world, where they were called *fidaws*. *Fideos* are still eaten in Spain, usually fried first and then cooked with a little liquid, something akin to a paella though made with extra-thin noodles. They can also be put into soup. Originally they were formed with the fingers into tiny little strands of pasta; nowadays people buy short strands of dried pasta, about the thickness of angel's hair.

Among the earliest Spanish cookbooks was first composed in Catalan by one Rupert or Robert of Nola in the fifteenth century and then printed later in a Catalan edition as *Llibre del coch* in 1520 and a Castilian edition in 1525. It contains a splendid soup of *fideos*, something like a cream of chicken noodle soup.

Potaje de fideos

Limpiarlos fideos dela suziedad que tuvieren: y desque esten bien limpios poner una olla muy limpia al fuego con caldo de gallinas o de carne bueno: y gordo: y que este bueno de sal: y quando començare de hervir el caldo echar enla olla los fideos con un pedaço de acuçar: y desque sea mas de medio cozidos echar enla olla conel caldo de las gallinas o de carnero leche de cabras o de ovejas o en lugar dello leche de almendras que esta nunca puede saltar: y cuezga bien todo junto: y desque sean cozidos los fideos apartar la olla del fuego: y dexarla reposar un poco: y hazer escudillas hechando açucar y canela sobre ellas: mas … muchos a y que con potages desta calidad que se guisan con caldo de carne. dizen que no se deve echar açucar ni leche: mas esto esta enel apetito de cada uno: y enla verdad con fideos o con arroz guisado con caldo de carne mejor es echar sobre las escudillas queso rallado que sea muy beno.[21]

Clean the *fideos* of the dirt they had, and being well cleaned place them in a very clean pot on the fire with broth of chicken or good meat. Also fat, and enough salt. When the soup begins to boil throw the fideos in the pot with a pinch of sugar. And when it's half cooked add to the pot with the soup of chicken or meat some goat's milk or sheep's or in place of those almond milk, this should never be skipped. And cook everything together. And when the *fideos* are cooked, remove the pot from the fire and let it rest a little. Then make bowls and sprinkle sugar and cinnamon over them. But … many hold that soup of this quality that is stewed with meat broth, they say ought not to have added sugar or milk. But this is a matter of personal taste. The truth is with *fideos* or with stewed rice with meat broth, better over the bowls is grated cheese so it will be very good.

Of all Renaissance-era cookbooks, nothing comes even close to the breadth and depth of Bartolomeo Scappi's magisterial *Opera* published in 1570. Not only does it have many noodle soup recipes, but it even has an illustration of a cook in the papal kitchens rolling out dough for pasta. We must imagine his patron, the elderly and saintly Pius V, who was renowned for his austerity, somehow lured out of his meditative trance as the aroma of this dish wafted into his private apartments and up his prodigious proboscis. (Incidentally, you can see his incorruptible body on display in Santa Maria Maggiore in Rome.) Although Scappi calls it a *minestra*, it isn't so much a soup as the ancestor of macaroni and cheese. I include it here because it's an excellent pasta recipe using the *troccolaturo* device, which he calls a *ruzzolo*, a notched rolling pin for cutting noodles. The noodles will work very well in soup too, though boiled less than half an hour.

To Make Minestra of Macaroni Roman Style

Make dough with 1 pound of fine flour with 4 ounces of white bread crumbs which have been softened in warm goat's milk, and 4 egg yolks, 2 ounces of sugar passed through a sieve, and made into a dough so that it's not too liquid, and having been worked for the space of half an hour on a table make into a sheet with a rolling pin, let the sheet be a little bit thicker than written above and let the sheet dry, with a ruzzolo of metal or wood, cut the macaroni and being made let them dry. If you want to cook them in simple water, cook them in a big pot with a lot of water and enough salt. And when the water is boiling, throw in the macaroni, because if you add them into cold water, they'll go to the bottom. This makes a dough for every sort of rolled-out pasta. When it's boiled for half an hour test them so it will be tender, and if not let it boil until they're finally well cooked. And being cooked get a big silver, pewter, or ceramic plate, sprinkled grandly with grated cheese, sugar, and cinnamon, and slices of provatura cheese. Place on top some of this macaroni, well drained of water, and above the macaroni sprinkle cheese, sugar, and cinnamon, and slices of provatura, and pats of butter. In this way there will be three layers, and douse with rose water, and cover with another plate and let it rest on hot coals or in a medium hot oven for half an hour, and serve hot.[22]

Scappi also has a recipe for tagliatelle that is made with 2 pounds flour, 3 eggs, and warm water kneaded on a table for ¼ hour. It is rolled out, wrapped around a pin, which is removed, and then the dough is cut into thin strips, exactly as Martino instructed. So far it is very similar to ours, except that he suggests it be cooked in a broth made of hare or crane or something like that and then sprinkled with cheese, sugar, and cinnamon. This one is actually a soup, and one wonders why long flat noodles went out of fashion in Italian soups, along with the sugar and crane broth, alas.

Italians carried their noodle dishes through Europe in the following centuries along with their art and architecture, music, and so on. The story of one expatriate is touching. We all know how noodle soup can be comforting, especially when one is stressed, and this is even more true when one is far from home surrounded by unfamiliar foods. As the great Commedia dell'Arte actor Tiberio Fiorilli, better known as Scaramouche, lay on his deathbed, his thoughts wandered to noodle soup. As an Italian who became famous in France at the court of Louis XIV, it was only fitting that in his last moments he should call for a hearty bowl, which in French was called *soupe de vermicelli*. A doctor burst into the scene and assured him that he might live another eight hours if only he ate something healthy instead. The actor commented "it's hardly worth the effort if you deprive me of a good dish of vermicelli, with which I can make my soup really ample." He then downed a bigger serving than usual and expired.[23]

There was a time in late seventeenth- and eighteenth-century France and England when pasta became fashionable, as did many things Italianate. Remember Yankee Doodle, who stuck a feather in his cap and called it macaroni? The Macaroni Club was a trend-setting group in London who wore outrageously large wigs and other attention-seeking fineries. Hence the irony when a hick American thinks a feather in his hat will do the same. This has nothing to do with pasta of course, but macaroni itself did appear in many cookbooks outside Italy.

Among the most important of these sources was François Massialot's massive *Le nouveau Cuisinier Royal et Bourgeois*. As the title suggests, this was an effort to translate the grand royal banquets to more humble settings where upwardly mobile city folk would try to pass muster with the titled ranks. Serving a fashionable vermicelli soup and acquiring the right clothes, manners, and accent were all ways for aspiring businesspeople to express their taste and discernment, not of course by cooking these dishes themselves, but hiring an expert cook whose dishes were sure to impress guests. This recipe is probably just what a wealthy householder would instruct his cook to prepare. It is very detailed but still workable today. The only baffling point is a two-hour cooking time, at which point one imagines the noodles would be obliterated no matter how low the boil. The first edition of this

A mixed stock made with an assortment of bones

book appeared in 1691; the recipe below is from the expanded three-volume edition. A *mitonnage* was a mixed stock of beef, poultry, and veal knuckle with vegetables, very much like the mixed stocks used in this book.[24]

Potage de Vermicelly à l'Italienne ou à la Provencale

The dough is made with fine flour, egg whites, and very hot water, for white vermicelly. Others make it yellow, adding sometimes powdered sugar, saffron, and egg yolks. You form the dough in little threads by means of a syringe pierced with many holes, so these little threads quite resemble worms, so they give this pasta the name Vermicelly, in French *vermicel* or *vermichel*; it is white or yellow, after it has been made you dry it in an oven, and save for when needed. Vermicel must be new, well dried, and a good color, white is more used than yellow, of it you make very agreeable soups; for which take the newest and least broken, wash carefully in cold water, and let it cook in a pot with good bouillon, about 2 hours, stirring now and then without breaking. Being cooked, remove them and garnish the plate in which you want to serve it, with a little ring of bread crumbs and then the vermicelli or cook a chicken in the *mitonnage* bouillon that you put in the middle and you dress the soup with the vermicelli and serve hot.[25]

The noodle soup fashion also spread to England, where one might find country housewives adding vermicelli to their pottage. Hannah Glasse, sort of the British Martha Stewart of the eighteenth century, recommends making it fresh rather than buying imported, and she offers some very interesting alternative ways to make vermicelli. The kind of sieve she is calling for is a hoop strung with horsehair or metal wires. If you push the dough through with a flat wedge or the palm of your hand, it will come out like little worms through the holes.

To Make Vermicelli

Mix yolks of eggs and flour together in a pretty stiff paste, so as you can work it up cleverly, and roll it as thin as it is possible to roll the paste. Let it dry in the sun; when it is quite dry, with a very sharp knife cut it as thin as possible, and keep in a dry place. It will run up like little worms, as vermicelli does, though the best way is to run it through a coarse sieve, whilst the paste is soft. If you want some to be made in haste, dry it by the fire in a quarter of an hour. This far exceeds what comes from abroad, being fresher.[26]

This type of recipe became so popular that it was also featured in taverns, as T. William's *Accomplished Housekeeper* of 1797 attests. The book was not originally designed for households but rather was composed with the cooks of the London and Crown and Anchor taverns, so picture this as something you might eat out in the city served from a capacious communal cauldron, though here reduced in size for ordinary households. This is one of several soups that are adorned with vermicelli. Scrag, by the way, is the neck of a sheep or lamb.

Vermicelli Soup

Having put four ounces of butter into a large tossing-pan, cut a knuckle of veal and a scrag of mutton into small pieces about the size of walnuts. Slice in the meat of a shank of ham, with three or four blades of mace, two or three carrots, two parsnips, two large onions, with a clove stuck in at each end. Cut in four or five heads of celery washed clean, a bunch of sweet herbs, eight or ten morels and an anchovy. Cover the pan close, and set it over a slow fire, without any water until the gravy is drawn out of the meat. Then pour the gravy into a pot or bason, let the meat brown in the same pan; but take care it does not burn. Then pour in four quarts of water, and let it boil gently until it is wasted to three pints. Then strain it and put the gravy to it. Set it on the fire, add to it two ounces of vermicelli. Cut the nicest part of a head of celery, put in chyan pepper, and salt to your taste, and let it boil about four minutes. If it is not a good color put in a little browning, lay a French roll in the soup dish, pour in the soup upon it, and lay some of the vermicelli over it.[27]

Around the same time, keep in mind that Thomas Jefferson had returned from France and Italy with a taste for pasta. There was a shop in Trenton, New Jersey, called Sartori's where he used to purchase noodles, but eventually he bought a little hand extruder to make fresh pasta himself.[28] Just a few years later, Virginian author Mary Randolph would introduce noodles to her readers in the form of both macaroni and cheese, and vermicelli for soup.

To Make Vermecelli

Beat two or three fresh eggs quite light, make them into a stiff paste with flour, knead it well, and roll it out very thin, cut it in narrow strips, give them a twist, and dry them quickly on tin sheets. It is an excellent ingredient in most soups, particularly those that are thin. Noodles are made in the same manner, only instead of strips they should be cut in tiny squares and dried. They are also good in soups.[29]

In the industrial era, machines made mass-produced noodles affordable and widespread. Freshly made noodles didn't disappear, certainly not in Italy, but durum semolina flour mechanically extruded into dried noodles suddenly became not only a convenience food but also relatively cheap and a perfect food for the working masses. Alexis Soyer, the great chef and author of the *Shilling Cookery for the People* says it perfectly in an entry on vermicelli and macaroni. The "restrictive" Corn Laws had kept the price of grain artificially high and restricted imports to protect farmers.

Pray Eloise, why should not the workman and mechanic partake of these wholesome and nutritious articles of food, which have now, in consequence of those restrictive laws on provisions having been repealed, become so plentiful and cheap? It only requires to know how to cook them, in order that they become as favorite a food in these northern climes as they are in the southern.* Boil three pints of the broth No. 1, break into it a quarter of a pound of vermicelli or macaroni; boil till tender, and serve. Macaroni takes twice as long as vermicelli doing.

*** Macaroni is now selling in London at fivepence per pound, and makes four pounds when boiled …[30]**

Let's figure out exactly how much money Soyer was talking about for a pound of pasta. A pound sterling in 1860 is worth about $113 U.S. dollars today.[31] Back then there were 240 pence per pound, so 5 pence would equal $2.35 today. That's pretty much exactly what an ordinary one-pound box of pasta costs now. One can easily imagine that feeding a family of four with a good soup, so Soyer's recommendation is sound.

By the twentieth century, especially after mass immigration, Italian pasta had also become a familiar and inexpensive food in the United States, available not only in boxes manufactured by U.S. companies, but increasingly premade in cans by companies like Chef Boyardee. Claiming authenticity, Progresso and other companies sold canned Italian minestrone and other noodle soups. At the same time, we can't forget that Chinese noodle dishes had also become mainstream, served in small inexpensive restaurants as well as in cans by companies like La Choy and Chun King. Wonton soup became as well-known as chicken noodle.

After canning technology, the most important breakthrough for noodle soup was the invention of freeze drying during World War II. It made perfect sense when shipping food for soldiers abroad, but after the war something needed to be done with the equipment. Enter companies like Lipton and the advent of instant soup. Freeze drying allowed small bits of chicken, tiny cubes of vegetables, and dried noodles all to go in a small packet. Add boiling water and you have soup. A similar story occurred in Japan, where ramen noodles were fried, making them relatively durable while also being precooked. Instant ramen was invented by Momofuku Ando for the Nissin Food Company in 1958. In the 1970s these appeared in the United States as Cup O' Noodles in their own Styrofoam cup, so they could be eaten at the office, on the go, or wherever people valued speed and convenience over flavor. Nissin's Oodles of Noodles followed shortly thereafter. Gradually brands of instant noodles could be found around the world, in some places become popular food where noodle soups had never really been before. Just think of the instant Maggi two-minute noodle soup that's become a street food in Delhi.

These modern conveniences are of little interest to us, but in chapter 8 we look at classic noodle soups from around the world.

TOOLS

In the course of researching this book I came to acquire a vast assortment of gadgets, some of which are well worth purchasing. I resolved from the start to avoid all electrically powered tools, partly because I wanted to get a sense of how noodles were made historically, but also because I had no interest in replicating an industrially mass-produced noodle like you can find in stores anyway. It's essential to get a feeling for dough with your hands, which can't happen if only a machine is interacting with it. Working, rolling, and cutting the dough all by hand means that the noodles won't be regular, measured, and identical, but they will absolutely taste like they were made with serious care. Hopefully these are the kinds of noodles you want to make at home too.

I have owned a classic Italian Atlas crank roller for thirty years, and it works very well. Though you may have to replace the clamp a few times, it should last forever, and it comes with two noodle width settings and a variety of attachments you can purchase. I have nothing against it, but I must admit I don't use it very often anymore: I much prefer to roll out dough myself and even cut it by hand with a knife. The whole process is meditative and relaxing, especially early in the morning when I'm barely awake and my muscles perform the basic actions without my brain even being engaged. More importantly, you have complete control over the dough. When you do this often, you can feel the subtle changes in dough texture, how it will roll out, when to add more flour, and when to coax it to be a little thinner. You will even be able to judge portions by eyeballing, and tell exactly how much flour will hold one egg, and how much dough will fit on your board. The entire process is a lot like meditation, especially in a quiet room where you can focus all your attention and become one with the dough. Let's start in earnest with the barest minimum equipment and later move on to greater complexity and cost.

ROLLING PINS

Honestly, almost any pin will work, so you don't need to run out and buy something new. But a smooth-surfaced, finished, and polished pin doesn't quite move pasta dough optimally. For the same reason avoid silicone, metal, or ceramic pins—flour just won't stick to them. Totally untreated wood works much better and only needs to be lightly floured. Handles are a matter of preference, but most pins with handles have a laminated surface, so if you can find an absolutely plain dowel of wood, unfinished and without handles, that's probably the best thing for pasta.

In Italy professional pasta ladies and many nonnas use a very long thin dowel-like pin on a huge table. Surprisingly, the dough is wrapped around the pin to roll out evenly—that is, you don't roll out the whole mass on the table and turn it over. Some now made by U.S. manufacturers are very impressive and expensive. Mine could double as a defensive weapon, is over 4 feet long, and seems much heavier that the ones used in Italy.

At the other end of the spectrum is a small Chinese rolling pin, about 8 to 10 inches long and 1 inch in diameter. These are used for rolling out small lumps of dough into circles by holding the pin in the right hand and turning the dough with the left on a small board. Normally the disks are stuffed for dim sum, but there are many other pasta shapes you can make this way.

There are also elliptical pins, which are excellent for pastry dough but don't offer much advantage for noodles. My hands-down favorite is a tapered French rolling pin. You just have to realize that it's not going to produce an even thickness of noodle if rolled in one direction, so you have to turn the dough around often and roll from many different angles. The advantage is that you can apply such intense force that no gluten strand can hold out against the pressure you exert onto it. That means that for most noodle doughs you don't have to wait around for the dough to relax. With my tapered pin I almost always roll it out immediately. Normally these pins are just the right size to handle a single serving on a large floured board.

BOARDS

If by now you have surmised that a large unfinished board devoted solely to dough is optimal, you would be correct. You don't want to use a cutting board with nicks and oniony aromas. It should be about 14 by 20 inches—the bigger the better—and it must be made of wood. Plastic would probably work, but there's nothing to love about it. Glass is just about the worst material for a board and will ruin your knives. Marble is also fine for dough, but not for cutting. Your board should also be completely flat, with no gutter or indentations. In Italy I'm sure you've seen people make a big mound of flour, drop an egg into the top of the volcano, and mix it in gradually with a fork. I love the idea but rarely fail to get flour all over the place, so why not just use a bowl and sacrifice the drama?

KNIVES AND CUTTING TOOLS

You'll need a good knife for cutting the dough. A standard chef's knife is fine, as is a sharp paring knife. A cleaver has other uses for shaping dough, more often for squashing than cutting. Many people roll up their dough and then cut it with a knife or scissors. I think the noodles come out uneven that way and often the dough ends up squishing and sticking together. I love just running the knife down the whole length of a sheet of dough, and eventually you'll find it's very easy to get an even width.

There are a few specialized cutting tools that are a lot of fun to use. In Japan for making soba there is a device that is sort of like a cleaver, but the blade extends down underneath the entire length of the handle. The idea is that when you press down, the pressure extends from the middle of the blade, and every part is cut evenly. The edge, unlike all French knives and even regular cleavers, is perfectly even, so every layer of stacked dough is cut cleanly. You can find inexpensive ones online, but a good one is quite heavy and can cost thousands of dollars.

Above: Cutting soba by hand is a meditative practice

In China there is a kind of sliced noodle made with a special square blade that's run quickly over a block of dough so that it seems to leap directly into the dough. I've never been able to find these blades, but you can get a similar effect with a cleaver. Better yet, a mandolin cuts a very fine thin relatively square noodle from a firm block of dough. It's the closest I've been able to get to a proper Fuzhou sliced (or shaved) noodle. The noodles themselves are called Dao Xiao Mian.

There is also a notched rolling pin that is designed to cut dough into medium-width noodles with the perfectly delightful name *troccolaturo*. I saw a wooden version on the cover of a Williams-Sonoma catalog, but in the shop they told me they have never seen such a thing. You can find them, but the wooden notches just aren't sharp enough to cut through most dough. Actually I'd seen this illus-

Below: The sharp edges of this notched rolling pin cut noodles perfectly

trated in Bartolomeo Scappi's *Opera*, printed 450 years ago, so I knew it had to work somehow. Turns out his was bronze, and you can actually find the exact same one online today. It will cut through anything. The notches are sharp and it's very heavy, so keep it wrapped up somewhere safe. Other special rolling pins can be used to cut ravioli and other shapes, and these would certainly be fun to play with for noodling.

Equally enchanting is the *chitarra*, whose name is cognate with guitar. It's a rectangular wooden box strung with metal wires, one side for wide noodles, the other for narrow. You just lay a sheet of dough on top of the wires. Roll it gently so the wires cut into the dough a little and prevent it from sliding around. Then just rub the rolling pin along the surface of the dough until it is completely cut through. The lovely squared-off noodles will drop down and slide out the side of the device. This is so much fun with kids.

There are also many pasta-cutting wheels with a long pedigree. They're also illustrated in Scappi. A straight-edged disk will cut even noodles, a wavy pastry cutter will give you wavy edges; there are even some with many little disks aligned so you can cut several noodles at once. A pizza cutter also works if you have one around.

EXTRUDERS

Some kind of extruder is required if you're looking for a rounded noodle form. Actually most noodles on Earth today are extruded. But you don't need to spend a fortune for an extruder. There are a few small handheld models that cost around twenty dollars. Many plastic versions are not quite sturdy enough to handle stiff dough, so metal makes more sense.

Among these there are two basic operating mechanisms. One works like a caulking gun with a cylinder connected to a pistol trigger that ratchets dough with great force through a die on the end. I found one at a cake-decorating supply shop, though I've also seen the same ones in ceramics stores. They're really designed for frosting or for soft clay rather than dough. The one I bought has Plexiglas dies that are laser cut. The holes were slightly too wide for pasta, but the company happily custom-made me a few new dies. The only major drawback is that toward the end of extrusion it's easy to crack the dies accidentally. Otherwise, the ability to hold and fire dough directly into the pot with one hand is really great. I think a powerful working pasta extruder like this is just waiting to be invented, maybe with metal dies or a safety catch to stop the mechanism toward the end.

A simple, inexpensive extruder suitable for everyday noodling

Most extruders use a screw press mechanism, and I have a plastic one that works fine. But my favorite is a small cheap stainless steel tube with a little bar on top that turns the screw downward and a handle on the side that you hold. They all seem to be made in China. Online reviews complain that the edges of the tube are sharp, and they are, so be careful. Otherwise, this contraption is very easy to clean, the dies screw onto the end and have no parts to fiddle with, and for the price it should be the standard go-to extruder for home use. The chamber also fits exactly one serving of dough.

There is also a much larger hand-cranked Italian extruder unit that clamps onto a table. It's made by Regina. It looks like a cheap plastic box, but it makes perfectly fine macaroni and many other shapes. The dies themselves disassemble and are easy to clean. I don't know exactly how long it will last, but so far so good. I have no idea why they aren't sold everywhere, but maybe they will be soon.

Finally to the greatest of all extruders, the bronze beast that weighs about thirty pounds: *il torchio ad bigoli*. It makes many different shapes beyond the long tubular bigoli. It's essentially a monster screw press with bronze dies powered entirely by human force. It has to be bolted to a table or bench. I think it could make spaghetti from a rock. The earliest documents describing these, then called an *ingegno* or engine, date to 1596 in Naples, and by the seventeenth century they seem to have been fairly common. You may have seen pasta described as bronze die extruded—well, this is the real thing. The coarse surfaces of the noodles are ideal for holding sauce. That's not a great concern in a soup, but they do seem to absorb more flavor in any context. The only problem is that it just about the most difficult thing to clean on Earth. You have to pick at the dies with a metal skewer, soak them for a long time, and scrub. It takes twenty seconds to make a batch of dough, but twenty minutes or more to clean. Many people leave the dies soaking in water all the time and I guess never bother picking at the holes to clean.

Il torchio, the bronze beast for extruding noodles, was invented in the Renaissance

If you are going into business, there are electric-powered extruders that would be fun to use. Online I found a beauty costing $10,000 that was the size of an SUV. There are smaller models, of course, and even attachments you can connect to your stand mixer. They just don't sound like fun to use.

There are also devices that are technically extruders though with no or few moving parts because they use batter rather than dough. You may already own a ricer or food mill, neither of which are designed for noodles per se, but they do work. The ricer is a metal chamber with a handle and plunger that fits inside that normally squishes or "rices" potatoes, that is, mashes them. Ironically, it also works with a rice dough for noodles. So too does a food mill. It has a crank on top of a bowl with perforated holes at the bottom. Then turn it and a little blade scrapes along the holes and forces the contents through. Ideal for tomato sauce and purees, but also for noodles.

A spaetzle maker is also a kind of extruder. Traditionally spaetzle are made with a wooden board and offset spatula, and I prefer to make them this way. But there are many other noodles that can be made in this device. It's basically a little squared metal chamber into which you pour batter; then it's shifted back and forth on a track over the holes directly over a pot of boiling water. The batter dribbles out, forming noodles in the water.

A passatelli press is another extruder. It's simply a concave metal dish with large holes and a handle mounted on top. You press it over a mound of dough made of bread crumbs to make a very noodle-like dumpling. It's also sometimes referred to with its other name and usage (ricing potatoes) as a *schiacciapatate*— one of the most delightful words in any language. With similar effect you can also use a large cheese grater. But with a grater you will need a very stiff dough, basically rubbed through the holes with the palm of your hand. In the end it looks a lot like passatelli.

In Thailand there's a similar tool made of tin: a cylinder with holes at the bottom and two rounded handles at the top. A metal plunger fits inside. It's designed for starch-based batters and isn't strong enough for a sturdy dough. If you have a tall pot you can put two sticks through the handles and perch it directly over boiling water. A similar device in China is like a pot with holes used to scoop up a similar batter, which is then held over the pot and thumped with one hand to make the batter go through. These only work with a special kind of thixotropic batter, discussed in chapter 8.

Although not designed for noodles per se, I have had great luck with a regular pastry bag and various tips that yield star shapes, ribbons, and an incredible range of forms. A squashed metal tip is perfect. You can also use squirty ketchup bottles and even squirt guns with a modified widened tip and a thin batter. I've even used whipped-cream canisters filled with batter, pressed gently enough so you don't create a fine mist. They're a little bit too powerful though. Even a sturdy plastic bag with one corner cut off works, and it saves you having to clean it.

STEAMERS

In Asia an entire class of starch-based noodles start with a batter but are then steamed so the starch molecules gel; then the large flat noodle is cooled and cut. Professionals use a large square tray set into a steaming box, which makes sense to maximize space. At home you can use a bamboo steamer with a flat-bottomed plate inside. Better yet, a flat-bottomed baking pan or springform pan works well too—one with a corrugated bottom makes really funky noodles. I've also used a rectangular glass dish for steaming; a small casserole would work too. I've even used a small dish set over a few chopsticks in the bottom of a pot with a little water at the bottom.

OTHER TOOLS

A few other tools are surprisingly useful in making noodles. First is the mortar and pestle. Many of the ingredients used throughout this book are best when pounded fresh at the last minute. There are also ingredients that can be pounded and put directly into the noodle for a marvelous effect in flavor and color. For dry ingredients, a coffee grinder works just as well, and you can keep one around just for this purpose.

I cover the details in chapter 6, but a coffee grinder in tandem with a dehydrator will revolutionize your whole idea of what noodles can be. Just about anything can be dried, ground, and put into a noodle. If you live somewhere hot and dry like I do, a screened-in frame set in the sun works fine. But a proper dehydrator is incredible—despite everything I say about not liking electric machines. As noisy and bulky as these are, you can put just about anything in it to dry: vegetable, fruit, meat, fish. Such ingredients ground up and added to a basic dough yield vibrant colors and spectacular flavors that beat any commercial colored noodle you can find. I discuss these in chapter 6, Noodles, but if you don't want to own a dehydrator, an oven set at 150°F works too, and a stone mortar for pounding can stand in for the coffee grinder.

There is also a relatively obscure class of noodles that are stamped. Corzetti or croxetti are the most familiar, and in Liguria they make lovely wooden stamps for round noodles impressed with stars, initials and other designs. It's a lot of fun if you can find them. But you can also stamp dough with anything. I'm surprised there aren't more commercial stamped noodle shapes. I leave this to your native ingenuity, but try rubber stamps, letters, or anything textured. You can roll dough over any textured surface too, like a screen or sturdy woven mat. I have even used a Sculpey roulette wheel to make one of the most beautiful noodles I've seen (see chapter 10). Many clay tools can double in the kitchen. And vice versa.

A gnocchi paddle is a little notched wooden board with a handle used to create ridges in dumplings made of potato, crumbs, or what have you. But they are also very useful for making ridged macaroni too. There are very inexpensive ones and beautifully carved examples to choose from. Many come with a small dowel used to form noodles, but you can use a chopstick too.

Gnocchi paddles can be used to form many fun shapes

In a keynote address at a conference held at the Culinary Institute of America at Greystone (in Napa), I made fun of chefs who use tweezers. Not half an hour later I bought a pair in the gift shop and now use them almost every day, not for plating tiny garnishes, but for plucking a single noodle out of the pot for tasting. Long chopsticks do work if you're nimble. Tongs do too, though they can brutalize a tender doughy strand. But my large bent-end stainless steel surgical tweezers work best. An Italian noodle fork works too. Some forks are just a wooden paddle with little dowels sticking out that somehow scoop up noodles from the pot; others resemble long spoons with tines on the end and holes to drain water out. A Chinese spider strainer, basically a wooden handle with a woven metal basket on the end, can also be useful for extracting noodles, along with other similar tools made for skimming the pot or removing ingredients. If you want a single noodle from the pot, you can't beat cooking tweezers.

Pinking shears are made to cut zigzags along fabric edges so they don't fray. They are also brilliant for cutting shell-shaped pasta. Somehow the combination of pressure and slicing action creates a beautiful noodle shape, especially if you're using several different colors in your dough. Small craft scissors aren't strong enough for dough—you need a heavy set of shears with strong teeth. Regular scissors can also be fun, just to snip pieces of dough into the water.

Needless to say, a colander is helpful to drain noodles, though an equal number of noodle recipes in this book are cooked right in the broth.

5

STOCKS

There can be no great noodle soup without a superb stock, so before we even touch a lump of dough, let's begin with soup bases. Please note I do not intend to quibble over the technical distinctions between stock, broth, bouillon, soup, etc. Much of what passes in common parlance makes no sense at all by strict culinary definitions. Usually broth is a liquid made with meat and seasoned, while stock is made with bones and is used either for soup or reduced for sauces and other dishes. It should have less salt for this very reason. Since this book contains only recipes for soup, all variations are seasoned like the sea, with salt that is, judiciously. And note that for all recipes I insist you salt according to your own preference, not mine. A recent study shows that most people don't follow recipes anyway, so why use the same amount of salt I do? You can use any of these soup bases in the recipes that follow, though I usually suggest one or another.

CHICKEN STOCKS

Chicken stock is the most prevalent of all soup bases. Taking the time to make it yourself is so important that I implore you to give it a shot before trying anything else in this book.

We have all tasted bouillon cubes, broth from a can or carton, soup concentrates, and other industrial prefabrications. And I do admit when I'm in a rush and the freezer stockpile is depleted, on such sad days I turn to a low-salt concentrate in a jar. It's OK in a pinch. But all these so-called time-savers are filled with chemically derived flavor enhancers— not necessarily monosodium glutamate (MSG), but a range of supposedly innocuous ingredients listed incongruously as "natural flavors" or something to that effect. This emphatically does not mean these flavors are extracted from whole ingredients as found in nature. The word natural is absolutely meaningless legally—much like the words fresh or healthy. Of course everything on Earth ultimately comes from nature, including poison. It is the combination of molecules into structures that imitate natural flavors but are ramped up to an extreme degree that I object to here, not because of the danger they pose to health, but because of the assault they make on our taste buds.

Taste a Dorito or, better yet, Cheetos. They don't taste bad; they taste very good. Too good in fact, which is why it's very hard to eat just one. They were developed in a laboratory to create an immediate burst of flavor in your mouth that then dissipates immediately in order to incite us to eat more, somehow not feeling the gustatory pleasure that comes from the slow lingering flavor and mouthfeel of say, real cheese. The more we eat, the more profit these companies make, the consequences be damned. The very same flavor enhancers are used in commercial chicken broths, which do indeed taste intensely chickeny, in a way that would be much more expensive to achieve using only chicken.

My point here is that these flavorings prevent us from tasting anything else. They so overpower other ingredients that it is no wonder some children don't like fruit and vegetables: they're not flavor enhanced.

I propose an experiment. Sip a bowl of soup every day for a few weeks, starting with a "flavor" packet from instant ramen. It may strike you as acrid at first if you're not used to it. But you will get used to the levels of sodium and chemicals in a day or two. Then every few days change to another less-processed broth, from canned to an organic carton, to a low-sodium concentrate. The idea is to accustom your taste buds to subtlety. It will take a week or more, and you might have to cut back on salty, sweet snacks while doing this, but eventually you will begin to taste the carrots and celery, the onion undertones, even the distinct aroma of bones and collagen in the skin. Then proceed to the following broth recipe. I promise you: it will be an entirely different experience, infinitely superior.

If you want to try a quicker version of this experiment, a similar phenomenon was recorded several hundred years ago by the theologian Jeremias Drexel in a book called Bitter Aloes. He proposed, for purely gastronomic purposes, fasting for an entire day, after which he insisted everything tastes more intense and vibrant.[1] He was absolutely right.

Now to chicken stock, but first I must address the chicken. If you have the wherewithal to purchase an organic free-range happy-as-a-chicken-can-be kind of chicken, you will note that they taste better, apart from any ethical position that may have led you to such a decision. On occasions when I roast a chicken or especially lightly poach it, this is a meaningful splurge. For half the price or even less, you can get a conventional chicken. There are many ethical and gastronomic reasons not to make this choice, but if you are making a few gallons of stock and end up buying whatever is on sale in bulk to fill your stockpot, I empathize with your choice. Normally I dislike buying chicken parts for the sole reason that it costs much more to have them cut it up for you, but again the big package of thighs on sale is sometimes an irresistible bargain. A whole chicken is always a good choice.

 **LIGHT CLEAR CHICKEN BROTH**

This is really the simplest of soup bases and takes so little preparation time that a recipe almost seems superfluous. As with everything in this book, please do not fret over quantities. If you have 2 stalks of celery instead of 3, it really does not matter. If you decide to throw in something else on a whim, it will not insult me. Consider this your opportunity to have fun in the kitchen, to experiment. In fact, I suggest you read this recipe once and never again. I omit a list of ingredients with exact quantities for the very reason that it simply doesn't matter. If you add more of anything, you'll get more flavor.

Fill a large pot halfway with cold water. My pot halfway filled holds 20 cups, which is 1¼ gallons or one imperial gallon. If you want to make a bigger batch, by all means do—just increase the quantities of everything. Place in the pot 1 whole chicken with an array of vegetables. Include 3 carrots, celery stalks, parsnips, onions, leeks—all cut up but untrimmed. Just be sure to wash any dirt from the leeks. Use fewer vegetables if your pot is too full. You don't need to peel the carrots or even remove the onion skins. Also add a few large sprigs of fresh dill, and perhaps a few stems of sage and parsley. A sprig of thyme works, some peppercorns, and that should do it. People often tie these up in a bouquet garni to remove easily, but I see no need since you're going to strain this later. Also include all the giblets except the liver, which would give the soup a livery flavor. And last, add 2 tablespoons salt. You can always add more later, but you can't take it out.

Heat the pot slowly, covered, but don't let it reach a boil. You want it to very gently simmer, with only the barest ripple on the surface. When muck accumulates on the top, skim it off meticulously with a spoon every few minutes. Then leave the pot on the stove for ½ hour. Remove the chicken to a large platter and let cool. Remove the meat from the breast and thighs and set aside, then put everything else back into the pot, including the bones and skin. Let this continue to simmer for another hour on the lowest possible heat.

Strain the contents of the pot through a large sieve with a double layer of cheesecloth into another large pot or bowl, pressing down gently on the solids with a wooden spoon. Some people use a paper towel rather than cheesecloth to make the broth perfectly clear, though it will end up tasting a tad like paper if you do this. The broth is clear enough with cheesecloth. Now return the broth to the stove in a clean pot and let it simmer further with the lid off. Resist removing any fat that rises to the surface: much of the flavor is right here. Taste the soup. Is it not intense enough? Then continue simmering to reduce it a little. Now add salt if necessary. Now you can return the chicken meat shredded to the pot, and add noodles and fresh vegetables for a perfectly simple lovely chicken noodle soup. Many variations can be found elsewhere in this book.

I usually put this stock into sturdy plastic single-serving (3-cup) containers and freeze for later use. You can use glass too, but be sure not to fill them up or they will crack. I have had bad luck with glass. Just defrost to use as your soup base. Rule 1: label and date everything before it goes in the freezer. This is a rule I regret not following almost every day.

🍜 LONG AND SLOW OVEN CHICKEN STOCK

This is a different creature entirely, and it is a stock since you include as many bones and parts as you can lay your hands on, but not meat that will be eaten in the end. For this wings are great, chicken backs, necks, and even thighs in large quantities. Use as many gizzards, hearts, and gristly bits as you can. You can buy a few whole chickens, but remove the parts you like to eat and use them elsewhere. Or better yet, freeze the carcass of every chicken you've eaten for a few weeks and then use them all in this stock. You can also use much more aggressive seasonings, so I include a whole head of garlic here, bay leaves, and sometimes spices like a few cloves or fennel seeds, which I adore. As for vegetables, use the same carrots, parsnips, and onion, but add more flavorful vegetable scraps. Actually anything you've trimmed will work, with the exception of crucifers: the cabbage family and stock make strange bedfellows. Any herb stems are perfect; save them in a big zippered plastic bag in the freezer.

So here clarity is not a great concern: you want flavor above all else. So fill your stockpot, season it well from the start with salt and pepper, and just place it in the oven at about 200°F and forget about it for at least 6 hours. Overnight or 12 hours is ideal. You will probably have to make a small batch to fit in the oven, but there is no labor involved at all.

When you remove it, let it cool a bit and then simply ladle off portions though a strainer into containers. It will be a deep gold. Let the containers cool and freeze them. Before using, I usually scrape off the layer of fat at the top and use it elsewhere. Browning onions in the fat is the serious schmaltz of the kind that makes Ethel Merman sing.

With this stock you can use a heartier noodle and more flavorful vegetables, and you can use it anywhere in this book that calls for chicken stock. When you taste this, you will never want to use a can again.

If you are a fan of the pressure cooker, there are new electric models that make an extraordinary stock. Simply put in your cut-up chicken and everything else, cover with water, and let it cook for about 2 hours under high pressure. You will have a nearly clear, intensely flavored, pellucid stock that you can strain right into your containers. Best of all, you don't fill the house with steam. It also works well with other stock types.

🍜 INTENSE ROASTED CHICKEN STOCK

Now we take the stock one step further. This technique is normally used with beef bones and the like, but chicken works just as well. Use the exact same ingredients as above, salted well, except this time smash the bones open with the back of your cleaver, place them in the oven and roast them for about an hour at 400°F. They should be charred, but keep an eye on them to make sure they don't burn, and lower the temperature if they brown too quickly. You can also use leftover roasted chicken, the bones, and any gristly bits too. Normally I add other kinds of bones to a roasted bone stock—pork, beef shins, duck necks. I return to this mélange kind of stock below. In the meantime, just scrape all the roasted bones into the pot, and be sure to deglaze your roasting pan with water or better yet wine, and pour it into the pot. The flavor is all here. Then simmer for a few hours more, strain, and use or freeze.

For you intrepid souls or those with little freezer space, all the above stocks can be reduced into concentrates too. Just continue simmering to reduce the volume by half, then you can store in smaller containers and add water later. You can even pour the concentrate into ice-cube trays, freeze, and then pop into a plastic bag, using a few at a time for a quick soup. In the end, I think reducing the stock just adds a lot more time and labor, but it does take up less space. If you are really keen, you can reduce the stock to a thick syrup and even dehydrate it into thin sheets for use in an instant soup (see chapter 10).

CHINESE CHICKEN STOCK

Throw away every rule aforementioned. In China a stock is made very different-ly and with a completely different flavor profile. First, take 1 whole chicken, prefer-ably with the feet intact (or add a few feet), put it into a pot of cold water, bring to a boil, and simmer for about 5 minutes. Remove the chicken, rinse it off, and discard the water. This is called feiseui, or "flying through the water." This way there's no skimming necessary. Then start all over again, with the rinsed chicken in water, slices of gingerroot, and scallions. Simmer for about 3 hours and then strain the broth into another container. This is the simplest form, intended for cooking, but since you want a rich soup, you can reduce this, add other aromatics and soy for greater depth of flavor. Definitely add some Shaoxing wine or sake. Dried mush-rooms, jujubes, or dried scallops can also be added. The chicken feet make the soup a little gelatinous and sticky without being viscous, which is really pleasant. I usually add a pork neck bone as well. When you use this stock as the base for a soup, a traditional clay soup pot makes a difference in the flavor, and it's fun too.

MEAT STOCKS

Here I offer one set of directions—regardless of whether you are using beef, veal, pork, or even lamb, the procedure is basically the same. You can of course mix different types of meat too, but I'll cover those separately below. For the time be-ing, use one type of meat for clarity and precision. Whereas veal stock is absolutely essential to a classical French kitchen, this is not something I prepare very often. Good veal bones are hard to find and are very expensive. And of course many peo-ple object to veal on moral grounds. It is, nonetheless quite different in flavor and texture from beef and is preferred for light sauces. For soups, it's not really crucial.

Lamb is also something few people use, but I like its bold and pronounced flavor. If you skim off the fat, it won't be overpowering. If you're doing a soup from Central Asia or even the Middle East, lamb stock is the best choice, so do give it a shot.

BASIC, SINGLE-MEAT STOCK

Buy enough meaty bones to fill a large roasting pan. The more connective tissue the better, so use joints, shins, necks, knuckles, and something with meat on it, like oxtails or shoulder. I often buy these in an Asian grocery store that charges about 5 bucks for a big bag, which comes to less than a dollar per serving of stock. Add to the pan carrots, celery, onion, garlic, herbs, and roast for about an hour at 350°F. You can roast everything hotter too—just keep an eye on it to prevent burning. Everything should be browned and a little charred, especially the vegetables, that's fine. Remove everything to a very large stockpot and cover with water. Deglaze the pan with wine and add that in. Now let simmer on the lowest possible heat for at least 10 to 12 hours. I do it overnight. Or you can just let it go all day if you are home.

Strain into single-serving containers, let cool, and then freeze. The fat will rise to the top and create a seal on each serving. I generally scrape off and discard the fat before heating in the microwave for about 5 minutes on high heat. It's now ready to use as your soup base. As long as you have good chicken stock and beef stock on hand in the freezer, you are set. If you're feeding a crowd, of course use it all right away.

OXTAIL STOCK

2 pounds oxtail segments

4 pieces lamb shoulder bones with a little meat (optional)

2 chicken legs (optional)

2 carrots

2 parsnips

4 fresh bay leaves with berries

2 small onions cut and unpeeled

1 head garlic cut in half across

1 cup red wine

Put all ingredients in an ovenproof stockpot and cover with water. Place in a 250°F oven overnight or for at least 12 hours. Add more water in the morning if necessary, and continue to cook another hour or longer if necessary. Strain. The meat will have given up all its flavor, so don't bother trying to remove or use any of it. In this stock, serve broad egg noodles, some shredded cabbage, and if you like a little sliced beef or ham. Although it sounds redundant, a boiled potato is very nice too.

This soup base should be crystal clear, focused, and clean in flavor, which is why you keep ingredients to an absolute minimum. As with a broth, the flavor should come from a large piece of meat as well as bones, which should not be roasted first. Start with 2 pounds beef shanks, sawed into small sections, and an equal weight of beef, trimmed of fat. Chuck is quite good, or even brisket—you want a cut with flavor rather than tenderness. The usual onions, celery, and carrots go in and a tied bundle of thyme, sage, and rosemary. Just place these into cold water, bring up nearly to a boil, and simmer. Remove the meat after 2 hours and reserve for another use; for example, thin slices are lovely in soup. Then gently simmer the rest for another 2 hours. Skim well, especially at the start, but also periodically throughout. When the stock is done, strain it through multiple layers of cheesecloth in a sieve.

In classic Italian cooking of Emilia-Romagna, brodo is served with tortellini. In general, Italians don't put long noodles in soup, but according to our definition of a noodle, this is also used with passatelli, tiny pastina, or stelline—which are little stars. This is noodle soup, and real comfort food.

Brodo can also be used as the base for any minestra, a thick soup with vegetables, beans, meat, and noodles. Not coincidentally, Pellegrino Artusi, author of the magisterial *Science of Cooking and the Art of Eating Well*, offered a recipe for brodo first, as if nothing in Italian cooking would be possible without it. That was in the nineteenth century. Rewind another four hundred years to the greatest Italian cookbook ever written, Bartolomeo Scappi's Opera of 1570, and likewise brodo is central to the entire tome. I offer his recipe in homage to the maestro. And in deference to his wisdom and preference of the era, this recipe calls for veal. The verjuice is unripe grape juice and malvasia a sweet golden wine. Scappi's is clearly an ancestor of the modern broth, but the technique and various options are mind-blowingly creative.

To Make a Broth of Veal Flesh in Another Way

Take a part of the tip of the breast, a part of the leg with the shank, cut as small as you can, powdered cinnamon, and a little salt, verjuice, and malvasia as the liquid, and add a little pulverized sugar after; place everything in a pastry casing, cook in the oven 2 hours, more or less according to the quantity, when it's cooked, remove the broth that's in the pastry, strained though a sieve, and with this broth you can make soup, and when you don't have flour to make the pastry case, use a pot and add inside these ingredients, being covered with its cover, well sealed with clay and egg white, place in an oven that's not too hot and leave it for 3 hours, check the pot often without uncovering, not having a pot nor an oven you can do it in a copper stew pot well tinned, or earthenware, placing coals more above than below, and with this broth you can make bread stew and a simple broth.[2]

Keep summer's heat out of the kitchen by making stock on a gas grill

OUTDOOR STOCK

Where I live in Stockton, California, it can hover over 100°F for several days in the summer, which makes even lighting the stove miserable, let alone turning on the oven or letting a pot bubble on the stove all day. So I came up with this solution. Follow the directions above for meat stock, but instead of roasting, brown your meat and vegetables on the barbecue first, then put them in a capacious stockpot with water and leave them to cook outside on the barbecue all day. It doesn't make sense if you have a propane tank, but if you have a gas line, you can just leave it on low all day. A barbecued stock tastes quite different from roasted and for some hearty noodle soups is truly novel.

MIXED STOCK

These are in my opinion the apogee of stock making for soup. It's rarely done this way in a classical kitchen because they want to be able to reduce stock and use it in various sauces without muddled flavors. It's a shame though. In the United States we like isolated varietal wines and tend to think of stocks the same way—chicken, beef, or fish, and so on—when in fact mixing can create much greater balance and complexity.

Since here you are going directly to soup, having many layers of flavor is ideal. I usually roast a mix of a few chicken thighs, duck or turkey necks, beef bones, a meaty hunk of pork, and vegetables, then simmer it all in water. A smoked ham bone goes perfectly too. Or I simply do a freezer dump: leftover bones, heels of Parmigiano, frozen stems, and vegetable scraps. There are no holds barred here, in fact you can also throw in shrimp shells. The leftover turkey carcass stock after Thanksgiving falls in this general category as well. I sometimes add a cinnamon stick and dried chilies, mustard seed, and coriander. This is entirely up to you. Many recipes in this book call for mixed stocks, perhaps with a couple of distinctive ingredients to highlight, such as lemongrass and galangal root in a southeast Asian soup, or tamarind, chilies, and lime leaves. I love serious complexity in a noodle soup, and it often begins right in the stock.

 **BONE BROTH**

For reasons that elude me, bone broth has become very popular nowadays, especially among paleo dieters. Chefs like to quip that they've been making this for centuries—and it's called stock. Actually it's quite different, though a milky white bone broth has been used in Asian cuisines for centuries. The key, unlike most other soup bases, is to use mostly bones and to boil them at full throttle for as long as possible. The marrow and connective tissue is really where all the flavor comes from here, so be sure to get several large beef bones cross cut, neck bones, knuckles, shank bones, and if you want some serious flavor an oxtail too, though you really don't want much meat in here. You can use aromatic vegetables too, though some people don't use any. They are more or less obliterated in the boiling process, but you're going to throw them away in the end, so why not? Many people blanch the bones first in boiling water, then rinse, which makes the final liquid whiter—in Asian cuisine this step is never skipped. Many people roast the bones too, but then I think you've really just got an ordinary beef stock, especially if you simmer it slowly, in which case French chefs are right. So my recommendation is to blanch, rinse, boil hard for at least 12 hours (adding more water when necessary) with a few aromatics. Be sure to salt—I once tasted an organic free-range salt-free bone broth with nothing added and it tasted like, well, bones.

 DASHI

This complex but relatively quick stock is the cornerstone of Japanese cuisine. Dashi is the base for miso soup and goes into a wide variety of dishes. But if you have been using the instant powdered stuff, you have never really tasted it in all its subtle alluring glory. I think it's actually best sipped on its own, hot but not scalding.

To start, good ingredients definitely make a difference. Giant kelp or kombu is key—these are big tough sheets of dark green dried seaweed. The best comes from Hokkaido in the north of Japan, where the meeting of disparate currents is said to cause the umami levels to rise higher than in plants gathered elsewhere. This results from the glutamates, which make your taste buds feel like they're wide-open and buzzing. This kombu can be very expensive, but you might want to splurge once in a while. You can also gather wild kelp at the beach or buy it in a natural foods store—the one from Maine is excellent, and so is Pacific kelp. The taste will be different from Japanese kelp but interesting nonetheless.

Next comes the katsuobushi. This is basically a filet of skipjack tuna that has been simmered, smoked slowly for months, scraped, left to dry, and fermented with mold. The result looks like a black piece of wood about the size of your hand. It's so hard it needs to be shaved with a special plane-like device. What you find in groceries is already shaven. Buy a big bag rather than little packets.

But you can also easily make your own. It doesn't come out as hard as professionally made, nor can you shave it as thin, but I have side by side tasted stocks made with the two, and the homemade is really good. Take a few pieces of raw sushi-grade ahi tuna. Although not the same species, this works well. Salt them on all sides and place on a rack or paper towel until dry, firm, and slightly sticky. This should take about 2 hours. Then put these in a smoker and make sure the temperature doesn't rise above 150°F. I use grape vine cuttings and local oak chips. After about 2 hours it will be black and smell wonderful. Then dry the pieces in a dehydrator overnight, or leave them out to dry in the sun. When they are very hard, get a sharp cleaver and shave them into the thinnest slices possible. They will be pink inside.

To make the dashi, whichever ingredients you are using: put about 6 square pieces of kombu in 4 cups water. If you want it stronger, use more, and vice versa. Let it soak 30 minutes. Then slowly raise the heat and simmer very gently for about 10 minutes—don't let it boil. Taste at this point: it should be subtly sweet, slightly vegetal, and taste only faintly of the ocean. Take out the kombu and raise the heat, bringing the water to a boil. Shut off the heat and throw in two handfuls of katsuobushi flakes. Let them steep for 2 to 3 minutes and strain through a fine-mesh sieve lined with cheesecloth. The stock is almost instant.

If you want to ramp up the umami to even another level, add dried sardines or even garlic. You can also reheat this stock, adding a handful of ground porcini mushroom powder, a heel of Parmigiano cheese, even some of the clear water drained from a freshly cut tomato. You want the stock to be clear, so strain again after adding more ingredients.

This stock is used in the recipes just below, but you can use it as the base for just about any noodle soup in this book. In other words, don't be afraid to use dashi in soups not strictly Japanese. It makes a great fish soup base, and vegetables like fennel and especially artichokes go wonderfully well with it. In some ramen soups, people mix pork stock with dashi, and you can even follow the above recipe using clear chicken stock instead of water, for a seriously intense base.

Home-cured and smoked tuna, used for making dashi stock

 ## PHỞ STOCK

Food historians argue whether phở is an adaptation of the French dish pot-au-feu, which was introduced to Vietnam in the colonial era, or whether it is an indigenous invention appearing around 1900. The French dish is a long-simmered meat and vegetable dish, having practically nothing to do with the Vietnamese noodle soup, so it seems pointless to argue. The word might simply be a version of the Chinese word *fun*, meaning flat rice noodle, in which case the dish refers to the noodle rather than the soup. Just make it. There are many versions, from the traditional Hanoi style to many others: this one will include bánh phở—the rice noodles found in all Asian groceries and practically anywhere now. They can be made fresh too—see chapter 6.

Phở, an aromatic spicy stock for Vietnamese soup

2 pounds beef bones with meat, such as shank or neck

1 pound pork, chicken or duck bones, or a combination of these

4 carrots, peeled and roughly cut

4 parsnips, peeled and roughly cut

4 stalks celery with leaves, chopped into large pieces

2 onions, quartered with peel

salt and pepper

5 star anise florets

5 cloves

1 stick cinnamon

5 black cardamom pods

1 tablespoon whole peppercorns

5 fresh lime leaves (available in Asian groceries)

4 slices galangal root

mushroom stems, chilies, and other vegetable scraps

The key to good stock and depth of flavor is roasting the ingredients first. You should get at least a few pounds of beef bones—neck and shanks intended for soup work really well, and as long as there's a lot of meat on them, you should be fine. You can also mix beef soup bones with pork bones, duck, poultry, lamb. Put these in a roasting pan with carrots, parsnip, onion, and celery. You can use peelings and scraps, but if you want a really clear soup it's best to use large clean pieces of vegetable that won't disintegrate in the long cooking. Sprinkle these with salt and pepper and roast at 400°F for 2 hours until the bones are brown and the onion charred. Put all the ingredients into an ovenproof stockpot, 8 or 12 quarts, and cover with water. The spice combination is the key to the flavor. A small handful of star anise is indispensable. Add cinnamon stick, cloves, black cardamom pods, and then a bouquet garni of parsley, thyme, and whatever other herbs you like. You are trying to add as much complexity as possible, so mushroom stems and chili peppers are great. So are lime leaves, galangal root, or gingerroot plus a tablespoon or so of salt and whole peppercorns. It is sort of a Vietnamese French stock. Put the whole pot, covered, in the oven, and set it to 250°F and forget about it for about 12 hours, overnight, or even longer if you like. Don't stir or mess with it. But do add water if it is depleted.

Remove the pot and let it cool for a few hours. Then gently pour through a fine-mesh strainer into another pot, leaving solids behind. All the flavor will have been extracted and the soup will be clear. You should have about half the volume of stock, so 4 quarts if you used an 8-quart pot. Freeze some in pint-size containers and reserve the rest in the pot to make your first batch of soup.

BÁNH PHỞ SOUP

Boil the rice noodles in water until cooked but still a little chewy. Drain and rinse with cold water and set aside. Add to your stock sliced carrots, red peppers, sliced cabbage, and whatever else you like. You can serve these on the side in little bowls if you like, too. Cut the meat off the bones of two or three sections of beef short ribs and then into thin strips. Sprinkle with fish sauce and lime juice and dust with a little rice starch or cornstarch. This seals in the juices once cooked. Add the meat to the soup and cook about 2 to 3 minutes. Then add the noodles. Toward the end, add 1 ripe tomato cut into chunks, 1 handful chopped cilantro—stems and all—and maybe bean sprouts. Then add the noodles, a good squirt of sriracha chili sauce, a squirt of fish sauce, and the juice of 1 lime. Turn off the heat to let all the flavors come together. Serve in a big bowl with chopsticks and an oversized spoon. For breakfast, definitely.

FISH FUMET

This is among the more elusive and difficult soup bases, to my mind. A fish not at the peak of freshness can make the fumet taste like a muddy wet towel. Even though Stockton (where I live) is a port city, supermarkets tend to carry filleted or filleted and frozen fish rather than whole fish. That's one of the casualties of a culture that discards bones, heads, and all the parts of a fish used to make soup. And then there's the question of species. You can be safe with a mild white fish like flounder and other flat fishes. Cod and snapper are good too, even something like bass. But anything even slightly oily that might taste fine from the pan can come out pretty rank in a soup base. With a class once we cooked a medieval Chinese soup recipe based on carp. Since it's a freshwater fish, we thought it should be good. I don't think I've ever tasted anything so murky, brooding, and foul in my life.

The other strange thing about fumet is that it only takes about 20 minutes' cooking time and you start with the fish bones, skin, and head on their own, soaked in water about 20 minutes to remove any blood, rinsed, and then simmered in fresh water and wine. When it's all in the pot, first skim carefully for a few minutes and then add the aromatics, which are chopped very fine or even shredded since the cooking is so quick. The simpler the better, so I usually prefer shallots and tarragon, maybe celery or fennel. I also like to use a dry white wine or rosé as part of the liquid. Strain through cheesecloth for clarity.

In most of the world they obey no such rules, use darker-fleshed fish, cook longer, scarcely worry at all about cloudy soup, and then throw in things like lemongrass, gingerroot, chilies, and other flavors that make you wonder who came up with rules in the first place. For a deeper flavor you can also sweat the bones and aromatics first in oil and even give them a little color. Add spices too—coriander seed seems to pair well—and if you want something vibrant add a peeled turmeric root or saffron. Any number of really assertive flavors pair perfectly well with strong fish stock, as evidenced in recipes throughout this book. You can use this fumet with any kind of fish or shellfish, too, such as oysters or clams. Just add the liquid from them.

Above: Fried oysters with egg, tomato, seaweed, and caviar in fish fumet

Below: Noodle soup in aspic at a ryokan in Kyoto

 ASPIC

To our current sensibilities, a meat or fish gelatin should be categorized among those grotesque foods eaten in the 1950s that should never be recalled except in terror and dismay. Perversely, earlier periods have been fascinated with them as well. The nineteenth century adored aspic, and in the late Middle Ages you might have been served a tricolor leche Lombarde that would have been perfectly at home in a suburban household in 1957. To tell the truth, an aspic is a just a marvelous solidified cold soup, but it has to be clear and well set to really work well. If you clarify the stock with egg whites and have used a lot of skin, or better yet a pig's foot, you will almost certainly have a firm aspic when chilled. Fish bones will also set an aspic. You can also use a packet of powdered gelatin, or agar-agar, which comes in powder form or in long puffy bars in Japanese groceries, called kanten. It's completely vegetarian (made from algae) and neutral in flavor, so

you can make a cold jelled vegetable stock in the summer, with bright vegetables suspended in the chilled stock. Now you are wondering what this has to do with noodles. You can serve a cold noodle with cubes of aspic. Or, as I discovered in Japan, the noodles themselves can be set in the aspic and cut into cubes, which is a really delightful trick. The lesson here—don't sell aspic short.

SHELLFISH STOCK

This is actually my favorite stock of all. Sometimes I wonder whether I buy crabs just so I can save the shells. In any case, any crustacean shell works here: shrimp, lobster, Dungeness or blue crab, crawfish. Save up as many as you can in the freezer, and you really only need the shells, smashed into small pieces. When you have about half a stockpot full, heat a bit of oil in the bottom of the pot and add the shells. Stir constantly until fragrant, about 10 minutes. Then add 1 chopped onion, 2 smashed cloves of garlic, 1 or 2 carrots, a few roma tomatoes, and 1 good pinch of cayenne pepper, and keep stirring. You can use Old Bay Seasoning in this too, but I prefer to experiment with herbs and spices. Thyme and bay leaves are great, as are a few cloves. Fennel is perfect. And if you want an extra fennulated flavor, add a glug of good French pastis or ouzo. Then add a glass of dry white wine. Cover the shells with water and simmer for about 1½ hours. Strain.

This stock goes perfectly with a thick chewy rice noodle, lime juice, chopped ripe tomato, cilantro, and a squirt of sriracha. If you add in some crab meat, maybe a garnish of red caviar, you will thank me. It can also be the base for a serious cacciucco Livornese or cioppino di San Francisco if you add in a range of other firm-fleshed fish, mussels, shrimp, scallops, and maybe squid or octopus. Then do something unorthodox and add noodles.

Shellfish stock with *mentaiko* (pollack roe), seaweed, mushrooms, and zucchini

VEGETABLE STOCKS

This section falls last not because it's the least interesting but because it's the stock you graduate to after you can appreciate the full panoply of other soup bases—or of course if you're vegetarian. It need not be the subtlest of stocks, but unless you can devote a lot of care and vegetable matter to it, this family of stocks tends to be on the lighter side. I recommend them therefore for summer fare, and cold soups are great just with vegetables.

BASIC VEGETABLE STOCK

Boil a pile of chopped vegetables—carrots, parsnip, celery, leek, onion, and scraps from just about anything. But much greater depth of flavor results if you first sauté everything in a pan with olive oil until golden brown. Start with the onions; the lower and slower you can do it, the sweeter they become. Red onions will give a vegetable stock deep color and flavor. Rather than sautéing, you can instead roast all the vegetables first. Trust me: a roasted parsnip is a thing of great beauty, and when used in stock it is sublime.

The advantage of vegetable stock is that it doesn't take hours—usually an hour or a little longer simmering in the pot is sufficient. Once the vegetables have sacrificed all their flavor, strain them out and add in fresh cuts of the same vegetables to serve in your soup. Or add in a different vegetable to create layers of flavor. For instance, a beet soup with a vegetable base is splendid—so too is asparagus. Then you can also liven up your base with something acidic, either citrus, a good vinegar, or surprisingly even pickle juice. See the recipe for şalgam suyu in chapter 10 if you really want to add a kick.

MUSHROOM STOCK

This stock starts with a lot of vegetables, but to these add as many stems from shiitake as you can save, scraps of other mushrooms, and if you're feeling grand, whole mushrooms coaxed into flavorsomeness in butter and then thrown into the stock, where they will be boiled to yield every iota of flavor. Soy goes well here too, and white wine to replace half the water. After you strain the stock and press hard on the scraps, add more mushrooms to the final soup. If you want a very quick mushroom stock, make a vegetable stock first, strain, then add a handful of porcini powder, boil a few minutes, and strain again.

SUMMER STOCK (SCRAP SOUP)

This stock is all about preventing waste. (Not about musical theater, though I encourage you to sing while making it!) So much food gets tossed out nowadays—

in the field, at the grocery, and even in our homes. Apparently the industry thinks we will buy only the most pristine unblemished fruits and vegetables, and they may be right about what sells. It's a shame though, because sometimes the ugliest fruit actually tastes best. But I understand why we're reluctant to eat damaged or old vegetables. The truth is, we shouldn't ship vegetables so far, or leave them on supermarket shelves or in our fridges so long. Barring the compost pile, the immediate solution is, in a word, stock. I'm talking pure vegetable stock suitable for vegans, a base for soup that is so refreshingly green and vibrant that it works perfectly with that bounty of summer vegetable scraps you are bound to have on hand. I like to use fennel tops, leek greens, bay leaves, celery leaves, and stems of parsley and thyme. Scraps from bitter leafy greens like chard stems are good too. You can use carrot tops and peelings from just about anything, including fruit. Hard cores of lettuce, corn cobs . . . literally any vegetable goes in. Unlike the Basic Vegetable Stock above, this is all scraps and just boiled. Fill the pot with scraps and cover with water. Boil for about 1½ hours and then strain, pressing on the vegetables to get every last drop. Simmer to reduce it by about half and then season with salt. It can be used as a soup base as is: add more vegetables, then green noodles—especially those based on green vegetables. Cold, it is equally compelling. You should never have to throw away vegetable scraps again.

6
NOODLES

IN PRAISE OF DRIED PASTA

There is no denying that dried pasta is just about the most convenient food product imaginable; it's easy to cook, virtually indestructible, and can be kept in your cabinet just for those occasions when you don't have a lot of time to fuss. Even as far back as the sixteenth century, Sir Hugh Plat recommended macaroni to the British Royal Navy as a food suitable for ships' provisions on oceanic voyages, arguing that it is durable, exceedingly light, cheap, and, among other virtues, "can be made as delicate as you please, by the addition of oyle, butter, sugar and such like."[1] He could have added that you can just toss it into soup as well. The majority of pasta available today from the inexpensive box of American macaroni to the artisanal import from Italy to the durable Asian rice noodle will be perfectly suitable for any recipe here.

But let me offer a few recommendations and descriptions of various pasta shapes nonetheless. Italians will tell you that the noodle shape must match the sauce, that some shapes are destined to hold sauces of specific viscosity and particulate inclusion, and that for some soups only a few shapes are even thinkable. In general smaller shapes like little stars or pastina go in very light clear soups. Ditalini (little thimbles) or elbow macaroni in *minestra*, tortellini in *brodo*, and so forth. Spaghetti can never go in soup. Why? Because Italians don't traditionally eat with chopsticks, and any pasta that can't be scooped up with a spoon is unsuitable. So be forewarned that I have no orthodox doctrine about which noodle can go into which soup.

Regarding quality, I am simply not a fan of short extruded cut shapes that look like SpongeBob, wagon wheels (*ruote* or rotini), radiators (*radiatore*), X-rated parts, or any other shape where the cut surface of the pasta absorbs liquid quickly, making the noodle mushy. On the other hand, these shapes all work perfectly fine: extruded hollow shapes like penne, rigatoni, curved macaroni; fusilli, and shells; and long spaghetti, linguine, and tagliatelle. They are all made exclusively of durum semolina wheat, and while there are subtle differences among various brands, I advise you to buy what you like at a price you prefer. Among Italian brands, I buy

De Cecco or Barilla, though Lidia Bastianich and Mario Batali both have brands that are really good but more expensive. There are many very expensive artisanal Italian brands, and sometimes they are great and sometimes downright awful. Price is no indication. You might prefer Ronzoni, Mueller's, or Buitoni for your soup. Of course, outside the United States you have your own favorite local brands.

In the past few years you also see dry noodles made from various alternative grains suitable for those with wheat intolerance, allergies, or celiac disease. Having suffered myself from the latter as a small child, I take these conditions seriously. But there may be many other factors involved in the rise in gluten intolerance. We use a super-high-protein wheat that contains high levels of glutenin and gliadin, which help hold large air pockets in bread and create stretchiness in noodles, but are actually fairly new in the human diet at these levels. We also mill wheat very differently than in the past, removing the germ and crushing the grains with steel rollers rather than stone mills. Since fermenting dough may play a large role in making wheat digestible, we have a few fermented pasta doughs here. In any case, the industry has suddenly flooded the market with non-wheat-based dried pasta, many of which are quite nice but can be a little gummy, so don't overcook them. Corn- and rice-based noodles are lovely. There is even orzo pasta made of rice, in the shape of rice, although the word actually means "barley" in Italian. I've also tasted pasta made of soybeans and one made of kidney beans that was nasty. Do experiment with these, but I teach you how to make your own from scratch.

For soup noodles around the world, it's best to stick with the classics that come from each country: German egg noodles, Spanish *fideos*, Greek *trahanas*, and so forth. For some soups it is preferable to use a dried commercial pasta, but I usually offer a homemade option for those who want to get their hands dirty.

Asian noodles present a challenge for many: the variety can be staggering, the brands may be unknown to us, the shapes are unfamiliar, and the base ingredients are different. Dozens of countries may share basic types but make the noodles very differently. The consensus is that most Asian noodles originate in China, but once lamian gets to Japan as ramen, or any noodle finds itself in Manila, Singapore, or Seoul, it can be a very different product. Let's review the basic types; in the recipes I usually call for something specific.

Dried rice noodles are usually flat ribbons in widths ranging from about ¼ inch to 1 inch. Most of them come from Thailand and may be labeled pad Thai noodles. In an Asian grocery store, a package may cost a dollar or so; the national brands sold in the supermarket are usually be three times the price. They are exactly the same. Actually the less expensive ones are usually longer and not cut to fit in a box but are folded over. There are also brands from Vietnam, Cambodia, and elsewhere in Southeast Asia. Buy a lot. These are just about the best quick soup noodle you can keep around. Throw them directly into any soup stock and bingo. There are also extruded round rice sticks that can range from spaghetti and vermicelli in thickness (they're often called the latter) down to fine threads. The finest widths are something that really can't be made without industrial machinery, so depend on them; they cook in nearly an instant.

The many kinds of Asian wheat noodles are almost always made of regular white wheat, not semolina. That makes them a little more brittle, but they often come curled up in a little nest. This includes all variety of Chinese lamian (which we often see spelled "lo mein"), curly, straight, and some exquisite pearly white flat noodles. There are pulled noodles, wavy ribbons, sliced squares, and just as many interesting shapes as found in Italy. Every other Asian nation has its wheat noodle as well: Filipino pansit, Japanese udon, and Korean jajangmyeon are all descended from Chinese types. These are all worth trying in your soup, and there are literally thousands of brands to choose from.

There are also dozens of noodles made from various starches: tapioca, cornstarch, potato, sweet potato, mung bean or cellophane threads—the list is endless. In all the recipes that follow, I offer the option to use a dried noodle or make it from scratch. However, some are so tricky—especially the superfine threads, that I suggest dried versions first. In many cases, the dried versions are exactly what people throughout Asian would use themselves.

The translucence of mung bean noodles is stunning

Now that I've said all that, freshly made noodles are infinitely more fun to cook, so let's dive right into the dough with the first of a few basic recipes.

WHEAT NOODLES

BASIC WHEAT FLOUR NOODLES

This is the most basic noodle recipe that can be adapted for use throughout this book and can easily be multiplied for guests. I offer you measurements now just to get you started, with the expectation that you probably find that you like to eat more or less than these amounts call for, especially if you're making it for dinner as the main course. Let me assure you: the measurements don't really matter and you will probably need to add a little flour or water to get the consistency just right anyway. Just for reference, 1 cup flour is about 4¼ ounces or 120 grams.

1 cup white bread flour or all-purpose flour, plus a little extra for dusting

1 large egg

$\frac{1}{8}$ teaspoon sea salt

1-2 tablespoons water to finish the dough

3 cups boiling water or stock

Place flour in a large, stable mixing bowl. Add egg and salt and mix with a wooden spoon. Gradually add water until the dough comes together. You may need no water at all or even a little more than 2 tablespoons. Gently knead the flour right in the bowl until it becomes a smooth ball. Since you haven't developed the glutens with rigorous kneading, there is no need to let this rest (other doughs are quite different). Place the ball on a well-floured wooden board at least 14 by 20 inches. If you only have a small board, divide the dough in two. Press the ball into a flat disk on the well-floured board, and with the rolling pin also well floured, roll out the dough, turning it every so often and making sure it doesn't stick. Don't worry about over-flouring this: that problem happens only with pastry dough, so give this noodle as much flour as it wants. Turn the dough over now and then too. The idea is to get the thinnest possible dough, and this amount should span the entire board perfectly. If you like, at this point trim the edges so they're even, but that's not essential. If you do trim, just save the scraps as *maltagliati* (lit., badly cut) for another soup.

With a chef's knife that fits comfortably in your hand, cut the dough free-form into long noodles using broad even strokes. To start, try making them about ¼ inch wide and 12 inches long. You should have between 50 and 60 noodles—the thinner they are, the more you'll have. This is more or less classic fettucine or tagli-atelle, and they go well in just about any soup in this book. Don't be put off by the fact that these are generally noodles eaten with sauce in Italy (*pasta asciutta*, or dry pasta) and we're eating them wet in soup. They are virtually identical to countless noodle types found around the world.

Dust the noodles once more with flour to make sure they don't stick, especially if you're not ready to eat them yet. If you are, put them directly into the boiling water or, better yet, boiling stock. You have heard that noodles should only be cooked in a great quantity of boiling salty water. That's simply not true if you're making soup. There are clear soups for which you'll want to boil the noodles sepa-rately and rinse them, especially Japanese udon, but for most soups, it's perfectly fine to boil the noodles right in the stock along with the vegetables. This is literally one-pot cooking.

OTHER WHEAT FLOURS

You can make a noodle out of any wheat, but the choice of flour type will ul-timately determine the final texture and mouthfeel of the dough. Hard winter wheat varieties that we generally get in the United States are just fine for noodles. If you want a chewy noodle, go with bread flour, which has around 12 to 14 percent protein, or even add a teaspoon of gluten to an all-purpose flour. For an everyday noodle, use only regular all-purpose flour, preferably unbleached and with minimal additives. If you can find Tipo "00" Italian flour, that refers not to the protein content but the level of milling, which is superfine in this case. It makes a lovely fresh noodle. The flour most commonly found in Britain is milled differently from U.S. flour and is lower in protein, which means that it works really well for hand-formed noodles. Even if they're somewhat thick, they'll still be edible. If you're lucky enough to find wheat flour in Germany, the taste and aroma can be exquisite. Germans take wheat and bread very seriously, and an egg noodle comes alive made with a fresh flour such as is available there. All these are meant to be eaten fresh, and although you can dry these noodles, they tend to be very brittle and break easily.

Some people suggest cake flour for both ordinary and pulled noodles. It has only about 8 percent protein. I've tested it many times and it can be used, but I just don't like the flavor. It's usually bleached, which involves treating with chlorine. I don't think it stretches well for pulled noodles, either, though apparently people do get decent results if you mix cake flour with all-purpose flour.

I am divided on the topic of whole wheat. It is supposed to be better for you, but I find most whole wheat flour you can find on the supermarket shelves to be stale and a little acrid. That flavor comes right through in a noodle. Having said that, you can make a magnificent noodle from fresh local whole wheat flour, as I've done in California, Oregon, other places around the United States, and a few places in Europe. So if you really like the flavor of whole wheat, then just ensure it hasn't been sitting on a shelf for ages. And if you can meet the miller, all the better. My instinct prods me to suggest milling whole wheat yourself, and I have tried using my hand-powered stone quern. It makes a decent whole wheat flour for bread, and the leaven and bacteria seem to do something great for the flavor of the wheat, but in a noodle it isn't that great. I once managed to source wheat grown within a few miles of where I live and milled it immediately, but the noodle was gritty. The same was true of the wheat I grew in the backyard in whiskey barrels. When it comes to flour for noodles, the professionals do a better job separating the coarsest parts of the grain, and the finer the flour, the better the noodle.

Durum semolina flour is a different creature entirely, not better or worse than other wheat varieties, just different in flavor and texture. Be sure not to buy coarse semolina, which is for baking. You want the finest milling possible labeled as suitable for pasta. This is what practically all commercial Italian dried pasta is made of; its yellowish color gives it away immediately. It dries firm and is ideal for shipping and long-term storage. Of course in many Italian soups, durum semolina flour is essential. Extruded shapes will almost always be made of semolina. At home there are many noodle types that really work best with semolina too, spaghetti above all else, though extruded macaroni shapes seem to work best with it too. Surprisingly, thanks to its high protein content, you can use semolina to make a pulled noodle; it just has to be kneaded a long time, with water added as you knead.

Grano arso (lit., burned grain) refers to the practice in Puglia in southern Italy of gleaning wheat from a field after the stubble has been burned. A proportion of these black, charred grains are mixed with other grains, ground, and made into a flour for noodles, which come out grayish. I've eaten noodles from Italy made of this flour and frankly they were pretty bad, though many people like the taste. But it led me to think that a smoked flour would be great if the kernels weren't charred. So I took whole fresh wheat berries—the kind they sell in natural foods stores for sprouting into wheat grass. They are often much fresher than dried wheat berries off the shelf, and because they're moist they absorb wood smoke. These I put into a metal vessel and smoked them for about 2 hours over smoldering vine cuttings, then ground that in a regular spice grinder. The flour was deeply malty, very smoky, but not acrid like the grano arso. It can be worked like any wheat flour, just with water, into a noodle. These served cold dipped into a soy-and-dashi-based stock was deliriously good. It sort of reminded me of good Scotch with a long aftertaste.

BASIC DOUGH TEXTURES AND TERMINOLOGY

A precise terminology is helpful in discussing the texture of doughs, which range in terms of density, tensile strength, or let's say stretchiness, and for lack of a better word, bounce. Some doughs spring back immediately when poked, which will make a chewier noodle. A *very firm* dough is ideal for slicing and grating and even pinching little shapes from, but it is a pain to roll out. A *semi-firm* dough is your basic rolled dough, which you want stiff and not sticky, but not rock hard either. These can be further divided into glutinous dough, which has been kneaded or worked a long time to make it stretchy; alkaline dough, which makes noodles that are both stretchy and slippery and a little yellowish; and a regular unkneaded basic dough. A *soft dough* will still be sticky and is best for extruded pasta, so it will go through a die easily. The trick is getting it just the right texture so that it goes through but doesn't stick together on the other side of the extruder. Sometimes these types of dough are best extruded right into boiling water. A *thick batter* is used for spaetzle and other poured or squirted noodle types. It should be like pancake batter or even thicker. Of course these must go right into the water or soup. A *thin batter* is mostly used for steamed noodles that are poured into a tray and are cut after cooking.

WHEAT'S RELATIVES

Nowadays you can find many of the ancient relatives of wheat not only in health food stores but on regular grocery shelves. They tend to be low in gluten, which is partly why they've caught on lately, but if they're fresh they can also be absolutely delicious. Genetically they're primitive forms of wheat, so if you have an allergy it's still best to avoid them. Otherwise, the low protein means they're very easy to work with and give you a lot of flavor compared to mass-produced wheat. Einkorn, or *Triticum monococcum*, is the simplest of these. Then there's emmer, which the ancient Egyptians loved; spelt, which was more common in Europe; and kamut. Treat these exactly as you would any other wheat flour—make into a dough as in any wheat recipe above and form into noodles. They probably will take a little more water or egg.

OTHER ANCIENT GRAINS

You will also notice a slew of other so-called ancient grains that are not relatives of wheat, so consequently are also a little harder to keep in a noodle shape without falling apart. However, they usually taste really good, and if you can find these already milled there's no reason not to give them a shot. Archaeological evidence reveals that millet is actually the first grain ever made into a noodle, about 4,000 years ago. You're already familiar with it: a tiny pale yellow seed that we normally feed to birds (i.e., birdseed). It can be cooked whole and was probably the first kind of polenta centuries before corn arrived in Europe. Unfortunately, it can sometimes taste really nasty. Some processors will explicitly state that they've washed the outer seed coat before milling, and I think this must make a big difference, because the taste can be really pleasant. Regardless of whether you extrude, roll out, and cut millet noodles, they really need an egg to bind them or they're too fragile to hold together in the pot. Rolling the dough is extremely difficult as well, so extrusion winds up being the best way. Amaranth is an ancient American grain whose taste is much sweeter, and the flour makes a similar slightly grainy but pleasant noodle. If you can find the fresh greens they're also very nice in the same soup. Quinoa is another grain from South America from which I've tasted both excellent flour and some rather bitter brands too. Try it once and if you like the taste, stick with it. Some people abhor the flavor of quinoa, so there's no hope for them. It does make a really beautiful noodle.

MORE GRAINS

Among all these grains I would also bring to your attention rye flour, which makes a gorgeous noodle, and oat flour, which is hearty and delicious. A range of other lesser known grains that make decent noodles

Chestnut flour makes an earthy noodle, perfect for winter

include teff from Ethiopia and sorghum. All these can be used to make noodles using the basic wheat techniques, and a few lend themselves to other forms as well. Buckwheat is not a wheat at all but a distant relative of rhubarb; it's used in Japanese soba and Italian pizzoccheri and is one of the most tasty noodle bases. It's usually combined with a little wheat to hold the noodle together. Various nuts also make excellent noodles, especially starchy chestnuts and even acorns.

STARCH NOODLES

Many noodles around the world, but especially in Asia, are made not from ground grain but from starch extracted from grain, tubers, or other plants. This is usually done by grating and soaking a tuber, straining out the liquid, and letting the heavier starch sink to the bottom. As an experiment, try it with a potato. Just peel it, grate it with a box grater. Then squeeze the grated potato with your bare hands into a bowl so the liquid is entirely extracted. Save the grated potato for hash browns. Then wait a few minutes and you'll notice a reddish liquid at the top of the bowl. Pour it all off. At the bottom of the bowl you'll see the residual potato starch. Add a little fresh water, mix, pour onto a plate, and microwave for 1½ minutes or steam for about 2 minutes. You'll have a wonderful chewy potato starch noodle that you can roll into a spring roll with fillings or cut up and throw into soup.

You can perform a similar experiment with regular flour as well. Mix flour and water into a dough and knead vigorously for at least 15 minutes. Then submerge the ball of dough in a big bowl of cold water and continue kneading for a few minutes. You will see the starch seep out of the dough. What you have remaining in your hands is the gluten. Amazingly, you can steam or even fry the gluten on its own; it becomes chewy and makes an excellent meat substitute. Let the starch remaining in the bowl settle for about an hour, pour off most of the water and then steam the batter as above. This is a classic dish from China called *liangpi*.

Nowadays there are industrial processes for extracting starch, so buying it in an Asian market is the easiest way. It's very inexpensive: for about a dollar you can buy a small plastic bag of powdery starch that will be enough for a batch to feed four people. The most typical starchy noodles you'll see in the store dried are made from rice, tapioca, potato, and a handful of translucent varieties from mung beans, sweet potatoes, and even more exotic plants like kudzu and arrowroot. There is also wheat starch for noodles. You'll often find fresh rice noodle sheets as well, but these are easy to make yourself. There are several basic techniques for making starch noodles regardless of the source, so let's start with a prototype of the simplest kind that is made in a similar way to wheat noodles but with a few interesting twists. No special equipment is needed for this.

BASIC RICE NOODLE

¾ cup rice flour (starch)
¼ cup tapioca starch
¾ cup boiling water
1 teaspoon oil

In a bowl add the starches and the boiling water. Mix with a spoon until it comes together like a dough. Add the oil and mix with your hands until smooth. It should be a very soft dough, but it won't stick to your hands thanks to the oil. Lay this out on a board and, without dusting with more starch, roll it out into a flat sheet with an untapered rolling pin. Cut into noodles of the desired length and then drop into boiling water for about a minute until completely cooked through. Drain and immediately run under cold water to stop the cooking process. Use them in a soup now or place them on a tray in the sun to dry.

This recipe works with most starches, although with rice alone it doesn't work very
well. Mung bean starch on its own is beautiful—it is also the basic recipe for extruded rice
noodles and it is the easiest dough to work by
hand into interesting shapes. Let your kids
roll out worms, or use two gnocchi paddles to
make grubs that look hauntingly real. Or just
call them cavatelli if you're put off by worms.

Another really easy way to form this
dough is by using the flat side of a cleaver and squashing it into shape. Simply take
an almond sized lump of flour, place it on a
wooden board lightly oiled, oil your cleaver
too. Lay the cleaver flat on top of the dough
with the sharp end facing you, with your right
hand on the handle and left on the flat top of
the blade. With a horizontal movement away
from you, squash the dough into a long ob-
long strip. Throw this right into boiling water; it's probably the easiest way to work this dough. It's also a classic technique for making dough used for filled dumplings.

A cleaver can be used to squash
a starch-based dough

BASIC STEAMED RICE NOODLE

Rice noodles often contain ¼ part tapioca starch to add extra chewiness, but they can also be made entirely of rice when steamed. Arrowroot or plain corn-starch also works. The recipe is so simple that it really doesn't need explicit mea-surements.

Combine equal parts starch and water (for one serving, 1 cup of each) and a pinch salt and 1 teaspoon oil. I use olive oil, though you will taste it. If you'd rather not, use a neutral vegetable oil like soy or canola. Stir very well and let rest for a few minutes. Arrange a bamboo steamer over a pot of boiling water. Or alternatively use a flat-bottomed casserole, tray, or anything else that will fit into your pot, and add a small amount of boiling water on the bottom with a pair of chopsticks in it so your vessel isn't touching the bottom of the pot. I have had good results with a springform pan, which holds the liquids intact, and then the sides can be released to pop the large round noodle out. You can also use a square sheet pan set into a wok with water at the bottom and covered with a lid. Whatever you use, rub it well with vegetable oil.

Mix your batter well again; it should be the consistency of heavy cream. Pour a ladleful into your pan so there is just a thin even layer at the bottom. Place it in your pot or steamer for about 5 or 6 minutes. This will depend entirely on the starch you are using. When the noodle is solid and firm, remove the vessel.

Lightly oil the top of the noodle to keep it from sticking to itself, and then gently remove it from the pan. Cut into noodles whatever length and width you like and set these aside while you do subsequent batches. Before steaming it, you can also add chopped green onion, chili flakes, crushed peanuts—whatever you like—to the noodle. These are often just rolled up and eaten for dim sum, but they make a really fun noodle for soup as well. Incidentally, they are called *fun* in Chinese.

FERMENTED RICE NOODLE

4 ounces rice starch (usually labeled "rice flour")
1 ounce tapioca starch
1 cup water
½ teaspoon salt
2 teaspoon oil

Mix all the above ingredients together except the oil, and let these sit out open on the counter for a day or two to ferment, pouring off the dark brackish water on top and replenishing it each day with fresh water and mixing well. This gives the noodles a pleasantly sour flavor.

Add the oil, stir well, and cook on low in a nonstick pan about 5 minutes until it comes together as a ball. Let cool. Dust with a little more tapioca starch and place in an extruder. Extrude directly into a pot of boiling water and cook for about 2 minutes or less. Remove the noodles and put them immediately into an ice-water bath. When you're ready add to soup, hot or cold.

Now here's a twist on the fermented rice noodle: follow the basic fermented rice noodle recipe, but let it go a full 5 days. Add to it 3 tablespoons moringa pow-

A basic rice noodle can also be dried and stored

A dark green tea noodle in a tamarind broth

der and 3 teaspoons rosemary-flavored olive oil. Heat the mixture gently in a nonstick pan until it forms a smooth compact ball. Extrude this directly into boiling water for 2 minutes and then plunge immediately into an ice-water bath. This goes best in a cold dashi stock or soy-based tsukemen. It's chewy, pale green, and just addictive. Moringa powder is made from the leaf of a tree with supposedly extraordinary health benefits. I don't know about that, but it makes a very pretty noodle. You can do exactly the same with Japanese powdered green tea, or a powdered herb like marjoram. Be bold and inventive!

CHILLED MUNG BEAN NOODLE

This is another variation of starch noodle technique that cooks the starch first and then lets it set up after cool. In Sichuan these are called *beichuan liangfen*. Mix equal parts (⅓ cup each) mung bean starch and water and let sit for 15 minutes. Then add 1¾ cup more water and bring to a boil in a pot. Turn down the heat and stir until the mass is transparent. Pour it into a flat-bottomed tray and chill in the refrigerator for an hour or longer. Cut the noodles with a knife, remove from the tray, and use in a soup.

PULLED NOODLES

This is the ultimate noodle, long, slippery, chewy, and in expert hands of such remarkable thinness that it makes you gasp in wonderment. You've probably seen Chinese experts do this with a long skein of dough, twisting it around, waving it up and down like a jump rope to stretch the dough and then twisting it around again. It is as much dance as cookery. The best experts can pull the dough into thousands of separate microstrands. However, after a few years of practice I'm still pretty mediocre at this. I can pull a perfectly edible noodle, but true artistry might take a lifetime to master. A few tricks will help you make a pulled noodle at home. Most importantly, you don't need to do this special dough twisting dance: there are many other ways to pull a noodle. But first let's discuss exactly what makes this dough stretch.

If you are making an ordinary flat rolled-out dough, there is no reason to knead it extensively. Exactly the opposite is true with a pulled noodle. You want to build protein chains so tough and so long that they will stretch without snapping. That takes a lot of kneading, pounding, and even braking. The latter term is a very ancient technique that involves squashing the dough with a stick—or brake, traditionally attached to one side of the kitchen wall over a large board. Bread makers used it to develop glutens in flour so the bread rises well and holds its shape. It also does wonders on making a noodle chewy. Remarkably, and inexplicably, the width of the brake makes a big difference. A rolling pin works fine, but if you use a dowel or other wooden device, it should be about an arm's diameter. In China a very traditional kind of noodle is made with a long bamboo pole; the noodle maker sits on the end and brakes the dough repeatedly, squashing a small section at a time, until it is folded over and the process starts again, sometimes with successively thicker bamboo poles. At home, simply squashing the dough with your pin, a little at a time, from one end to the other will work. Fold it up and start again.

Also important is alkalinity. Legend has it that a source in China with naturally alkaline water made the perfect slippery noodle. Most Chinese noodle makers use a product sold by the Koon Chun company in Hong Kong and labeled "potassium carbonate and sodium bi-carbonate solution." You can find the bottle with its bright yellow label in Asian groceries in the United States. A tiny bit of this in a batch of noodles turns them ever so slightly yellow and gives them a faintly soapy flavor. Even ¼ teaspoon in 1 cup flour for 1 serving is sometimes too much for my taste, so I often use less. In Japan they use a powder called *kansui* (sodium carbonate and potassium carbonate) to make ramen, but I've never found it in the United States. You can also take ordinary baking soda and bake it for an hour at 250°F, and food science author Harold McGee assures us that it is a strong enough alkaline to be used in noodle making.[2] Chemically it's sodium carbonate after baking, the same as what in Chinese is called *jian*. There are also now available a few brands of lye water from the Philippines used to make pansit noodles. The Lucia brand is made from soda ash (sodium carbonate) and sodium silicate; the Tropica brand is sodium hydroxide. Each one works the same way, with a few drops mixed into the dough.

There is also a burned and mysteriously processed mugwort powder called *penghui* widely used in central China to make Lanzhou lamian. It's not available in the United States, so I can't recommend it. If you happen to find it, use the slightest amount very diluted in water, and rub some of the liquid into the dough after thorough kneading, which causes it to loosen up. Be sure not to add it directly to the dough or to use too much—doing so will produce an alkali burn on your tongue and palate.

Having said all that, you can make a pulled noodle without alkaline water too—it won't have the same texture, but it will be good all the same. To form the noodles, you can pull each individual strand separately by hand into long strips and toss them right into the pot. But the method I like best replicates that used in Japan for superfine sōmen noodles and involves two long sticks. In Japan huge racks facilitate stretching noodles this way, but at home you can have a friend hold one end while you stretch. You need to make a batch for two in order for this to work properly.

Above: Hand-pulled noodles resting before cooking

2 cups all-purpose flour
1 teaspoon salt
1 teaspoon wheat gluten
1 cup water
1 tablespoon oil for hands, more or less

Mix the flour and gluten first, then add the water and salt. Oil your hands and then knead roughly for a good 20 to 30 minutes. Let the dough rest at room temperature for at least 6 hours. Use both hands to roll the dough into a cylinder, twisting it in opposite directions as you roll it out into a long, twisted snake. Let it rest for another hour or longer. Then stretch the snake into one long noodle and wrap it around two big cooking chopsticks or other long sticks. My son and I did this and managed to wrap the thick noodle around the two sticks about 20 times, which would later become 40 noodles. He grabbed one stick and I grabbed the other, and we gently stretched by slowly walking backward away from each other until we were about 8 feet apart. That's a single noodle about 320 feet long. If you have a place to hang them, you can pull them even thinner and longer, just an inch or so every hour. In Japan they dry pulled noodles this way too. The noodle my son and I made was long and thin enough, so I just cut the ends and put the noodles directly into boiling water. The neatest thing about these is that in profile they aren't flat like a rolled noodle or round like an extruded one. They're sort of elliptical, and the surface is super smooth.

If you would rather pull the noodles individually, just cut your coil into shorter lengths and take each length right to the pot of boiling water. Pull each into noodles maybe a few feet long and drop them right in.

Another very traditional way to make these noodles—which is really a single noodle—is to coil a very long noodle inside a cylindrical basket and pull directly from the coil into the water without breaking the noodle. A very long noodle is meant to ensure longevity. It's an amazing thing to watch, especially if the noodle maker can toss the noodle a great distance into the pot. This is mostly for theatrics, as the noodle itself tends to be a bit uneven and clunky, or at least the few times I've had it.

If you'd like to try an easy pulled noodle, see the recipe for *uyghur laghman* in chapter 8 on classic dishes.

Pulled noodles are not only found in Asia though. In the town of Nuovo on Sardinia there is by many accounts one remaining woman who knows how to make traditional *su filindeu*, which translates as God's threads. It is very simple, but there's probably a good reason no one else can do it: the incredible skill required. It is made from a semolina dough, kneaded for a long time, rested, and then pulled into tiny threads, which are laid on a huge round mat (the *fundu*) and then repeated with three layers of noodles, each in a different direction. The whole circle is dried and then broken into pieces. These are cooked in sheep broth. It is said to be the rarest pasta in the world.

OTHER NOODLES

ALKALINE NOODLES

If you do like alkaline slippery noodles but don't want to pull them, here's another way to do it. Take 1 cup flour and 1 egg white and add ½ teaspoon alkali water and more water to make a stiff dough. Knead and brake the dough for at least 15 minutes in a sturdy freezer zippered plastic bag. Once it's flattened, fold over a few times, return it to the bag, and start again. This prevents your dough from going all over the place. Let rest for about half an hour, roll out, and cut. They will be very chewy. You can also substitute other types of flour here—semolina or a proportion of another grain. Boil and then be sure to wash these in cold water, which for some reason is essential to bring out the chewiness. Then add to soup of your choice.

BATTER NOODLES

A spaetzle recipe appears in chapter 8 on classics, but if you want to make an extruded noodle using a piping bag with a flattened tip, or some other device, here's a basic recipe that is truly the easiest noodle to make, period. You can even mix the ingredients in a zippered plastic bag, cut off a corner, and squeeze it directly into the soup. Mix 1 cup flour, 1 egg, and enough milk to create a thick batter. You can add ¼ teaspoon baking powder to make it a little lighter. Using wine instead of milk also makes it light and tasty. You can add herbs and spices—dill is a favorite of mine in a noodle—or any kind of powdered flavoring. Most importantly, if you have different tips for your bag, usually used for cake decorating, you can make some lovely shapes. I have added beaten egg whites to get a super-light fluffy noodle and even used a *pâte à choux* dough, which is slightly absurd as it makes something like a fluffy boiled pastry or gnocchi Parisienne soup noodle. But, if you'd like to experiment, make it with ½ cup water and ½ stick butter, boiled, with ¾ cup flour added. The whole is cooled and 2 eggs are stirred in well. Either pipe this into soup or drop tiny little nubbins of dough into the soup from a spoon. People will be perplexed.

More interesting: you can work other finely ground ingredients into your batter and pipe them. Finely ground salmon makes a fantastic noodle, as does shrimp

Above: A squashed cake decorating tip and piping bag make a great noodle

or any other fish. Ground meat or, if you really have guts, pâté, can also go into a batter noodle, but I think meat is better when put directly into the soup, not in a noodle. You can also add ricotta or another cheese and make the batter just a little thicker, add mashed potato or bread crumbs, and cut them into little cylinders as you squeeze the bag. It's a neat trick for making soup gnocchi.

Whatever you include the key is to have a tip that's not too big or your noodles will be too thick. The best results I've had were with a tip that I squashed with pliers and pinched at the edges so they came to a point. The noodles had a ruffled edge and a slightly wider chewy middle. Also avoid the tiniest round tips because the batter just gets clogged in them.

Above: A salmon-based noodle made with a piping bag and star tip

Below: The unusual shirataki noodle has no calories

 **SHIRATAKI**

This is the strangest noodle I have ever made, and doing it from scratch is more like an alchemical experiment than an exercise in cooking. Among everything in this book, this is one recipe where the procedure and measurements really need to be followed precisely or it won't work. I'm not sure if that makes it any less fun, because these are seriously bizarre. First of all, they have no calories. They also have no flavor. Weirdest of all, they don't get mushy the longer you cook them, and if you want to store them, you have to put them in water (unlike virtually any other noodle on the planet). You can actually buy these in a Japanese grocery in a block, green or white, that can be cut, or in noodle form in a little plastic bag filled with water. To make them at home you'll need to order a few odd ingredients. Konjac flour is sold under the Miracle Noodle brand. The calcium hydroxide is also used to make tamales, so you can find it in any Mexican grocery.

1½ tablespoons glucomannan, also called konjac flour
2½ cups water in a small pot
¼ teaspoon calcium hydroxide (cal, or pickling lime) dissolved in 1 tablespoon water
large pot filled with water not quite at a boil

Whisk the powdered konjac and water in a small pot and let it sit undisturbed on the counter for 10 minutes. Cook on medium heat on the stove, mix for 4 minutes, and let cool. Add the cal dissolved in water and stir in well. The whole thing suddenly becomes a solid mass. Gather this together and put into an extruder and extrude directly into the water, which is not boiling. Agitate the water a little so the noodles don't stick together. Raise the heat and boil for 30 minutes. Then rinse in cold water and store in water in the fridge until ready to use.

You can use these traditional Japanese noodles in just about any hot soup. They stay chewy and don't really absorb flavors, either. My favorite way to eat them is in a cold soup with fruit, even in a glass of sake with some lychees or mangosteen. They seem to offset the fruit nicely with texture. I have also extruded shapes of shirataki noodles. A fusilli die makes strange ragged tubes that look and feel in the mouth very much like squid. There are many possibilities. If you don't have an extruder, you can also pinch off little shapes and toss into water. The thickness doesn't seem to matter as it's not really cooking from the outside inward, like most other noodles. Curiouser and curiouser.

Cold noodles in sake with fruit

ADDING DEHYDRATED FOODS

I never thought I'd be endorsing a machine of any kind, but of every tool used in writing this book, the dehydrator is one gizmo I would have trouble doing without hereafter. Drying is of course an ancient preservation technology, and a few years back I built a screened-in wooden rack that slides between the openings in my trellis so I can put fruits and vegetable and even meat on the pitched, south-facing roof of my house, which gets direct sun most of the day. Mind you, I live in the Central Valley of California, where for a good half year there is no rain or even humidity, plus intense heat. In the summer it can get well above 100°F. Basically, I live in a dehydrator. If you don't, setting your oven to somewhere between 125 and 150°F and placing the food on metal racks will work fine. But the dehydrator—despite all the noise and who knows what kind of electric bill—can literally dry anything. It doesn't get very hot but mostly blows air around. The model I have is called Excalibur, which I am told is the top of the line. And I believe it.

In tandem with the machine I often use a small inexpensive coffee grinder exclusively reserved for noodle making. In small batches I grind the dehydrated vegetables into a fine powder. You can use this as a seasoning, and in fact I have had amazing results with tomato powder, pickle powder, even squash powder used as a condiment on sandwiches. Dehydrated and ground pickled Moroccan lemon is unfathomably good. But when you put these powders into a noodle, the results can be phenomenal—vibrant colors and intense flavors that hold up in a soup. These make every commercial colored dried vegetable pasta I've eaten pale in comparison. Homemade powders are also much better than taking cooked vegetables and working them into a fresh dough, as is often done with spinach. When you dehydrate the spinach, you can get much more into the noodle for much deeper

flavor and color. As a general rule I use 50 percent vegetable powder and 50 percent wheat flour bound together with egg. The amount of egg you'll need is completely variable, and there's no way to measure how much of a given vegetable you'll get after dehydrating and grinding anyway. You can also put a vegetable powder into a rice noodle or noodles made of other starches, but I've found that sometimes it can compromise the structural integrity of the noodle, so you are better off grinding them coarsely and adding just a small amount for visual effect.

Above: Gemelli produced by twisting red and green pepper noodles together

Below: Dehydrated vegetable powders mixed with starch can be worked like modeling clay

The exception to this is mung bean starch. If you add vegetable powder to an equal measure of this starch, and add water, you will get a vibrantly colored dough with a texture like modeling clay that is frankly the easiest noodle to roll out, and many colors will stay separate if you align them and roll between sheets of plastic wrap. I did this once with red cabbage powder, artichoke, squash, and tomato in stripes, and the noodles looked exactly like a Dr. Who scarf. The whole flat sheet was boiled in a paella pan and cut into noodles afterward.

The beauty of using dehydrated and ground vegetables is also that so many things you never imagined could be put into a noodle suddenly work in a snap. An entirely new world of possibilities opens up. Let's start with one that I consider the holy grail of vegetable noodles.

ARTICHOKE NOODLE SOUP

2 pounds baby artichokes
2 or 3 large artichokes
vegetables for stock, like carrots, parsnip, celery, fennel, onion

For many years I tried to get an artichoke into a noodle. I cooked the hearts and worked them into a dough. The flavor was lost. I scraped the leaves and tried the same. I thought of cooking pasta in the artichoke water, or maybe making a puree and adding noodles. None of these works. Instead, trim baby artichokes: peel the stems, remove the outer leaves, and snip off the top. Then slice them very thin and sprinkle with lemon juice so they don't discolor. Dehydrate them. It won't take more than a day, because there actually isn't much water in an artichoke. Crumble them into your coffee grinder or pound in a mortar into a very fine green powder. Add roughly the same volume of wheat flour and enough egg to bind into a firm dough. Roll out and cut into whatever form you like. Long thin noodles cut with a *chitarra* seem to work well (see chapter 4). The flavor is hauntingly bitter.

Cook these in a vegetable stock that has been made with artichoke trimmings and stems from 2 or 3 large artichokes. I like to add some fennel or oregano, which seems to intensify that lovely expansive stimulant effect on your taste buds caused by artichokes. The ancient physicians called it an aperient, which opens all the passages in the body, aiding the circulation and flow of nutrients. An aperitif is supposed to do the same, which is why it's made with bitter greens and sometimes even—artichoke. In fact, the Italian liqueur Cynar is made with artichokes.

Artichoke noodles: the most intense artichoke dish on Earth

Save the artichoke hearts, dice finely, and sauté in butter until just softened but not browned. Then serve the artichoke noodles in the artichoke stock, add a touch of milk or cream, and garnish with your pieces of artichoke. A few drops of dark, mysterious Cynar might not be amiss either. Or maybe even Fernet.

SALAD NOODLE SOUP

The most beautiful noodle soup I have ever made was a salad. I literally took all the ingredients in a salad and made them into noodles. They were six distinct colors and flavors: tomato, lettuce, carrot, cucumber, celery, and purple cabbage. Each was cut into thin slices or shredded, dehydrated, and ground into six separate and arrestingly beautiful powders. If you grind them fine they will amalgamate with the noodle in color, but you can also leave them just a little coarse for a speckled effect. As above, mix with equal parts flour and moisten each with egg to make six separate doughs. Working in order from lightest to darkest, roll each out into separate sheets and cut into noodle shapes. Because this is a salad and you want it to taste as such, I recommend serving this cold in a light vegetable broth, but add a drizzle of oil and vinegar to remind everyone what it is. But it is good hot too, in a chicken broth—you can go a little crazy and add croutons, bacon bits, Parmigiano, anchovies, blue cheese. Choose whatever you feel really should go in a salad, but keep in mind that the more you add, the less the flavor of the vegetables will shine through.

UNUSUAL NOODLE INGREDIENTS

This section describes various extraordinary and unusual ingredients that you might want to put into a noodle. Some are actually quite traditional, others simply tasted so nice that I must to commend them to you. No special equipment is needed for any of them, though you might want a dehydrator for a few. Let's start

Top Left: Dehydrated salad vegetables

Top Middle: Vegetables powdered in a coffee grinder

Top right: Powder mixed with egg and flour to form dough balls

Bottom Left: Dough rolled out into noodles

Bottom Right: Final salad noodles ready for soup

with one that I wanted to work so badly but was simply so dreadful that I include it merely so you can gawk.

 CRICKET NOODLES

In the fall of 2015, cricket products suddenly hit the market with a vengeance. Students in my Introduction to Food Studies class brought in cricket flour cookies, muffins, and power bars, and at a Food Tech conference we met entrepreneurs who raise crickets for human consumption. It's sustainable, high protein, affordable—many convincing arguments were presented as to why we ought to be eating crickets. None of the commercial products were that bad, though most were laden with a lot of chocolate so the flavor of the cricket wasn't terribly discernable. So I went online and ordered 100 percent pure genuine organic cricket flour. Of course I sang: "When you wish upon a bowl, makes no difference, dough will roll …" When it arrived I opened the packet and a rush of recognition hit me, so familiar, so palpable. Not Jiminy. You know that very distinctive acrid smell you note in pet shops? It's not pets, it's the crickets they feed to lizards and the like. As I worked in some wheat flour and water, the aroma became more intense. I could almost feel it seeping into my skin. I think if you did this frequently you might become a cricket. I did manage to make noodles, boil them, and taste them. It was one of the most singularly vile things I have ever put in my mouth. Do not try this at home. This is the only thing in this book I advise you to *not* make.

POTATO CHIP NOODLE

I admit a few weaknesses of which I am very embarrassed. Good potato chips are one of them, especially right when I get home from work with a nice cocktail. I try to make a bag last a whole week, but my kids usually devour them. This recipe was inspired by a complete accident, and frankly I'm amazed it worked. The process of making them may put you off potato chips for a while, but the final product really does taste like chips. First, in a moment of distraction you have to accidentally tip a bottle of really good strong beer directly into your bag of chips. I think I had Drake's Denogginizer. The chips should be just moistened enough to be ruined.

¼ of a 8.5-ounce bag Low-Fat Ruffles Potato Chips

a good glug of excellent high-alcohol super-hoppy IPA beer

1 egg

¼ cup potato starch or rice starch

water

2 cups dashi stock

Take your ruined chips out of the bag and crush them up with your fingers along with one egg. They will be surprisingly greasy and will smell rather unpleasant. Persevere nonetheless. Add about ½ the amount of starch, which should be somewhere around ¼ to ½ cup. Add enough water to make a batter about the same thickness you use to make pancakes. Pour the batter into a nonstick pan—there's no need to grease it. Cook on low heat until the mass begins to solidify, then turn it over and cook on the other side. Remove the big round noodle, let it cool, and then cut it into thin strips. Or you can cut it into rounds to replicate a chip shape. For reasons that elude me, this tasted really nice in a dashi stock, though I imagine any stock would do. Garnish with a sour cream dip made with instant onion soup mix. No, I'm kidding.

FLAMIN' HOT CHEETOS NOODLE SOUP

I don't know how these things came into my house, because they are just about the most falsely engineered junk food I can think of. What possessed me to turn them into a noodle I can't rightly say, but the technique actually yielded a noodle that looked and tasted exactly like the original snack, but in noodle form. This is the sort of thing you come up with on a weekend when you are so bored

A traditional dish of noodles made with blood

you would do anything for entertainment. These are pure unmitigated evil.

Grind 2 cups of the aforementioned Cheetos. Add 1 cup flour and 1 egg to make a lurid reddish dough that will be soft and sticky to the touch. Avoid touching it if you can because, yes, the coloring will come off on your fingers. Extrude these through a ricer or food mill directly into chicken stock, and they will come out exactly as they went in except smaller: short little brightly colored squiggles. To serve, I suggest you add lots of hot sauce to the bowl, maybe a few thinly sliced raw Thai chilies, lime juice, and sliced shallot. Then a good handful of chopped cilantro. Wait—did I actually eat this one?

BLOOD SOUP OR *BLUTKNUDELN MIT ZUPPE*

I am not including this recipe to gross you out: it really is a traditional dish in the German-speaking Alps and the south Tirol, where it is also called tagliatelle al Sangue. It really is delicious too. For years I was under the impression that it was impossible to find blood in the supermarket, but lately I have been able to find a regular supply of fresh pig's blood in the Asian supermarket. Perfect for late-night cravings (just kidding again). It will come coagulated, which is fine. Blood actually scrambles when you cook it, much like eggs. So it also acts as a perfect binder for a noodle but also adds a really deep rich flavor. The best way to do this is to put about 1 cup blood in a bowl and add the flour to it until you get a firm dough. Roll this out and cut into wide strips. Boil them directly in your broth.

The first time I made these I paired them with very untraditional dashi stock, some wakame seaweed, and fish cakes. It was very good, but I think a better choice is a stock based on pork itself. Or if you're using beef blood, then use beef broth. If you use perfectly ordinary vegetable garnishes like carrots and onion, they don't compete with your tasting the full flavor of the noodle. So keep the garnishes simple and unobtrusive.

ACORN NOODLES

A regular ritual of mine is to collect acorns from the park near my house. They just happen to be sweet from a white oak and need no leaching to remove bitter tannins. I get a lot of looks from people and angry squirrels poaching their acorns, but I remain undeterred. Most acorns require soaking in water, as explained below. Gather your acorns and put them in a cool, dry place where bugs are not likely to get to them. Native Americans wrapped them in pine boughs and put them on stilted platforms. Wait a few months until they're dry. Or put them in the oven on very low heat for about a day—they'll dry out and get just a little brown, which only adds to the flavor.

Remove the shells, then crush the acorns by hand in a mortar until very fine, or use a powerful blender like a Vitamix. Taste the flour. If it's bitter, put the acorn flour in a big bowl, cover the flour with water, and swish it around thoroughly with your hand. Let the flour settle, and pour off the water. Repeat several times until the flour tastes sweet. You will next need to lay the flour out on a cloth to let it dry in the sun. If your acorns are sweet to start with, just use them ground as flour.

The amount of other flour you will need to add to this is entirely dependent on your acorns, so I suggest taking a small amount of acorn flour and adding a small amount of egg and a little regular flour to see if it holds together as a dough. Equal amounts of acorn and regular flour should work fine, but if you can use a greater proportion of acorn flour, the better. You can either roll these out or extrude, whichever you prefer.

Pairing these noodles with native wild ingredients makes the most sense. So if you can get venison with bones, by all means make a stock and serve with slices of the venison. Steaks of farmed deer can be found frozen, and these can be quite good. Ground bison is also readily available if you want to add meatballs to the noodles, or simply add the ground bison to the stock for a chili-like texture. I think tepary beans would also go well. On the other hand, these noodles are reminiscent of good soba noodles, so serving them in a soy-based stock would also work well.

SAGITTARIA NEW YEAR'S NOODLE

If you look around the produce aisle in an Asian supermarket around late January or early February (Chinese New Year), you might find a box of some strange-looking roots, not unlike lily bulbs. There's even usually a little green sprout at the top. In Chinese these are called *see goo*; the Latin name is *Sagittaria*, named for the arrowhead-shaped leaves. They make one of the most interesting noodles I've tasted.

> 1 dozen Sagittaria roots
> 1 egg
> 3 cups turkey stock
> ¼ pound ground turkey
> 1 stalk celery
> 1 carrot
> 10 brown mushrooms, sliced

Peel the *Sagittaria* roots and parboil boil them in water for just a few minutes until soft. Chop them finely—the resulting texture is something like potato. Place these in a low oven or dehydrator until completely dry, and then grind them into a fine powder. These can be made directly into a noodle moistened with egg. No wheat flour is necessary. Either roll out or extrude into noodles and boil in your stock.

I happened to have on hand a really nice turkey stock that went perfectly with these nutty noodles. Cut up the vegetables into big pieces, cook in the stock, and add the noodles, which will just take a couple of minutes. Then serve. You could just as easily combine these with a rich Chinese chicken stock, a dash of soy, and some water spinach or other leafy green vegetable. Those would represent money in the new year. And if you contrive to make really long noodles, they will foretell longevity.

DIOSCOREA OPPOSITA NOODLES

Another interesting root that you can make into a noodle is colloquially known as the Chinese yam or *shan yao*. It's named for the ancient botanist Dioscorides, who was the first in the Greek-speaking world to identify it. You cannot mistake the roots, which are long and white and have little dark spots from which sprout a few root hairs. When you slice it, the root exudes a mucilaginous goo, which is why it's been used in Chinese medicine as a demulcent: it soothes irritated membranes in the throat and elsewhere in the body. For this very reason you can buy dried root slices in any Chinese pharmacy or even many grocery stores, and the powdered form is also not hard to find. I just like making them from fresh roots.

Peel and slice the roots and leave them to dry in the sun, oven, or dehydrator. Grind them finely. Add egg white alone to bind into a flour, because the whiteness of the noodle is truly charming. To roll these out, you'll need two sheets of plastic wrap. They're simply too tricky to roll out without support. Peel off the top sheet, flip over and peel off the other, then cut the dough into noodles and very carefully transfer to your stock. They taste a little like potato but are quite sweet and not at all slimy once cooked.

What to pair these with is entirely up to you. I used a white bone broth that had been boiled a long time to reduce, and the meat and potato aesthetic was nice, especially with some ground beef and a little kale. A regular beef broth would work nicely too, but there is no reason not to use whatever you happen to have on hand. This is a noodle as versatile as any other. Any place a potato-like flavor goes, so will these noodles. Fish stock and cod would be perfect.

TIGERNUT NOODLE

I'm not sure why tigernuts have suddenly appeared as a health food, but they are so sweet and delicious that I have to mention them. In Latin they are called *Cyperus esculentus* and are actually a tuber. In Spain and elsewhere they are used to make *horchata de chufa*, a lovely milky drink. I suggest buying the flour online, as the dried nuts are tricky to process. They definitely don't work alone as a rolled-out noodle. So essentially either hydrate with eggs and make little pinched pasta shapes that will hold together in a soup, or mix with flour and egg to make noodles. The little globs I made went very nicely in a Catalan-inspired soup that started with a soffrito of onions, garlic, and tomato, with chicken stock poured on and the noodle bits cooked right in the broth. But if you want to stick with a certain theme, these were also among the earliest cultivated plants in ancient Egypt and even in prehistoric Connecticut. I'm not sure what either of these periods suggest, maybe ibex broth for the former and for the latter wooly mammoth?

Lastly, I encourage you to mix flours to invent new noodles of your own. One I stumbled on is a simple hybrid of wheat flour and rice starch held together with egg and a little oil. I don't think such a noodle is made anywhere, but it is very easy to roll out and cut. It's a great noodle for beginners, and I am certain there are many other combinations if you're game for experimentation.

7

GARNISHES AND SEASONING

In this chapter we discuss the vast range of foods that can be used to embellish a noodle soup and the ways they are used to enhance the overall aesthetic appeal of the final dish visually, in terms of texture and mouthfeel, and of course as flavor enhancers. There are two basic approaches to adorning your soup. First—and this makes the most sense in terms of efficiency—is just throwing ingredients into the pot along with the cooking noodles. Timing here is much more important than you might suspect, because some vegetables or meats take a long time and would still be undercooked if you put them in with the noodles to cook, while others take just a minute and should be tossed in only at the end. Others are best added to the bowl right before serving or even placed in a separate bowl so diners can add them as they please.

An entirely different approach to garnishes is used primarily in Japan but can apply equally well to any soup is what we might call the *bol composée*, in which the vegetables and meats are carefully arranged and kept separate partly for dramatic effect, but also so diners can choose which additions can be eaten in an order that suits them. If everything is dumped into an indiscriminate mass, it becomes harder to fish out individual ingredients and taste them separately. For this reason the garnishes are usually much larger as well: whole slices of meat, large pieces of vegetable arranged discretely just as they would be on a plate. For instance, in a beautifully garnished bowl of udon, you might find carefully carved vegetables that would become totally lost if cooked all together. Sometimes ingredients are layered, hidden beneath one another so they are discovered gradually by the diner. If you think of your bowl as a stage, why would you want all the characters out at once? Introduce them slowly. Get to know them as the drama unfolds. This is not merely a visual trick—sometimes even tastes within one bowl can be gradually introduced as one plunges its depths. It may be for this very reason that in many

Japanese soups you will have soy at the bottom, another stock on top, and a third drizzled in right before service. Presumably, if done correctly, the dish changes as you are eating it.

You might also think of your bowl design as a landscape. Ideally the colors, textures, and volume of the ingredients should vary. Arrange them to alternate height, too, so you might have a mountain of noodles, a valley of vegetables, a river of broth passing through, a small hamlet of pork at the bottom. All the parts should be balanced in proportion and form, though not symmetrical. There should be straight lines and curves, rounded and angular shapes. Your eye should be led in a clear path through your bowl, as well. The time you spend in arranging can lend immense visual appeal to your meal. Of course once you dig in, everything goes topsy-turvy, but remember we eat with our eyes, too, and there is nothing as lovely as a well-arranged bowl of soup.

On the other hand, sometimes it is precisely the melding of ingredients that makes the overall experience rich and satisfying. For example, because you want the flavor suffused through the entire broth and joined intimately with the carrot and celery, dill merely sprinkled on chicken soup before serving, rather than cooked in the broth, would be visually misleading and disappointing in taste. In other words, garnishing soup is serious business.

Seasoning is no less serious, because without it your soup will be wan and flat. Seasoning literally begins and ends with the sea: salt, that is. As with all other seasonings, it goes in at the beginning, middle, and very end. The creative cook will probably want to avoid all commercially premade seasoning mixes, which constrain you to someone else's preferences and even brash stereotypes of what someone thinks should be "Mediterranean" flavor or "curry powder." Surprisingly, dried ground spices and herbs play a relatively small role in soup seasoning because they cloud or even muddy the soup. Whole herbs and spices are preferred at the stock-making stage, and if ground are usually only sprinkled on at the last minute. Fresh herbs are infinitely more interesting. As for the range of condiments that can be used in your soup, as you see in this chapter, the list in virtually endless, and they can turn a dull soup into something truly magnificent if used judiciously.

VEGETABLES AND FRUITS

A soup without vegetables is too sad to even imagine. There will almost always be vegetable flavor in your broth of course, but you want something else floating around with the noodles in the interest of contrasting color and texture, and of course added flavor and nutritional value. We proceed taxonomically because every family of vegetables works differently in a soup and adds very different notes.

Think of your root vegetables as the bass notes. They add sweetness, profundity, and yes, a bit of earthiness. There is almost no soup that is not improved by the addition of some carrot or parsnip. How you cut these is also vitally important. If you have a fresh noodle that would take three minutes, you need to cut your root vegetables very thinly so they cook in the same time, or alternately start cooking them in the broth earlier. Or you can cook them in a pan or roast them in the oven until perfectly tender but not falling apart, and then put them in the soup later. But of course if you don't want to dirty another pan, or if you want something lighter in flavor, just carefully time when you put in your root vegetables. A tiny dice, or *brunoise*, is about $1/8$ inch squared and is ideal for your quick soup. A julienne or fine strips take a little longer, usually about 5 minutes, and if you've cut relatively thick diagonal slices or cut in larger pieces then they should be cooked in the broth until tender with just a little bite, before the noodles go in. Or at the very last minute you can grate some carrot into your soup, which produces a fetching result.

There are also many other root vegetables you can use. Beets, yellow or Chioggia, can be visually stunning; red beets will turn the whole soup red, which is classic in borscht. Celery root and turnips add their own distinctive flavors in soup. Starchy roots like potatoes and sweet potatoes aren't heretical, but they do seem redundant, adding another carbohydrate to the noodle carbohydrate, so I generally avoid them unless called for traditionally. Some roots are untraditional but fantastic all the same in soup. Jicama works surprisingly well. Lotus roots are simply gorgeous, especially in thin slices and cooked minimally so they still have crunch. Most of the starchy roots mentioned I've turned into noodles themselves.

Later in this section I also include squashes. I hesitate to cook these very long, though a few squares of pumpkin in a soup can be very nice. Zucchini get mushy, and there is nothing worse than noodles in what appears to be a pureed vegetable soup. There is something cognitively dissonant about it, but if a thick amalgamated soup with slurpy noodles is your thing, then go for it.

Rounding out the bass section are root bulbs. They are essential, almost indispensable, and there is hardly any noodle soup that is missing at least a hint of allium at some point. In fact, the onion family usually plays a part in the stock, in the soup as garnish and often at the very end for decorative effect. Roast or boil onions and garlic in the stock. Garnish with leeks and shallots, and flourish with scallions and snipped chives. These aren't hard and fast rules though. Some stocks take scallions happily, and a finely sliced pickled onion can be a thing of beauty on top of a soup. And need I mention a little tangle of crispy fried onions floating above your noodles?

The mid-range notes are provided best by cruciferous vegetables and leafy greens. In contrast to those aforementioned, they are usually not part of the stock. In fact, the cabbage family should be kept far from your stock unless you like smelling brimstone. But cooked in the soup gently, so there's still a little crunch, any member of this family will glorify your soup. Cabbage is *Brassica oleracea*, and it's great for soup. So are all the forms found in Asia, like bok choy, and what they call baby bok choy is adorable. This family also includes broccoli, cauliflower, kohlrabi, collared greens, and yes, even that darling of the modern plate—kale. They're all different shapes of the same plant and are all perfect in your soup, cooked so still firm but not raw. To this list should also be included fermented brassicas, and you will be amazed at how good a little sauerkraut or kimchi can be in a soup.

Unrelated but equally useful are other leafy greens, such as broccoli rabe, which is just about the perfect vegetable on earth. Just finely shred a few leaves

and throw them in, and the depth of flavor is astounding. Escarole provides an equally interesting bitter note, as can finely shredded Belgian endive. You might perhaps balk at the idea of lettuce in soup, but it really is delightful and not uncommon in soups around the world. Would you ever have imagined that noodle soup is the ideal destination for your leftover undressed salad the next day? Chard goes nicely in a soup too, though keep in mind it's a form of beet, so it may color your soup. On the topic of spinach leaves, I am torn. Many people like spinach a lot, and in terms of flavor I have to agree. But the oxalic acid in spinach can leave your teeth feeling chalky and unpleasant. When spinach is cooked with fat or baked into something this effect is less noticeable than in a soup. When there are so many other leafy greens to be found nowadays, why use spinach? Try sorrel instead—it has a wonderfully sour flavor that sings in a soup. Dandelions and wild sow thistle are also delicious in a soup or worked right into the noodle.

Sow thistle is a flavorful addition to noodles

Legumes can also fill out the middle range of your soup composition. Obviously, long-cooked beans are deeper and sonorous compared to fresh green string beans, which add a much lighter, higher note. For all dried beans, including lentils and chickpeas and even dried field peas, you can play it safe by cooking them separately and then adding them later. There's nothing worse than adding a bean to a soup before you remember that you'd already added acid—vinegar or lime juice—which will prevent the beans from cooking through. If you're absolutely sure about the timing, then I say go ahead and cook the beans with other vegetables. If you cook them separately, it's up to you whether you add the cooking liquid to the soup. Much of the flavor will be there, though some will argue that so are the indigestible sugars that cause gas. If that's a worry, then leave out the beans. But the combination of a bean and noodle is really a match made in heaven. Nutritionally they are also perfect partners if you think of historic combinations like *pasta e fagioli* or miso soup with noodles.

The *Solanaceae* occupy the alto range in your soups. They're not always necessary, but some representative really perks up the whole, and most often I find tomatoes do the trick. They can be cooked long in your stock or even serve as the base. Tomato soup with noodles? Why not? Or even a smidgen of tomato paste in your soup. But I prefer tomatoes best just chopped coarsely and placed in the pot for a minute or two at the end, just barely cooked and still distinctly coloring your soup. In the summer I can't resist a great local tomato, specifically for garnishing a soup. Bell peppers can also be used this way, or they might be part of your trio of sautéed vegetables to start. A few strips of red, orange, or green pepper, or a combination of these, is beautiful in any soup. Needless to say, chili is also absolutely fundamental—see below under seasoning. Eggplants are Old World cousins in the *Solanaceae* family. They need to be cooked through, though there are a lot of soups in which they're really nice, especially in surprising forms such as baba ghanoush.

For the soprano section are your bright acidic and spicy notes. Citrus may not seem so important, but whenever you think a soup needs just a little lift, hit it with some lime. I adore the flavor so much that I have to resist putting it in when not called for. Likewise lemon is lovely, even orange juice, tangerine, grapefruit, calamondin (also called calamansi), Japanese ponzu. Would you believe that even kumquat does interesting things for a soup?

This upper range is also filled in with flavorings that come in at various points in the score but aren't always noticed as distinct elements in the soup. They can be aromatics, herbs, or even bottled sauces. They can give the entire soup character, some at the very last minute before serving or used ad lib on the table.

As a flavoring element, gingerroot is crucial in many Asian soups. It goes into the stock, or is cooked in a kind of mirepoix with shallots and added after, but you can impart ginger flavor into your soup in other surprising ways. I often grate it finely and then squeeze the liquid directly into the soup. It prevents solid pieces of ginger from spoiling a clear soup. To add aroma you can also just put in a few slices, which are not eaten. In soups, slices of comparatively tough galangal root are usually served this way, especially in Thai cuisine. It's sort of like ginger but more pungent and mustardy. Turmeric root will give your soup a bright yellow hue. Nowadays you can fairly easily find whole roots, which are highly preferable over dried ground turmeric. In fact, that goes for all root spices.

Latin and Italian cultures boost flavor by deploying a sofrito method: chop the base ingredients fine and fry in oil before adding to the soup. The basic principal is used in most other cuisines. The southern European classic is carrot, celery, onion, and a spoonful of tomato paste browned together before adding liquid. The same principal can be used with gingerroot, shallots, and tiny hot chilies fried in coconut oil, then adding a spoon of shrimp paste. Or try peeled turmeric, lemongrass, and crushed garlic, followed by a little tamarind paste. Mix and match any triad of vegetables and, if you like, add a concentrated paste to the mix to intensify the flavors.

If you're using dried and ground spices, most are best when toasted with the vegetables first or added as just a pinch at the end. That even goes for pepper, as well as coriander seed, cumin, and a range of other spices that go into a soup as a flavoring element at the end. Think of sumac or za'atar sprinkled on at the last minute. Or a dusting of smoked paprika. Or the ubiquitous Renaissance favorite, cinnamon and sugar. Still I think most spices are better off if used whole during stock making and then removed so that only their flavor and aroma remains. Saffron definitely needs long infusion to achieve full flavor and color, as does annatto, the preferred coloring in South America. Likewise long infusion for mastic, which is the dried exudate of the lentisk tree grown on the Greek island of Chios. You might recognize it as the flavor in retsina wine, but it too has appeared in soups histori-cally. If you want to get really obscure, the favorite seventeenth-century aromatics, ambergris and musk, have also been used in soup.

Herbs are another matter entirely. Many work fine in your stockpot, especially stems, sage, dill, bay leaves—and thyme. But most herbs should be chopped at the very last second and added to the pot or even atop each individual bowl. This is es-pecially true of those delightfully aromatic herbs that lose color if cooked, includ-ing cilantro, parsley, and basil. In fact, I will go so far as to say that the perfection of your soup will diminish in precise proportion to the amount of herbage it lacks. Without a sprig or two of an herb, expect a boring flat bowl without excitement or verve. Other herbs can stand in of course: tarragon, chervil, young dill sprigs, a frond of fennel tops, and even more obscure verdure like hyssop, summer sa-vory, borage, tansy, and bee balm; even hyper-bitter rue adds such an interesting note. Most of these you will have to grow yourself because they're almost never sold fresh, or even dried for that matter. Oh, and don't forget all the mints, which may seem odd, like chewing-gum flavor in a savory soup, but they are worth try-ing. Also, there are many herb-based sauces made fresh that work as a dollop in a soup—think of aioli in a fish soup, or pesto.

Bottled sauces have their place too. Some can be made at home with great labor, but for the purposes of soups, most are much better handled by experts. You can make fish sauce and soy sauce if you are truly adventuresome, but there are great brands to choose from to have ready at hand for a last-minute flavor boost. Most important—and bear in mind the havoc these powerhouses can wreak on your palate if abused—is chili sauce. A squirt of sriracha, a few shakes of classic Tabasco, Crystal, or Cholula. Not to mention a green chili sauce or smoky chipotle. Even the ludicrous sauces made from habaneros and Bhut jolokia labeled with skulls and other frightening logos are actually splendid if you add a single drop to a pot of soup. All these hot sauces are your piccolos and highest wind instruments. If you really want to make some at home, throw some chili peppers in a blender with salt. Let it sit in a jar for about a week to ferment. It will be delicious, used ju-diciously. But the bottled brands can be mighty fine.

For a really good chili oil, I suggest leaving a good handful of red Thai bird chilies out to dry. Or buy them dried. Then pass each one briefly over an open flame, the same way you would toast a marshmallow, just for a second on each side. Let cool, remove the stem, and shake out as many seeds as you can. Chop the chilies and heat gently in a pan with ¼ cup oil, 1 finely chopped garlic clove, and 1 teaspoon salt. Be careful not to burn, and don't breathe in deeply over the pan! Let this cool, pour into a jar, and let sit for a few days for the flavors to amalgamate. This makes enough to halfway fill a little glass spice jar and lasts quite a long time. A dab in a soup is plenty.

A few other indispensable sauces you simply must have on hand are soy sauce and fish sauce. The pungent aroma of the latter is thrilling to the core and should not be omitted in south East Asian soups, even if you are faint of heart. Worcester-shire sauce can also be put to good use, and I have been surprised how nicely a little prepared mustard perks up a soup. You definitely need a few miso pastes of varying hues and a tub of Korean *gochujang*. There are even some places where stranger condiments are actually not out of place—rose water in some medieval and Middle Eastern soups, for example.

Among these condiments I would also keep around vinegars of every variety, including balsamic, apple cider, rice wine, and malt. Chinese black vinegar is magical. You never know when you might need a dribble. Various types of wine, beer, sake, and hooch can be used in soup too for added flavor. A splash of sherry in your consommé, or port in your beef stock, can be divine. Oils can also be used for flavoring, especially toasted sesame oil, and in a thick Italian minestrone a drizzle of olive oil works perfectly too. On Japanese ramen you'll often find *mayu*, which is garlic cooked slowly in sesame oil until black, then blended into a bitter condiment.

There are a few interesting items you can add on the top of your soup at the end. A sheet of nori seaweed is traditional in Japan. Elsewhere you might see fried noodles, which add a wonderful textural element, sort of like all those bells and whistles you find in the percussion section. They are more noticeable than any other ingredients because they seem slightly out of place. Nuts I would include in this category. Just crushed can be interesting, but if you toast them in a dry pan, then throw in a little salt, sugar, and spices, the resulting crunchy bits add so much to a soup. Peanuts in a Southeast Asian soup, walnuts or hazelnuts in a European soup, and need I say that a pecan toasted with maple sugar makes not only an incredible snack but also a wonderful garnish for noodle soup. You can garnish your soup with almost any form of crunchy snack food. Fried pork rinds are exquisite and traditional in some noodle soups. I hesitate to suggest anything that will go soggy immediately, and for this very reason I don't think fried tempura bits go well in a soup though they are very traditional, and neither does popcorn. But a corn nut sure does, as do a few sturdy tortilla chips. Whatever stays crunchy will furnish the perfect decorative element.

Fruits can also be used to decorative effect, though obviously they fit much better in cold summery soups than in hot meaty ones. Still, you would be surprised at how well dried fruit like raisins or prunes align with the flavors of meat and some spices. Apricots with pork are sublime. This was a perfectly common flavor combination centuries ago. Next time you have a beef broth, soak a handful of raisins in sweet wine, add a cinnamon stick and orange peel to your broth, and you will understand the aesthetic.

TARE

Another species of garnish associated most with Japanese noodle soups could be profitably employed elsewhere: the *tare* (pronounced *tar-eh*). This is essentially a lump or pool of some intense flavoring placed at the bottom of the bowl that slowly melts into the soup as you eat it. You might find, for example, a lump of miso, so the soup is presented clear but then turns opaque, saltier, and more fla-

Braised beef presented elegantly in a simple soup

vorful as you eat it. The idea is brilliant, but why stop there? Imagine a lump of anchovy paste, shrimp paste, tomato paste, roasted mashed garlic, a wad of thick hummus, or refried beans. A spoonful of ajvar, a Serbian combination of onion, roasted pepper, and tomato that makes a soup magical, and the whole point is that it's a surprise—you don't see or taste it at first.

Traditionally, the *tare* in a bowl of Japanese ramen can also be a liquid, either *shoyu tare*, a soy base often combined with sake, mirin, sugar, sesame oil, and other flavorings. Miso is the fermented bean paste; *shio* translates as "salt" but often includes dried fish, seaweed, and other ingredients to create an umami-rice concentrated essence. Hakodate is the city most closely associated with this kind of ramen flavoring. These are the basic ways ramen soups are categorized as well, though the exceptions are so varied that no rule seems to apply.

PROTEINS

Just as with vegetable garnishes, the proteins can take just about any form your mind may dream up, from a few slices of leftover steak tossed in the pot to an elaborately prepared piece of meat braised, or smoked, or cured in some wonderful way. These turn an ordinary noodle soup into an entire meal, and although they're not necessary, I think a little protein, maybe 3 ounces per bowl, does improve it immeasurably. I offer many varied techniques in the recipes that follow, but here I want to inspire you to think creatively on your own, using everything from completely humble ordinary meats to extravagances for rare occasions. I also speak in general terms here about techniques that apply equally to flesh, fowl, and fish. Or to be more specific, these work with pork, beef, lamb, chicken, turkey, duck, and any fish or shellfish.

The slice is the most elegant way to garnish a soup bowl, and if you've had a really good bowl of ramen, you know just three or four slices of meat fanned across the top can be exquisitely minimal and delicious. These can be braised pork belly, thinly sliced boneless short rib or filet mignon, a leftover chicken breast—just about anything you can get consistent, even slices from. Usually these are cooked ahead of time, since the time in the bowl is minimal. Sometimes you'll see a breaded cutlet of pork or chicken sliced and added to the bowl. The crumbs will obviously get a bit soggy, but the advantage is that the meat won't be dried out, as it so often is with modern industrial animals that have minimal fat. Of course, if you can get free-range, happy animals, all the better. A neat trick for breaded garnishes follows here.

Fussing over design can be very diverting

BREADED CHOPS AND LEFTOVERS SOUP

A good shoulder chop of pork on the bone, lamb, or even chicken breast, breaded, and fried in a pan until golden brown is a wonderful thing. I have found that not only do I almost always have some leftover meat, but there are inevitably leftover crumbs and eggs from the whole process. This recipe solves both dilemmas. The quantities here are for a family dinner, with maybe 1 or 2 leftover servings. You can of course do this from the start without leftovers.

    3 chops or chicken breasts
    salt, pepper, and dry herbs
    1 egg beaten
    2 cups dry bread crumbs, preferably from good-quality stale bread, or panko
    1 egg
    1 tablespoon butter
    1 tablespoon olive oil

Season the chops well with salt, pepper, thyme, or whatever herbs you like. Sage with pork, and rosemary with lamb are both classic. Dip each piece in the egg (without dredging in flour) and then, on a big plate, press each into the bread crumbs to coat all sides. Set aside. Fry the meat in the fats on medium heat until firm to the touch and deeply colored on the outside, about 15 minutes for chicken and 20 to 30 for thicker chops. Let rest at least 10 minutes. Eat for dinner, putting aside a few slices for the next day. Mix the leftover crumbs with the leftover egg and season, add a little butter or olive oil and a drizzle of wine from your glass, maybe some grated Parmigiano, and press together firmly to create a stiff dough. Wrap it tightly in plastic wrap and put in the fridge overnight.

The next day, heat a rich broth to a gentle boil. Grate the hard crumb dough into noodles by squashing with the heel of your hand, through the grater and directly into the soup. Add a few leftover vegetables for good measure. In a few minutes, the soup will be done. Ladle it into a bowl and garnish with the slices of leftover chops, arranged in whatever fashion tickles your fancy. If you want to add fresh herbs or the like, no one will complain.

If you are not intent on fanning out the slices in this way, consider the technique of velveting, which keeps the meat much more juicy and tender. Slice the raw meat very thinly, season with salt or soy or whatever you like, and then dust with tapioca starch or some other starch. Just before putting the soup into bowls, slide these slices into the pot. They'll cook in about a minute or less, and the starch seals all the flavor inside. Trust me on this: they shouldn't be cooked long. If you prefer, you can fish them out and arrange on top of the noodles, though that seems silly.

Another classic technique for adding protein to the pot is to finely chop the protein (meat, shrimp, or whatever) by hand, roll into little balls, add a little starch to keep them moist, and plop them into the soup. These will take just a few minutes to cook. If you prefer to make a classic soup meatball, in Italy they would add crumbs, maybe egg, Parmigiano cheese, and herbs. In China the soup balls tend to be more finely chopped and larger, with shallot and gingerroot and other flavorings. Any way you like it is fine. Of course you can use ground meat, but the texture won't be as interesting. If you are really lazy, as I sometimes can be, just open a package of ground beef or turkey, take a few little misshapen pinches and toss them directly into the soup. It will still be quite nice.

You can also cook tougher cuts of meat much longer in the soup base that will ultimately become your noodle soup. Think here about stew meat, pork shoulder, or anything that needs long, slow cooking. If you like, you can remove a large piece of meat, shred it, put it back into the pot, and then add your noodles to cook at the end.

There are other procedures, however, that are worth the time and effort to make a soup magnificent. Tying up a piece of meat like pork belly or using a whole brisket, braising it long and slow in a pot, and then removing it, letting it cool and slicing it thinly for the top of your soup is both classic and remarkably good. I also like curing meat to make a quick homemade ham or corned beef, which go so nicely in a soup, as do a range of lightly smoked foods, not just ribs and chops but fish like trout and halibut. You can of course buy these at the store to add to your soup, but just beware that a little goes a long way. Smoke can be delightful in a noodle soup, but there is a fine tipping point where it suddenly becomes cloying and overpowering. So think literally a few slices of pastrami or a small portion of smoked salmon—just as garnish. Your star must always be the noodle, not the protein.

Many types of protein can also be added in dried form. Trust me: jerky doesn't work very well unless you shred it finely. But dried squid is really nice, and dried scallops are absolutely classic. Bacon, I assure you, makes everything wonderful, even a noodle soup, finely crumbled on top. Resist the urge to put in something really intensely flavored, like barbecued ribs or pickled herring, or anything that will suffuse the soup so intensely that you won't be able to taste anything else. Or use just a soupçon for extra punch.

Last, we must consider the dairy-based garnish. There are many soups into which a spoonful of sour cream, yogurt, or crème fraiche is both traditional and a great idea. The creaminess slowly melts into the soup as you eat it, whether it's a cold borscht, a hot beefy goulash, or even, though this may sounds strange, a fish-based Asian soup. Milk or cream itself can go into most soups to add richness and finesse. Cheese is a little trickier, because you want it either amalgamated into the soup or melted on top. And here too, Asian soups are not out of the question—in Japan they put a slice of American cheese on top of a bowl of ramen. I didn't say it was good, just that it is done. Grated Parmigiano is great on a noodle soup, or anywhere come to think of it. I also see no reason not to float a raft of noodles with melted cheese on top, as is done with French onion soup. Just be careful tossing cheese directly into a soup, where it might separate, become unpleasantly stringy, or who knows what else.

GLOBAL CLASSICS

(8)

In this chapter I offer noodle dishes from places around the world similar to what you might find if you traveled to that place or ate in a restaurant specializing in that region's cuisine. With historic dishes I provide a modern version rather than repeat what you might find in a historic cookbook. As elsewhere, I've tried to avoid modern conveniences, even though in many places they are commonly used in the home and even in restaurants. If you prefer to use a shortcut such as a dried noodle or a premade stock, by all means do. Full instructions for the more complex recipes from scratch are included in case you decide to go gung ho. Note also that some of these recipes call for basic procedures explained elsewhere in this book—check the contents or index. When a noodle is unique to one particular context, the recipe appears here. They are arranged in no particular order.

GERMANY: SPAETZLE

This is a basic batter noodle made with similar ingredients to a pancake batter, though a little thicker and actually worked up to develop protein strands in a way you would never do with a pancake lest it become tough. In Germany the traditional way to do this is with a *Spätzlebrett*, a little wooden board with a handle, but you can just use a small cutting board. The key is to put the batter on the board and, using an offset metal spatula, scrape long thin noodles from the edge of the batter directly into the boiling water or soup. Some boards come with a *Schaber*, a metal wedge like an angled bench scraper, which also works nicely in place of the spatula. You can keep wetting the spatula or scraper with the hot broth too, so the noodles slide off easily. It sounds difficult, but it is actually very easy, and since these are slightly irregular in shape it really doesn't matter if you're not expert at this.

Begin with 1 cup flour and 1 egg in a large bowl. Add enough milk to create a thick batter, plus a pat of melted butter, 1/8 teaspoon baking powder, a few gratings of nutmeg, and freshly ground pepper. With a rubber spatula, beat the batter for about 5 minutes until strings of dough form easily as you let it drip into the

Ohn-no khao swè perfectly balances salty, sour, spicy, and savory flavors

bowl. It should be thick enough to remain on the board without running off. Scrape the batter off the board into the soup. You can use a regular chicken soup, but a rich pork stock is ideal. Add 1 heaping tablespoon paprika or better yet your own dehydrated and ground red pepper. Slice some cabbage into the soup, and add a dollop of sour cream at the end. With this combination, caraway is really good in the batter and a glug of Riesling instead of milk. Be prepared to fall off your chair.

BURMA: *OHN-NO KHAO SWÈ*

Although you will find the name of this dish transliterated a dozen different ways, the name simply means coconut milk chicken noodles. It is sometimes hailed as the national dish of Myanmar (Burma), alongside mohinga, the wonderful fish noodle soup. Each is equally deserving of the honor. A probable descendant of *ohn-no khao swè* is the khao soi found in northern Thailand, where it evolved into many different forms. There are quick and easy ways to make *ohn-no khao swè*, but pounding the ingredients to extract their flavor makes a big difference, as does a good fresh chicken stock. The recipe works best with fresh medium-sized rice noodles. See the Basic Rice Noodle recipe in chapter 6 or purchase them in an Asian grocery. Dried noodles also work. This soup is also often made with thin egg noodles. The unique flavor comes surprisingly not only from the coconut, but from chickpea flour, which can be purchased or made from dried chickpeas whizzed in a powerful blender or food processor. You can also garnish this however you like, with hard-boiled egg or pickled mustard greens.

4 ounces fresh medium-size Basic Rice Noodles

¼ cup plus 2 tablespoons peanut oil, divided

1-inch piece fresh peeled gingerroot

1 small garlic clove

1-inch piece fresh peeled turmeric

1 small red chili pepper

1 skinned boneless chicken thigh, cubed

2 cups chicken stock

1 tablespoon fish sauce

1 tablespoon chickpea flour dissolved in ½ cup water

boiling water

3 fluid ounces coconut milk

1 handful chopped cilantro

¼ lemon

1 small shallot, chopped

Start by taking a handful of noodles and frying them in ¼ cup hot peanut oil for a few seconds, just until they puff up. Set them aside on a paper towel to drain and cool. Then pound gingerroot, garlic, turmeric, and chili in a mortar into a fine paste. Fry this paste gently in 2 tablespoons oil about 5 minutes. Add the cubed chicken and stir. Let it stick a bit to the bottom of the pan and cook through. Then to the chicken stock add the chicken mixture, fish sauce, and chickpea flour slurry (stirred well so it doesn't clump). Stir and let this gently simmer for about 10 minutes.

Put the fresh noodles into boiling water and let cook about 10 seconds, then drain in a colander and run under cold water to stop the cooking. Or cook and drain dried noodles according to package directions.

When ready to serve, add coconut milk to the chicken soup and bring to a boil.

To assemble, put the noodles in the bottom of a bowl and pour the chicken soup over it. On top add the fried noodles, cilantro, lemon wedge, and shallot. Add a little more ground chili if you like it spicier, as well as other garnishes.

 JAPAN: SOBA

These seem like the simplest of noodles, but perfecting them may take a lifetime. There is no reason not to make them fresh at home though. They taste so much better than dried soba noodles, which have a muted buckwheat flavor. You don't want to overpower their flavor either, so a simple *tsuyu*, or cold dipping sauce, is all you need. *Tsuyu* is a combination of dashi stock (see recipe in chapter 5), soy, and mirin. Nothing else. If you have a special cleaver for cutting soba, it does help but is not necessary. A bamboo slatted tray or zaru is also nice, to set the cold noodles on. The more proficient you become making these noodles, the greater the proportion of buckwheat to wheat you can use. Too much, and the noodles are too brittle, but too little and the flavor is not intense enough.

Mix ¾ cup buckwheat flour with ¼ cup all-purpose flour. Slowly drizzle in water until you can form a firm ball of dough. Knead thoroughly for about 10 to 15 minutes to incorporate the water, and then let the dough rest for 15 minutes. Roll this out into a large very thin sheet on a well-floured board. Watching professionals do this is impressive. Then cut this into the thinnest, even strips you can with a cleaver, using straight downward pressure. There's no need to make them too long either, or they will break in the pot. Keep them well dusted with flour so they don't stick together. Boil a very large pot of water without salt and add the noodles, not stirring around too much or boiling too vigorously, for about a minute. Remove and plunge into a bowl of ice water, swishing around with your hands to remove the starch. Gently drain in cold running water and set on a plate or a zaru draining mat with a little bowl of the dipping soup on the side. You can also shred a few sheets of nori and put that on top. Some people also serve chopped scallions and wasabi on the side, but there's no reason to overdo it.

You can also serve soba hot in a full bowl of the same dashi stock with soy and mirin. A dash of toasted sesame oil and a few sesame seeds go perfectly with it. When you are serving this hot, it's best to keep it simple, without added garnishes.

NETHERLANDS: GROENTESOEP MET BALLETJES

The name itself might be the best part of this soup. It just means vegetable soup with meatballs. The Dutch don't exactly have a great reputation for cooking, but I think this soup vindicates them. It's simple but good.

3 cups chicken stock or vegetable stock
1/8 pound ground pork
1/8 pound ground beef
1/4 cup bread crumbs
salt and pepper to taste
4-5 pieces broccoli
a handful of chopped cabbage
4 ounces dried vermicelli or fresh thin egg noodles (Basic Wheat Flour Noodle)

Groentesoep met balletjes is sturdy Dutch fare

Bring the stock to a gentle boil. Mix the two meats with the bread crumbs and season very simply. Roll the combination into little meatballs, small enough for a single bite. Toss these directly into the soup, followed by the broccoli, cabbage, and noodles. They should all finish cooking about the same time, unless you're using fresh noodles, in which case cook everything else for 5 minutes and add the noodles for the last 2 or 3 minutes.

CHINA: *SUAN LA FEN*—HOT AND SOUR SWEET-POTATO NOODLE SOUP

When people think of the globalization of the food supply after 1492, the first ingredients that come to mind are tomatoes, potatoes, and corn from the Americas going across the Atlantic and being slowly adopted in Europe. Or we think of cattle, pigs, and wheat going from Europe to the Americas. But equally important was the exchange between East and West. The adoption of new ingredients in Asia happened so swiftly and decisively that few contemporaries seemed to have even noticed. Think of the chili peppers, brought by the Portuguese to the west coast of Africa, then the Ottoman Empire, to India (where European botanists thought they originated), and then finally to China. Szechuan cuisine seems impossible without chilies today. Many ingredients crossed the Pacific as well, carried by the Spanish from Acapulco to Manila, from where they ultimately traveled to China—that route is probably how sweet potatoes got there.

Sweet potatoes are hardly an ingredient we associate with Chinese cuisine, but they became so important in marginally fertile soils that some scholars, such as Sucheta Mazumdar, speculate that the sixteenth-century population boom in China was due largely to the introduction of the sweet potato. China still grows the vast majority of sweet potatoes on Earth. Moreover, leave it to native ingenuity to transform such an unlikely root vegetable into noodle form.

Sweet potato noodles are made from the starch, and although you can buy them dried, they require very long soaking and then further boiling to make them palatable. I have had terrible luck with them—sometimes they even become tougher when added to soup, especially when combined with acidic ingredients. All the more reason to make this soup with fresh noodles. Should you doubt the thoroughly New World pedigree of this dish, consider the peanuts that garnish it—which also originate in South America.

These noodles are among the weirdest things on Earth. The batter seems to defy Newtonian physics, being solid in your hand under pressure, but a drippy glop if left to its own devices for a second. The technical term for this is thixotropy. The idea is to let the dough drip through something with very large holes directly into boiling water, thumping the device with your hand a little to encourage it. A ricer (without the lever) works, as does a colander with very wide holes. My best results have been with a German spaetzle maker while tapping the dough with my fingers, though you can also buy a device made in Thailand with holes of the perfect size and a tin plunger that fits inside.

Here's how they are made. This serves two people—it's too difficult to make a small amount. Put 300 grams or 3 cups minus 3 tablespoons sweet potato starch in a bowl. Put the subtracted 3 tablespoons into a pot and add 1 cup water. Cook gently, stirring all the time, about 10 minutes, until you have a thick slimy glop. Let that cool. Then add ¼ teaspoon alum (potassium aluminum sulfate)[1] to 1 cup room-temperature water to dissolve. Add that to the starch in the bowl and stir vigorously. Then add the glop. Pour this batter into your container with big holes right over a pot of gently simmering water. Thump so it drips down and makes long noodles. It's a bit tricky, but even short, slightly misshapen noodles are nice and chewy. Remove the noodles after a minute and rinse under cold water. These are the same as dangmyeon noodles in Korea.

Continue with the rest of the noodles, then proceed to the soup.

¼ pound ground pork

1 garlic clove, chopped

1 small knob gingerroot, peeled and grated

5 or 6 Szechuan peppercorns, coarsely crushed

3 cups pork or chicken stock

1 teaspoon soy sauce or to taste

1 teaspoon chili oil or to taste

1 dash toasted sesame oil or to taste

1 teaspoon Chinese black vinegar or to taste

1 handful fresh cilantro, chopped

¼ cup roasted peanuts and or soy nuts

Brown pork in a pot along with garlic and gingerroot. Add Szechuan peppercorns and toast briefly. Add the stock and bring to a boil. Add the other liquid ingredients. Ladle into a bowl, top with noodles, and garnish with cilantro and peanuts.

 ## FRANCE: CONSOMMÉ MADRILENE

This is a classic French technique put to new use. It sounds like very little bang for a lot of buck, but I think it's worth the effort if you're making a cold soup and really want to see the ingredients. More importantly, this strange clarification process somehow concentrates and intensifies the flavor of the broth, which is the real star here. The most important thing is to start with a good strong chicken or veal stock—remove every bit of fat by freezing the stock and scraping off the fat, which you can save for another use.

3 cups chicken or veal stock

1 egg white

2 small carrots, peeled and diced

2 stalks celery, diced

2 shallots, diced

2 ounces ground beef

vermicelli

tomatoes

Bring the stock to a simmer in a small pot (or a large one if you are multiplying the recipe). Mix together the remaining ingredients in a bowl and temper them by adding a little hot stock by the spoonful, maybe 6 or 7 spoons. Then add it all back into the stock and stir gently. Cover the pot and simmer at the lowest possible heat for 1 hour. You will notice a raft floating on top with all the egg, meat, and vegetables and impurities suspended in it. Carefully drain off the clear liquid into a fine-mesh sieve lined with two paper towels (don't use scented ones). Discard the solids. Chill the clear consommé, and remove any fat from the top.

Arrange in a bowl a mound of fine vermicelli, cooked and chilled, the most buxom summer tomatoes chopped into a fine dice, perhaps a few slices of cold roast chicken or pork, and actually anything you would put into a summer salad goes fine in here. I have even garnished it with globs of pesto, which tastes great but ruins the clearness of the soup after a few bites. A dab of rouille would go nicely too, or a dollop of thick yogurt.

THAILAND: BOAT NOODLES *KUAI TIO RUEA*

For this start with a mixed stock with part pork as well as aromatics like cinnamon, star anise, pepper, lemongrass, galangal. It's not completely different from phở but is not based on beef. What makes it unique, first, is that it should be served in a small bowl, traditionally right off a boat. Second are the garnishes, which can include a wild array of ingredients. What I had in Los Angeles at the Sapp Coffee Shop—which I am told is the best in town—included pickled bean curd, basil, fried garlic, a large and smoothly amalgamated meatball, pig's liver, spleen, tendon, pork cracklings, and probably a little vinegar and fish sauce. Everything was held together with a little beef blood, not in a cube but mixed into the broth and cooked. There were also some standard rice noodles, bean sprouts, and probably sugar. The combination does sound a little overwhelming, but it's very satisfying.

ITALY: MINESTRONE

This just means a big soup, and it's very easy to make, though if you ask any two Italians they will argue over what exactly should go in. What follows is my preference—if you'd like other things, go ahead. It is also absurd to offer a single serving, so extend this as necessary.

1 stalk celery, diced

1 carrot, peeled and diced

1 small onion, peeled and diced

2 tablespoons olive oil

1 large ripe tomato

3 cups beef stock

¼ cup borlotti beans or other bean, cooked until tender in water, drained

fresh oregano leaves, stemmed and roughly chopped

4 ounces uncooked small elbow macaroni

¼ pound ground beef

1 tablespoon bread crumbs

salt, pepper, herbs

extra virgin olive oil

grated cheese

Start by sautéing your *soffritto* vegetable trio in olive oil until translucent. Remove the peel of the tomato by cutting a little X in the base, dropping it in boiling water for a minute, and then running it under cold water—the peel should now come off easily. Remove and discard the seeds, then chop the tomato and add it to the pot. Add the stock and cooked beans. You can also use fresh beans, such as cranberry beans, and cook them right in this soup, which will take about 20 minutes. Add the oregano, and finally add the macaroni. These can be dried store-bought or made fresh, but dried is most common. Before serving, make tiny little meatballs with the ground beef and bread crumbs, seasoning with salt, pepper, and herbs, and then just drop them in the soup. Ladle into bowls. Before serving, drizzle a little olive oil on top and, if you like, a few raspings of Parmigiano or pecorino.

The variations on this are endless. Leftover meat can substitute for the meatballs. Surprisingly, this whole thing works just as well if you use fish stock and balls made of ground fish instead of meat, and then you can garnish with other fish as well.

 ## SINGAPORE: CURRY LAKSA

This dish from Peranakan or Nonya cuisine (a combination of Chinese and Malay cuisines) can be found in Singapore, Malaysia, and elsewhere with countless variations. This version uses thick rice noodles, which can be purchased dry or homemade (Basic Steamed Rice Noodle). The word *laksa* itself is intriguing. It is said to derive from Sanskrit *laksh*, via Hindi. It seems also to be related to the word *lakshen* for noodle in Yiddish, probably through Central Asia.

Sambal

1 tablespoon fermented shrimp paste—*belacan* (or dried shrimp)

4 dried red hot chilies, soaked in water and drained

1 tablespoon oil

Curry

2 peeled turmeric roots

1 teaspoon dried coriander

1 clove garlic

2 shallots, peeled

¼ teaspoon peppercorns

1 stalk lemongrass

1 tablespoon *belacan* (Malaysian shrimp paste)

2 tablespoons oil
½ can coconut milk (about 6 fluid ounces)
3 cups shrimp or mixed shellfish stock
3 tamarind pods

¼ block firm tofu
peanut oil
4 large raw shrimp, peeled
¼ pound thick rice noodles, cooked separately
handful bean sprouts

Begin by making a sambal, or chili paste, by grinding the *belacan* and chili peppers and frying lightly in oil. Set this aside. Then make a spice paste by grinding all the curry ingredients in a mortar or food processor. Fry this in the oil until fragrant. Add the coconut milk and shrimp stock (see Shellfish Stock recipe in chapter 5). Soak the flesh from the tamarind pods in hot water for ½ hour and then push through a strainer to make a paste. Add it to the soup. Let this simmer and reduce slightly. Cut the tofu into slices and fry these in a little oil in a nonstick pan slowly so browned on all sides. You can also use tofu puffs, which are prefried. Parboil the shrimp for just a minute. To assemble, put noodles in a bowl, pour the soup over, and garnish with pieces of tofu, shrimp, and bean sprouts. Last, add a bit of the sambal, however hot you like it. You can add to this chicken, cockles, or quail eggs. Feel free to use whatever you have around.

A great vegan variation is to leave out the shrimp paste and shrimp, substituting a regular vegetable stock (see chapter 5) for the shrimp stock. You can add more vegetables to make it more substantial and lively as well. In fact, if you are using dry noodles and a store-bought vegetable stock, this can be put together in a few minutes.

MEDIEVAL ITALY: PASSATELLI FOR MARY

These are somewhere between a noodle and a dumpling, although historically no one in Italy would have made this categorical distinction. In fact, the word *macaroni* was a generic term for all pasta shapes, many of which were what we would now called gnocchi, made with bread crumbs rather than potato. There's a scene in Boccaccio's *Decameron* in the land of Bengodi where the macaroni are rolled down a mountain of Parmigiano cheese into the mouths of the hungry people below. An extruded modern macaroni would never roll like that. In any case, passatelli do look and behave like noodles even though

Passatelli are a cross between a noodle and dumpling

they're based on bread crumbs. You can make these with a proposer passatelli maker—a metal disk with holes in it and a handle on top—or you can just use a cheese grater with wide holes and squish the dough through with your fingers.

3 beef marrow bones
1 cup finely pounded stale bread crumbs
½ cup Parmigiano-Reggiano cheese, finely grated
pinch grated nutmeg
½ teaspoon freshly grated orange peel
1 egg
3 cups stock

Roast the marrow bones in a 350°F oven for 1 hour until well browned. Scrape out the marrow fat and let cool. Take good stale bread crumbs and either pound them fine in a mortar or whizz them in a powerful blender—you want this as fine as flour. Add to the crumbs the remaining ingredients except the stock and mix together into a very firm ball. Add more bread crumbs if necessary. Let this thoroughly chill overnight. The next day you will have an absolutely solid ball of dough. Grate it with a cheese grater into long strips, directly into a pot of stock, either beef or chicken. Cook for about 2 minutes and serve.

If you are using the passatelli maker, you can skip the chilling overnight stage and just place a ball right on a board and squish the device downward and forward over it to make lovely noodle shapes. Another way to do it is with a meat grinder, which will make slightly more ragged strips. Other successful variations on this type of noodle can be made with panko bread crumbs, and even good cheddar in the noodle, though obviously unorthodox.

In the Middle Ages a common image was Joseph cooking a pot of soup for Mary after she had just given birth. The logic, according to humoral medicine of the day, was that the body needed a restorative (the word *restaurant* has the same meaning, and early restaurants did serve soups) that both contained concentrated nutrients and was easy to digest—thus soup. Broth makes perfect sense, but so does a soft noodle like these. We are never told in the paintings what Joseph was cooking, of course, but they do often look remarkably like passatelli.

PENANG, MALAYSIA: DUCK SOUP NOODLES

This state's major city, Georgetown, was founded by the British in 1786 as a trading center. Consequently, it attracted influences from throughout not only the Pacific but India and the rest of the world as well. This admixture of cultures continues to make Georgetown a vibrant culinary center today. These noodles are a common sight among hawker stalls, though derived ultimately from China and found elsewhere. The dish is unique in that it contains a slew of medicinal Chinese herbs. I wasn't able to identify several of these positively, but a few are not too hard to find. Dong quai (*Angelica sinensis*) appears to be typical, as do astragalus, codonopsis, and Solomon's seal. I was worried about the dosage though, so I offer a nonmedicinal version using only ginseng and goji berries, which are also commonly used. The noodles are called *mee sua* (misua), which are a very thin wheat flour noodle originally from Fujian province in China.

1 duck
1 tablespoon salt, divided
1 teaspoon cracked pepper
¼ cup goji berries
1 ginseng tea bag or other form of ginseng
¼ pound *mee sua* noodles
2 spring onions
a few bean sprouts

Cut up the duck into sections, removing the breast meat and the thighs. Put all the other parts (use all the giblets except the liver), lightly salted, in a baking pan and roast for 1 hour at 350°F until brown. Pour off any fat and save for another use. Put the roasted bones and other parts in a pot. Deglaze the pan with water and pour that in the pot and cover with water. Gently simmer for 2 hours, skimming the debris from the pot every now and then. Strain through a cheesecloth-lined sieve, discard solids, let cool, and refrigerate in a container. When cold, remove any remaining fat on top of the container.

You can serve up to 4 people if you use both breasts and thighs, but cook all the pieces and reserve for another soup later if you have fewer people. Sprinkle the pieces with remaining salt and pepper and fry these in a hot pan with reserved duck fat until the breasts are barely cooked through, and still pink, with the skin crisp. Remove them and set aside, loosely covering with a piece of tinfoil. Cook the thighs an extra 15 minutes until well done. Alternately, you can also slowly braise the thighs in the stock, but the breast meat will only dry out this way.

To assemble, heat the duck stock and add the goji berries. Add a ginseng tea bag or another form of ginseng; if you use the tea bag, remove it after about 5 minutes. Slice the breast meat into thin slices, remove the bone from the thigh, and thinly slice the meat. Right before service, add the noodles, which will only take a minute or two to cook. Serve with slices of duck meat in the bowl and a sprinkle of green onion.

 ## VALTELLINA, ITALY: PIZZOCCHERI

In the north of Italy on the Swiss border, buckwheat flourishes, as it does in many places with extreme climates. This noodle dish is a great way to use this resource and to generate internal body temperature to stave off the cold. The classic version is not a soup, but it comes so close and tastes so good this way that I hope you will try it.

1 cup fine buckwheat flour

¼ cup wheat flour

1 egg

2 cups chicken broth

a few leaves savoy cabbage or Swiss chard, shredded

1 small waxy potato, peeled and cubed

½ clove garlic, smashed

4 sage leaves, shredded

1 teaspoon butter

2 ounces coarsely chopped Casera cheese, Fontina, or young Parmiggiano-Reggiano

Mix buckwheat and wheat flours and add the egg. If you need a little water, add that too to make a firm dough. Roll out the dough and cut into wide noodles about 4 inches in length—longer noodles would break easily when boiled. Set the noodles aside and boil the broth. Add to it the shredded greens and potato. When the latter are barely cooked through, add the noodles. Fry garlic and sage gently in the butter. To assemble the dish, place the noodles, potatoes, and greens into a bowl with a little broth, add the crumbled cheese, and top with the garlic and sage. I have also included mushrooms in this dish and used beef broth instead of chicken. It's remarkably hardy and will have you yodeling in no time.

JAPAN: HAKATA RAMEN

Ramen is where this book began and more or less where it ended, as well, in the form of a pilgrimage to the city of Fukuoka to find what is acclaimed as one the great ramen dishes of Japan. Supposedly the word *ramen*, which first appeared in the late seventeenth century, is an adaptation of the Chinese word *lamian*, or pulled noodle. Whether that is true or not, the noodle itself did come from China and was said to have been introduced by the scholar Zhu Zhiyu, who presented it to the feudal lord Mitsukuni. Unusually, the noodles in this version are not cooked with *kansui*, the alkaline additive that makes them slippery and yellowish (see also under Pulled Noodles in chapter 6). That's more typical in Tokyo and the north.

Throughout the city of Fukuoka, one half of which was once the separate city of Hakata, you will find yatai, or stalls, most of which are no longer street stalls but are actually sit-down restaurants. But there is a collection of them in the industrial north part of the city near the fish market. There you can perch on a wobbly bench while you are served a steaming bowl of tonkatsu ramen. Watching closely, I think I understood what was going on. First, a little tare based on soy sauce is put at the bottom of the bowl, then the milky white pork bone broth, followed by a little drizzle of what I think was melted pork fat. It sounds strange, but the three don't actually meld completely together but instead suffuse throughout the bowl as you eat it. Precooked thin straight noodles go on top with a thin slice of pale braised *cha siu* pork belly and then a bowl of finely sliced green onions on the side, which are requisite. The dish doesn't look glamorous, but the flavor is remarkable. You could make these noodles by hand (see Basic Wheat Flour Noodle in chapter 6), but I don't think anyone in Japan does. There was no egg on this version, but I think it's perfect—boiled 5 minutes so the yolk is still liquid, and white barely set.

¼ ounce dried straight ramen noodles

4 pounds pork bones with a little meat (trotters, shoulder, or knuckle)

vegetables for the stock: onions, gingerroot, leeks, unpeeled garlic, chopped coarsely

soy sauce

melted pork fat

a 5-minute boiled egg, shelled and halved

1 thin slice of braised pork belly (see recipe in chapter on garnishes)

I would make a big batch of this broth and freeze whatever you don't use. Put the bones in a pot of cold water and bring to a boil. Boil about 5 minutes, then drain and rinse, scrubbing well to remove any dark bits. Return to the pot with fresh water. Place vegetables in a pan with fat and brown them thoroughly, then add to the pot. Bring to a boil and let boil about 10 hours, replenishing with water if necessary. You shouldn't need to skim the pot much, but maybe a little at the start. Strain this into another pot through a fine-mesh sieve.

Cook the noodles and rinse well before assembling the soup as described above. How much fat you add is entirely up to you. I'm not fond of sticky lips, so a teaspoon is plenty for me. But a restaurant called Gogyo makes what is called *kogashi shoyu-men*, which means burned ramen. What they do is take a ladle of melted pork fat and splash it into a searing hot wok, where it flames up dramatically. A spoonful of this is added to the ramen gives it a kind of charred barbecue flavor that's alluring. I would only try this outside, unless you have a good hood over your range and a fire extinguisher handy.

In Japan there is also a delightful custom of arranging a kind of half pipe flume from lengths of bamboo, pouring water into it, or arranging it under a waterfall and then sliding the sōmen—very thin noodles—down it. It's called nagashi sōmen, or flowing noodles. People stand all along the flume and try to snatch noodles out with chopsticks, and then dip them into mentsuyu, a dipping

Hakata ramen served at a yatai

sauce of mirin, sake, soy, and dashi. If you have large bamboo growing, saw down a few poles, then use a cleaver and a rubber mallet to split them. Carve out the nodes so you have smooth half tubes, then arrange the poles against a fence or over chairs—however you like to make a long course. The longer the better. Rig a garden hose to the high point so you create a stream, and then launch your noodles down it. Put a bucket at the end with a colander over it to catch those that escape. This is a great idea for a party. If you didn't have bamboo, you could take a really long split plastic pipe and create a flume too.

POLAND: ZUPA OWOCOWA

(ADAPTED FROM A RECIPE BY KRYSTYNA POWLUCSUK)

In the mountains in late July when the berries begin to ripen on the side of the road, pick the darkest, sweetest blackberries, at least a small basket, about a pint. Cover with water and cook these gently with just a little sugar and a slight suggestion of ground cinnamon and cloves. Mix 1 teaspoon potato starch with ½ cup cold water until you get a slightly thick smooth creamy liquid. Add this to the fruit, and stir so the soup is slightly thickened. Chill the soup thoroughly, or it can be at room temperature, but not hot. Add to this cooked and chilled extra-fine vermicelli. On top dollop a little sour cream.

YUNNAN, CHINA: CROSSING THE BRIDGE NOODLE SOUP

The story of this soup goes that a scholar wanted to find a place to study uninterrupted. So he chose an isolated island reachable only by a narrow foot bridge. Every day his wife would come and bring him a bowl of soup, which was cold by the time it got there. Being ingenious, she decided to bring the noodles separately and take the broth in a different container covered in a layer of fat, which would keep the heat in. When she arrived, they were mixed at the last minute, making a perfect bowl of hot noodle soup. The soup itself is simple: a good broth, an egg, some thinly sliced beef, tofu skins, ordinary round rice noodles, cilantro, and green onions, and then to top it off a tad of hot chili oil and a shot of vinegar. To replicate the aesthetic of the soup, serve the noodles and broth separately, to be mixed at the table. If you want to add the layer of fat, go ahead.

SWITZERLAND: CHARD NOODLE SOUP

1 bunch Swiss Chard, stems removed
water
1 cup flour
1 tablespoon olive oil
3 cups chicken stock
grated Swiss cheese

I would never have imagined that Swiss chard could be so remarkably aromatic, but it is. Just chop the leaves finely and cook them down in olive oil. Add a little water and then mix with flour. It makes a beautifully flecked dough. You can roll this out and cut, but I prefer to shape these by hand. Take two small gnocchi paddles. Place a thumbnail-sized lump of dough on one and with the other facing the opposite direction, roll them apart, applying light pressure. What you have in the end is called cavatelli, but it goes by various other names elsewhere. It looks rather like *gnocchetti* but is indeed a noodle, shaped like grubs. If you want to lighten these, a couple tablespoons of ricotta in the dough would not be out of place at all, but then squeeze the water out of the greens and add an egg to bind it together. How to serve these? I think in a simple clear chicken or vegetable stock, nothing else but a good grating of hard cheese, from Switzerland of course. How about Appenzeller or raclette? The noodles will tinge the soup slightly red.

With this same technique you can make noodles from just about any cooked leafy green—kale, mustard greens, or broccoli rabe, which is divine. If you prefer to make a really hearty meal of these, a few pieces of sausage would go nicely.

MOROCCO: HARIRA

This is marvelous soup eaten especially to break the fast in the evening during Ramadan, but you can eat it any time. The key is to include a range of filling ingredients entirely of your choosing, though it's the combination of beans and noodles that give this soup real heft. Usually harira contains fava beans, chickpeas or lentils, onions, tomato, and lamb. The spices also make it unique: turmeric makes it yellow, gingerroot and paprika give it bite, cinnamon and cumin makes it a little aromatic, and parsley gives it a brightness, along with lemon juice. The fat normally used is a fermented butter called smen, in which the onions and lamb are cooked, but ordinary butter works fine. To finish it all, broken dried vermicelli make this a proper noodle soup. I haven't given measurements here because it really doesn't need any—add exactly what you like, tasting as you go.

Start by frying the onion in butter. Cut the lamb shoulder into fine strips, add it to the pot, and brown. Then add all the spices and let them toast a bit. Add water, lentils, crushed peeled tomatoes, and diced celery. Cook just until the lentils are cooked through. Add the other beans, which have been cooked separately in water and drained, plus the broken vermicelli. Test to see when the vermicelli are done. Before serving add a handful of finely chopped parsley and the juice of 1 lemon.

ITALY: PASTA E FAGIOLI

(AKA PASTA FAZOOL IN THE UNITED STATES)

This is one of those simple comforting soups you can either throw together using canned beans, tomato sauce, and dried pasta, or lavish more attention to with fresh beans, and so forth. It's good however you make it. Many people cook the beans directly in the pot, which sometimes works fine, especially if they're fresh. If the beans have been sitting on the shelf for ages, it's a better idea to cook them separately in salted water, drain, and add to the soup so they are cooked through and still retain their shape.

    1 slice pancetta, diced
    1 small onion, chopped
    1 carrot, peeled and chopped
    1 stalk celery, chopped
    3 cups chicken broth
    1 cup cranberry or cannellini beans, cooked
    ¼ pound ditalini or small macaroni
    grated cheese, chopped parsley, olive oil optional

Gently heat the pancetta in a pan to render the fat. Add the onion, carrot, and celery, and cook in the fat with the pancetta, but don't brown. Add the chicken broth, beans, and small pasta, and simmer until the pasta is cooked but still firm. At the end you can sprinkle Parmigiano, parsley, and a drizzle of olive oil over.

SALENTO, ITALY: SAGNE 'NCANNULATE

This noodle technique is delightful. Use a regular egg-based dough, or something colorful made with dried squash, a green vegetable, or even beets. For a spectacular effect, make several different colors (see the Using Dehydrated Ingredients section in chapter 6). Just roll out the sheet of pasta, and use a pastry cutter with a fluted wheel to cut wide noodles that will have wavy edges. Then hold one end of each noodle down, and with the other hand twist—the edges will line up and create a hollow cane. Try not to crush these—just set aside and let dry to preserve the shape. Boil gently and add to whatever stock you like.

TIBET: THENTHUK

This is a hearty soup for winter, one of many versions which are generically called thukpa, which means soup. This is a wide flat noodle that's pulled and absolutely simple to make. This is a vegetarian version, though you can also add lamb, beef, or yak, browned at the beginning. In Nepal it would have more aromatic spices, which you can also add: coriander, cumin, and asafetida. If you're climbing mountains, make it as rich as you can with fat—a knob of fermented butter perhaps.

1 cup flour
water to make a moderately firm dough
¼ cup oil
1 clove garlic, peeled and chopped finely
1 knob gingerroot, peeled and chopped finely
1 turmeric root, peeled and chopped finely
1 tomato, chopped
3 cups water
handful spinach leaves, chopped
½ cup chopped cabbage
1 small potato, peeled and cut into slices
salt to taste

Mix flour with water and roll into a long coil, coat with oil, and let rest 1 hour. Start the soup by frying garlic, gingerroot, turmeric, and spices if you like; then add the tomato. Add 3 cups water and simmer. Add remaining vegetables and salt to taste. When the vegetables are cooked, flatten the coil of dough with your well-oiled fingers so it is a long flat strip, about 1 foot long or more. Then pinch the end and pull off rectangular noodles and throw directly into the pot, letting them cook a few minutes.

 **IRAN: ASH-E RESHTEH**

This direct descendant of medieval soups has relatives all around the world, wherever you see thin noodles and beans together. I think the best way to do this is with a lot of greens so the texture isn't too heavy, but the soup should be thick. It's traditionally served as part of the New Year's Nowruz celebrations. Note, this uses no stock and it's vegetarian. If you want to make it vegan, substitute a non-dairy yogurt or cream.

1 small onion, chopped
1 clove garlic, chopped
olive oil
½ cup dried black-eyed peas or other small beans, lentils too if you like
½ cup dried chickpeas
1 teaspoon salt or more to taste
5-6 leaves kale or 1 handful of spinach, finely chopped
¼ pound thin noodles
¼ cup strained yogurt or kashk
1 tablespoon mint oil (mint leaves and olive oil—not essential oil of mint, which has medicinal uses, nor mint extract)

Start by frying onion and garlic in olive oil in a pot until very lightly brown. Add the beans and chickpeas barely covered with water and no salt. After a ½ hour, when the beans have just begun to soften but are not yet cooked through, add the salt. (If you're pressed for time, just use canned beans instead.) Then add all the greens and cook another 15 minutes or so. Last, add the thin noodles. Angel hair pasta is fine, as is any homemade noodle. Right before serving it is traditional to stir in kashk, which is a fermented dairy product that has been dried and reconstituted. If you can't find it, strained yogurt comes close. The mint oil can be made by pounding a few peppermint leaves in olive oil; drizzle this over the top at the end.

 PERU: SOPA CRIOLLA

Peru is one of those places that so thoroughly mixed cultures from around the world, ingredients, and culinary traditions that these have now become seamless. The noodle soup tradition goes back to colonial times, and fascinatingly there is also a large Japanese community that brought an entirely different set of noodle soups. This recipe comes from the first admixture.

¼ pound beef chuck, round, or sirloin, chopped finely by hand

2 tablespoons olive oil

salt and pepper to taste, cumin, and dried oregano

1 small red onion, chopped

1 clove garlic, finely chopped

1 small hot ají amarillo (yellow chili), finely chopped

1 large tomato, chopped

3 cups water

1 small potato, peeled and cubed

4 tablespoons evaporated milk

¼ pound angel hair pasta

1 egg

corn on the cob, cut into rounds (optional)

Fry beef in olive oil until well browned. Add salt, pepper and a pinch each of cumin and oregano. Add onion and garlic and keep frying. Add ají, the hotter the better. If you can't find this kind of chili pepper, a yellow scotch bonnet will also blow your top off. Use a small piece if you are timid. Then add the tomato. Continue to fry gently until everything is cooked down. Add water and potato cubes, then milk. Fresh milk would be fine too. Cook until the potato is soft. Add the pasta and boil until cooked. Before serving you can either poach an egg right in the soup or break it in and stir vigorously like an egg drop, whichever you like. Or fry the egg sunny side up and top the soup with it before serving. I really like a few slices cut from a corn on the cob in there too—just cook it for a few minutes at the end after the pasta goes in.

 INDONESIA: CENDOL

Similar cold refreshing noodle drinks are found throughout Southeast Asia and are made with a green rice noodle colored with pandanus leaf. It's hard to find, so I think coloring the noodle with any green vegetable is fine, and certainly preferable to food coloring. After that, it's mostly up to you what to add.

> 1 batch regular rice noodles colored green (see Basic Rice Noodle recipe, ch. 6)
>
> 1 can (14 fluid oz.) coconut milk, or fresh coconut, grated, steeped, and squeezed
>
> 1 tablespoon palm sugar
>
> cooked red beans
>
> fresh tropical fruit like mango, papaya, jackfruit, durian

Cendol, here made with white rice noodles, is cold and refreshing for summer

Form the noodles and chill. Dissolve the palm sugar in the coconut milk and then chill. Arrange the noodles in a glass dessert dish or cup and garnish with beans and fruit of your choice. All the ingredients should be ice cold, and you can add ice as well.

 POLAND: KLUSKI LANE

This is a kind of poured noodle, similar to spaetzle, but this has a thicker batter that's either drizzled into the soup from a fork or poured from a pitcher at a height. If you can manage to pour a thin steady stream, you get long noodles. They are really good boiled in water, thoroughly drained, then fried in butter. They're often served as a side dish just like that, but you can also add some chicken broth.

POLAND: CZERNINA

This soup is rather more complicated than kluski and a lot more interesting. Just be sure to pronounce it right: *cha NEE nah*. It's a black soup made with duck blood. If you don't have a live duck to kill, use pig or beef blood from your local butcher. Arguably the most comforting soup for heartbreak, czernina is traditionally given to a young man if the parents of his loved one reject his marriage proposal.

> 3 cups pork or duck broth
>
> 1 cinnamon stick, a few cloves, allspice, whole peppercorns
>
> 1 handful dried fruit, including raisins, apples, pears
>
> ½ cup pork blood
>
> 2 tablespoons apple cider vinegar
>
> 4 ounces thin dried wheat noodles

Start by heating the broth with the spices tied in cheesecloth until suffused with spice, about 45 minutes. Then add dried fruit. In a bowl, add vinegar to the blood and mix thoroughly until smooth. Add some broth into the blood mixture to temper, and then add it back into the soup. Simmer gently and finally add the noodles and simmer until they become soft. There's a similar soup in Sweden called svartsoppa—again meaning black soup.

GREECE: TRAHANAS OR TARHANAS

These are a simple kind of tiny noodle bit invented I am sure as a way to store flour and milk, found not only in Greece but throughout the Balkans, Turkey, Armenia, and Iran. The word might be related to the Greek word *trakton* and Latin *tracta*, both of which mean to "draw out" or roll out a sheet of dough. These were cracker-like sheets that were broken up and added to various dishes as a thickener, quite possibly an ancestor of the noodle. My favorite is in the ancient cookbook, attributed to Apicius, which has a recipe for minutal of apricots and pork thickened with tracta. There are other etymological speculations, but by the Middle Ages the dish certainly took a form very similar to what is eaten today, not exactly a cracker thickener or a noodle, but somewhere in between.

The quick and easy way is to mix a good thick Greek yogurt with flour until you get a soft dough. You can use regular flour, semolina, or even crushed bulgur wheat. Each gives you a very different final texture. Roll this out into sheets and place them in the sun or warm oven. Then, when completely dry, smash them up into small pieces and store in a jar.

When ready to cook, lightly cook the dried dough bits in olive oil. Add either milk or broth, and vegetables if you like, but these aren't necessary. Maybe crumble some feta on top and add a sprig of dill.

For the sake of experimentation, if you have access to raw milk you can also make these entirely from scratch the way the ancients did. If left on the counter, pasteurized milk will rot and curdle and is definitely not edible. If unpasteurized it will become host to bacteria, which will sour it—the pH drops, making it inhospitable to pathogens and essentially preserving it. Start with whole wheat grains and grind them in a stone hand quern or other mechanical milling device. This gives you exactly the right texture—modern milled flour is too fine for this recipe. Mix this coarse whole wheat flour into the raw milk and add salt. Knead to incorporate all the flour, and you will have a rough dough. Draw it out on a wooden board and leave outside in the sun or warm oven. It will turn sour and dry thoroughly. Break these up about the size of granola and store until ready to use. I would cook these in broth with wild bitter greens.

SLOVAKIA: PULLED NOODLES

About the time I was trying to perfect my Chinese lamian—to little avail, I might add—I happened to take a boat from Vienna to Bratislava for fun. As I was wandering through the market on a very cold windy day, I came across a woman (wearing a babushka) with a wad of dough in her hand, pulling long thin noodles and tossing them into a huge pot of soup. She seemed a little agitated after I stood staring for about 10 minutes, at which point she said what I can only assume meant "they're just noodles," then laughed a little and asked if I wanted some. They were just noodles, but how did she get them to do that? It turns out all you need to do is vigorously knead a basic dough of flour and water for about 30 minutes. Slap it down on the board a few times, squash it with your rolling pin. The glutens like this kind of abuse. Put the dough in a big bowl, cover it with oil, place a cloth on top, and forget about it for at least an hour—two is even better. Then pinch off a piece and roll a long coil between your palms. From the tip of this, pull long strands until they break off. You might be able to get fairly long noodles with a little practice. Throw them right into the soup. An ordinary rich chicken stock is perfect, and nothing else. But if you want to add a little cabbage, that would be nice.

SHIRAZ, IRAN: FALOODEH

This is more of a dessert than a soup per se, but it's a really fascinating use for noodles—it's the original snow cone. You can use store-bought dried rice angel hair pasta, but it's not hard to make at home. The garnish can be any type of fruit, but grapes befit the origin of this dish.

1 cup water

1 cup sugar

3 tablespoons rose water (not essence)

1 cup rice starch

3 cups water

1 cup dark red wine grapes or shiraz wine

grapes to garnish

Over medium heat, dissolve the sugar in the water; then cool and add the rose water. Chill thoroughly in the freezer. Mix the rice starch with water and cook in a nonstick pan over medium heat, constantly stirring, until a firm ball of dough results. Let this cool at least half an hour. Extrude this into a bowl of ice water and let rest there without agitating too much. Meanwhile, crush the grapes and reduce over medium-high heat into a syrup, or alternately cook down the wine into a thick syrup. Let this chill thoroughly. Mix the sugar syrup into the noodles and return to the freezer. After an hour, scrape with a fork as if you're making a granita, and return to the freezer. Do this a second time to get a fine frozen slush. When solid, put into dessert glasses, pour over the grape syrup, and add a few more grapes as garnish. In lieu of the grapes, you can be more traditional and use lime juice and berries.

SPAIN: FIDEUÀ A BANDA

This is a slightly irregular way to make this dish, so perhaps it shouldn't be called classic, but in Catalunya, people have been playing with recipes for a long time, so perhaps this isn't too far off the mark. Legend has it that this noodle dish was invented in Gandia by Joan Batiste Pascual, who was better known as Zabalo, a century ago when he was feeding fishermen paella and ran out of rice. Actually, this technique of frying the noodles first goes back many centuries and is descended ultimately from the Middle East, arriving to Spain courtesy of the Moors, who ruled Spain after AD 711. Nowadays people use a thin short vermicelli-like noodle, but you can also make this from scratch.

1 cup flour
1 egg
pinch of salt
1 tablespoon olive oil
1 small onion, finely chopped
1 carrot, peeled and diced
1 stalk celery, diced
1 teaspoon fresh tarragon, chopped
1 quart fish stock or shellfish stock
pinch saffron strands
5 shrimp, peeled or any other shellfish
a handful of squid chopped into rings, tentacles separated
1 small piece of firm-fleshed fish, chopped into large cubes

Make a very hard dough from flour, egg, and salt; let this sit uncovered for 1 hour. Then grate it into strips by pushing it through with the palm of your hand, that is, not like you would grate a piece of hard cheese, but by sort of rubbing it though the holes in an upward motion. Let these strips dry completely. In a paella pan or other large, shallow pan, heat the olive oil. Toss in about 4 ounces of the *fideos* and cook gently until lightly browned all over. Then add in onion, carrots, celery, and tarragon, and cook until opaque. Slowly add in the fish stock in which the saffron strands have been soaking. You can also cook the shrimp shells in the stock for extra flavor. Cook this on low without stirring until the noodles have soaked up the stock. I like to cover the pan and turn the heat down, though normally people will just keep adding stock until everything is cooked. A few minutes before serving, bury the shrimp, squid, and fish in the noodles and let them cook through. Here is the really untraditional twist: arrange the noodles and fish in bowls and pour on more hot stock so you have a noodle soup. If you can find it, squid ink will turn the entire dish black. I had it like that not long ago in Girona and it was amazing.

XINJIANG, CHINA: UYGHUR LAGHMAN

These noodles can be found all through Central Asia, the former Soviet Republics, and into Russia. The word is likely a variation of *la mian*, and it is a pulled noodle similar to the Chinese version that seems to have traveled along the Silk Road with traders. The technique is a little different from that used in China, as well as a lot easier. This is the pulled noodle for beginners. The batch is for 3 or 4 servings because the dough itself is much easier to work in this volume.

3 cups all-purpose flour
1 egg
1 teaspoon salt
1 cup water
1 cup olive oil, or as needed

Put the flour into a large bowl with a stable base and add the egg and salt. Start working the dough by grabbing fistfuls, squeezing, and then pressing them into the bottom of the bowl. Sprinkle on a little water with your fingers now and then. Work this ragged dough, constantly adding water a little at a time, for 15 minutes. Very slowly it will come together as a dough, but it should be very stiff and a little difficult to work with. Press down on the dough with your fists. Then cover it with plastic wrap and leave it for 1 hour. After that time, roll out the dough with a rolling pin on a wooden board to about ½ inch thick and 12 inches long. Rub oil all over the dough and cut it into strips about ½ inch wide. Oil these well, cover, and let them rest in a bowl about 15 minutes.

Now technique is essential. With your well-oiled fingers horizontal to a wooden

The coiling stage of handmade *laghman* noodles

board, roll each strip out back and forth slowly moving your hands apart so the 1-foot-long strip is gradually perfectly evenly round and about 3 feet long. You'll have to let it drape over the side of the board and pull it along as you roll it. The diameter will be about ½ inch (the same as a Sharpie marker). Coil these on a plate starting from the inside and working out, keeping them well oiled all the time and layering when you get to the outer edge of the plate. You will get about 12 coils in two layers. Cover these in plastic and let rest for about an hour.

Here's the final stretch. Using the same finger rolling technique, with oiled hands, start at one end of the noodle, roll back and forth with one hand and pull *very* gently with your other hand. Pulling in the same direction all the time, make your way all the way down the noodle. Then start again, again going in the same direction. It should take two or three runs of pulling and stretching to get your noodle to about 10 feet long. It sounds difficult but really isn't.

If you are feeling adventuresome, wrap the entire length of your noodle around both hands with a motion that's kind of like doing the backstroke, catching the noodle strand between thumb and forefinger, until there's a skein of noodles wrapped between your hands as with the string in the cat's cradle game. Then gently pull, smacking the noodles on your board every now and then. This looks a lot like the Chinese technique. Frankly, this is where the noodles usually break on me, so I think it's better just to keep rolling and stretching on the board to get them thin enough.

Boil these in three batches, which means about 4 superlong noodles per batch. After about 2 minutes, drain in cold water, and set aside with a drizzle of oil. It takes maybe 30 or 40 minutes to make the whole lot, but with a little practice you'll be amazed at how easy and fun this is. After all this, you will only have about 12 noodles, equaling about 120 feet in total.

For a Single Serving

¹/₃ batch *laghman* noodles

Soup

¼ pound lamb shoulder or mutton in fine strips
salt and pepper to taste
3 tablespoons oil
½ each red and green bell pepper, in thin strips
½ onion, sliced into thin strips
1 large tomato, chopped
3 cups water or lamb stock
¼ cup squash in small cubes
¼ cup potato in small cubes

Season lamb with salt and pepper and brown in a pot with oil. Add peppers and onions, and brown; then add the tomato. Add remaining ingredients and simmer until cooked through. Place noodles in a bowl and pour the thick soup on top.

KOREA: DONGCHIMI-GUKSU

This cold soup has a base of fermented radish water, a kind of kimchi, which should definitely be made at home. In Korea they use a large football-shaped white radish that's available in the winter, but you can use daikon, and I've used little red radishes too, which make the broth pink. Start by chopping but not peeling the radish. Roll the pieces in salt in a bowl and then put them into a quart jar in the fridge for 4 days without adding any water. The radish creates its own liquid. Then take a square of cheesecloth and put into it 1 unpeeled chopped knob of gingerroot and a few chopped garlic cloves and add that to the jar, or separate into several jars if necessary. Add a few chilies pierced with a knife, 1 chopped onion, and 1 unpeeled Asian pear. Cover the whole thing with water and let it ferment at room temperature for 3 days, then put it in the fridge until ready to use. As a variation on this I've added green chilies, scallions, turmeric to make it yellow, watercress, radish leaves, and even slices of chayote. Whatever you like to pickle would be good in this soup.

To serve, put some cooked and chilled noodles at the bottom of a bowl. Years ago in New York's Korea town I had a cold soup with extra long noodles that were cut at the table with scissors. I think it may have been this soup. In any case, use a thin long starch-based noodle or rice noodle, not wheat (see any of the starch noodle recipes in chapter 6). Pour some of the pickling water on top to create the broth, then add some of the chopped pickled radishes, maybe finely chopped cucumber on top of that, and finally half a hard-boiled egg on top. The flavor of this soup is sour, salty, garlicy, spicy, sweet—actually every flavor you can imagine—yet still really refreshing, surprisingly enough even when it's cold outside.

NEW ORLEANS, LOUISIANA: YAKA-MEIN

How exactly this variation of a Chinese noodle soup came to the African American community of New Orleans remains a mystery, but anyone who has set foot in this gorgeously louche city, has drunk a bit too much, and then needed something to perk up with the next day, will certainly appreciate that it's here. Many despair that yaka-mein is in danger of disappearing, at least among restaurant fare, but it's easy enough to make yourself even if you're not on the second line behind the main parade.

Under no circumstances measure the ingredients. Boil beef stewing meat in water with green bell pepper, onions, and celery. Remove beef and shred finely, then return to the pot. Season with Creole seasoning, either a prepared mix or a combination of chili pepper, cumin, Worcestershire sauce, soy sauce, and Louisiana hot sauce. Add cooked linguine and any quantity of hard-boiled egg, finely chopped, per serving, then a healthy mound of chopped green onion on top. In place of the beef you can use pork chops or actually any leftover protein.

HUNGARY: CSIPETKE

These are one of the easiest noodles to make and also perfectly delightful. They can go into a wide range of soups, including *gulyásleves* or what is known in the United States as goulash. It is not a beef stew on wide egg noodles, but actually a soup, which goes wonderfully with these little *csipetke*. The goulash makes enough for about 4 people, so either make more noodles to serve more people or freeze the leftover soup.

2 onions, finely sliced

2 tablespoons lard

2 tablespoons sweet Hungarian paprika

1 pound beef stew meat, such as chuck or beef cheek

salt and pepper

8 cups beef stock

2 carrots, peeled and cut into large sections

2 parsnips, peeled and cut into large sections

1 cup wheat flour

1 egg

sour cream

In a large pot, begin by cooking onions in lard, very slowly until they are caramelized and very sweet. Don't be afraid of pork fat: it adds an incredible depth of flavor and is no different from any other animal fat, including butter. Just don't use the hydrogenated stuff that comes in a block. If necessary, just melt a piece of fat yourself. Once the onions are caramelized, add the paprika and stir well. Season the meat with salt and pepper, and add to the pot on low heat until it is lightly colored. Add beef stock and simmer gently for 1½ hours. About halfway through add carrots and parsnips.

Make a dough with the flour and egg. Pinch off tiny little pieces of dough, squash them with your fingers, and put on a well-floured plate. When ready to serve, toss these directly into the soup. Serve in bowls with sour cream on top. And of course you should have Béla Bartók playing in the background.

GREECE: AVGOLEMONO WITH ORZO

I vaguely remember my grandmother making this simple dish in lieu of matzo ball soup. I would take this any day of the week. Start with a basic, straightforward chicken soup. It can even be flavored with dill. Boil orzo pasta in the soup. This shape gets its name from the fact that it looks like a kernel of barley, but it's actually make of wheat. You could make these fresh by hand too. Break 2 or 3 eggs into a bowl and add the juice of 1 lemon. Use 2 lemons if you like things really sour. Very slowly ladle hot soup into the eggs, stirring vigorously the whole while so the egg is amalgamated into the soup. This is called tempering, not unlike distempering as a culinary term used in the Middle Ages. You don't want the eggs to scramble. Once the bowl is close to being full, add it back into the soup. Serve immediately hot with a big spoon and an inordinate quantity of freshly ground black pepper.

BATANGAS, PHILIPPINES: PANSIT LOMI

Filipino cuisine is a remarkable combination of indigenous, Chinese, Spanish—or rather Mexican—and U.S. traditions. These influences follow the waves of traders and conquerors who arrived here, and rather than maintaining distinct dishes from each, all the flavors seem to have been thrown together, with incredible results. This soup is a good example. The noodles came with Shanghai merchants, and the pork products came via the Manila galleons from Acapulco. If there were Spam in this, we could add U.S. pedigree too. The noodles are round fresh egg noodles made with lye, which leaves them yellow and slippery. Labeled *miki* noodles, these are sold in Asian groceries; or, you could make thick fresh extruded egg noodles yourself, adding lye water or baked baking soda (see Alkaline Noodles, chapter 6).

1 onion, sliced

1 clove garlic, chopped

6 thin slices chorizo sausage

1 small piece pig's liver (optional)

3 cups pork stock

a few small meatballs made from ground beef

1 small slice ham, diced

¼ cup sliced Napa cabbage

¼ pound *miki* noodles

2 tablespoons cornstarch or other type

cold water

1 teaspoon each soy, fish sauce, calamondin (calamansi) juice, or lime juice

1 small jalapeño or other chili pepper, chopped

1 handful chicharrón (fried pork rinds)

Sauté the onions and garlic in oil. Once nicely browned, add chorizo and pork liver, and continue frying until brown. Pour in the stock. Bring to a boil and then add meatballs, ham, and cabbage, and stir well. Then add the noodles. Make a slurry with the starch and cold water and add that to thicken. Season with soy sauce, fish sauce, calamondin juice, and chili pepper. At the very end, crush the chicharrón and add to the top of each bowl. Eat while hot with a spoon and fork rather than chopsticks, another sign of the mixed ancestry of this dish.

This is going to sound strange, but for most Americans the prototype chicken noodle soup for the past century and more has come in a can manufactured by the Campbell's Soup Company. There have always been great versions from scratch, whether you had a grandmother that was Jewish, Amish, or something entirely different. But the flavor in the can is really what most people think of first. Like the Andy Warhol image, the soup inside has also become iconic, and so comfortingly familiar to most people in its predictability and monotony that if you start thinking about it, much like the can in the image, it becomes quite frightening. For many years I was given this soup to take to school for lunch in a blue wide-mouthed Snoopy Thermos. It was poured from the can, heated with a can full of water, and dumped into the Thermos. Several hours later it was still fairly hot, thanks to the miracle of insulation. The noodles had squared edges, they were short and over-cooked. There were stray particles of "dehydrated mechanically separated chicken," cube-shaped carrot pieces, maybe celery and onion. There were also, alas, many other unspeakable things that went in. All the same, it was the epitome of comfort food for me and I'm sure many other Americans. My younger son has exactly the same relationship to it, and he still enjoys it unless I'm around to make something from scratch.

It may be an exercise in futility, but I want you to try to replicate the flavor and texture of this dish without opening a can. It can be familiar, taste great, and be homemade from scratch. The instructions will be obvious to some, but if you've never done it before, it's actually very simple. If you don't have a lot of time, just take some good chicken stock, add egg noodles, celery, carrot, and onion. That's all there is to it. But I want to get closer to the original, which of course isn't loaded with all the chemical flavorings. This recipe serves about 4 people; there's really no way to make a single serving.

1 whole chicken
12 cups cool water
1 tablespoon salt
3 cups flour
2 eggs
water for dough
3 carrots, peeled and diced
3 stalks celery, diced
1 onion, finely chopped

With the chicken on a cutting board, run your knife down one side of the breast bone and with even strokes separate the meat from the bone. Pull off the skin. Set the breast meat aside. Don't worry about the pieces being very neat. Do the same on the other side. Next remove the thighs and legs from the carcass and separate them from each other. Cut off the wings and cut each section, separating the upper part, middle, and wing tip. Then cut the backbone in half. Add the water to a pot and then all the chicken parts, including the skin, neck, and giblets, but not the liver. Add salt. Gently heat the stock, but don't let it boil. Let it simmer for about 1½ hours.

Place flour and eggs in a bowl and mix thoroughly, adding enough water to make a soft dough. Place the dough on a well-floured board and roll it into a sheet about ¼ inch thick. Cut into strips a little bit wider than ¼ inch, and finally cut noodles into 6-inch lengths.

Strain soup through a sieve into another pot and taste for salt. There will be a little fat on top, which is good. Resist the urge to season with herbs or even pepper. But do add in all the vegetables. Then cut the breasts into tiny pieces, salt lightly and dust with flour, and add that to the soup. Stir well so the pieces don't stick together. Cook vegetables until soft, and then add the noodles. Cook them also until soft. You might miss the "flavoring" as an ingredient—whatever that is, MSG, and of course the yeast extract, soy protein isolate, and sodium phosphate. But this is actually a really decent noodle soup.

 ## DELAWARE: SLIPPERY DUMPLINGS IN SOUP

If you're not from southern Delaware, an area across which you can throw a rock, you've probably never heard of these. Despite the name, they really are not a dumpling, but an odd square noodle. Make a big batch of these to cook in a big pot of soup, and you'll be able to feed the whole state.

3 cups flour
½ teaspoon baking powder
1 teaspoon salt
1½ teaspoons shortening
chicken stock
carrots, celery, and onion, prepared and chopped small

Mix together all the ingredients and moisten with chicken stock until you have a fairly soft dough. Roll out on a floured board and cut into squares about 2 by 2 inches. Cook these in chicken stock with vegetables. The noodles are actually slippery, just as in the name.

ITALIAN AMERICAN: CIOPPINO, OR SEVEN FISHES CHRISTMAS SOUP

Many Italian Americans and others observe the tradition of serving seven fishes or often many more on Christmas Eve. The idea lends itself beautifully to a large presentation of cold noodle soup for a good number of people. In the middle of a large flat-bottomed dish or casserole, arrange a mound of noodles. In sepa-

Cold fish soup is a new take on traditional Seven Fishes for Christmas

rate sections, arrange as many different types of seafood as you can: precooked peeled shrimp, slices of fresh cooked or raw tuna, cooked shredded crabmeat, balls of cooked *baccalà* (Italian for bacalao) bound with egg and bread crumbs then breaded and fried, rings of squid, pieces of steamed fish like halibut or flounder. The greater the range of shapes, textures, and colors, the better. Sea urchin roe would be fun, as would a little caviar. Divide each section with a band of chopped raw red pepper and cooked broccoli or something else really green to make it look like Christmas. If you really wanted to have fun, you could make holly-shaped green noodles out of spinach and little round red noodles from dried bell pepper for the berries and strew them about (see any of the noodle recipes using dehydrated vegetables, chapter 6). Before serving, add well-chilled clear shellfish stock (see chapter 5). Let diners serve themselves with a big deep spoon and small bowls.

The exact same thing works hot too, it's just a bit more tricky to keep the fish warm while you arrange it all. Of course it doesn't have to be neatly arranged—everything in the pot is fine. For a hot version, I would use a stronger tomato-based stock, something akin to a cioppino from San Francisco, which is often served on pasta. If you go in that direction, you definitely also want crab and shrimp, maybe clams, mussels, and other shellfish. For the pasta, a short ziti is ideal, especially since picking around shells and slurping long noodles is a little too much to ask people to manage without mayhem.

SOUTH KOREA: BUDAEJJIGAE

This is a thick soup invented after the Korean War, when Americans stationed near Seoul introduced canned U.S. ingredients like Spam and hot dogs. That means it really can't and shouldn't be made from scratch. Please realize, I am not giving you this recipe to make fun of it. It is a real dish invented out of desperation. Keeping with the spirit of the dish, I suggest in fact that no ingredient be fresh, and if you can find everything in a convenience store, all the better. It's all cooked in a pot and brought to the center of the table; if you can keep it on a hot plate, great.

In a wide fairly shallow pot, arrange slices of Spam, diagonally cut hot dogs, a big mound of jarred kimchi, a block of ramyeon noodles per guest (or ramen), a mound of canned baked beans, and American cheese singles. Cover this with water and add a bouillon cube or the flavoring packets from the noodles. Canned chicken stock would also be fine. Heat until noodles are cooked, and add as further seasoning some *gochujang* chili paste, soy, mirin, and whatever else you can find to satisfy your hunger. You may be tempted to add spring onions, mushrooms, and something resembling a vegetable, but I urge you to resist.

SARDINIA: FREGOLA SOUP

Tiny cylinders of semolina flour, called fregola, are ideal for soup because they stay firm and chewy. The key here is baking the freshly made pasta. A wood-fired oven will impart a smoky flavor, but a regular oven is fine too. There are baked pasta forms in Asia too, and the nutty flavoring is so exquisite that I'm surprised the practice isn't more common. These come from Sardinia but are similar to pasta in North Africa and to Israeli couscous.

1 cup fine semolina flour

½ cup water, more or less

1 onion, sliced

½ fennel bulb, cored and sliced finely into strips

1 tablespoon olive oil, plus more for drizzling

1 large tomato, chopped

3-4 cups water

½ pound manila or cherrystone clams, cleaned well and soaked in cold water 15 minutes to remove any grit

Make a dough using the flour and water only. Knead for about 5 minutes until you have a very firm dough, then let it rest about 15 minutes. You shouldn't need to add any flour to your board or the pasta, which would only burn in the oven anyway. Roll it by hand on a wooden board into very narrow coils about the width of your phone charger cable, and let these dry for about 15 minutes. Don't worry if they're uneven. Cut the coils into tiny cylinders and let dry further so they don't stick. Arrange on a baking sheet and bake in a slow oven, 200°F, for 20 to 30 minutes. A few pieces will become dark—that's fine, but don't let them burn. These store well in an airtight container, so do make more if you have the time.

For the soup, fry the onion and fennel bulb in the oil. Add tomato and salt to taste. Add water, stir, and bring to a boil. Add the fregola and cook through. Before service, add the clams. Discard any that haven't opened. Serve in a shallow bowl and drizzle over a little more olive oil. The soup is flavored very delicately so you can taste the pasta, but you can also use bottled clam juice if prefer a stronger broth. A sprinkle of chili flakes is nice too.

Fregola are a tiny baked Sardinian pasta

🍜 SURINAME: SAOTO (SOTO AYAM)

This soup originates in Indonesia and takes a million different forms across this vast nation of islands. It is also found in Suriname, which like Indonesia became a Dutch colony in the seventeenth century. The soup has a much longer pedigree before the Dutch arrived, of course, but it is fascinating how certain dishes and all the ingredients travel around the world with the people. In this case, it was workers sent to South America, not exactly enslaved, but more or less. It's wonderful that their recipes survived. This is basically a chicken noodle soup, but all the condiments you can add in make it spectacular. In Indonesia it's also often served with white rice, but cooked cubes of potato or taro are more fitting.

1 whole chicken

Spice Paste Mixture (Sambal)

3 knobs fresh turmeric root, peeled and chopped

2-inch piece of galangal root, peeled and chopped

1 teaspoon whole coriander seed

1 teaspoon whole cumin

1-inch knob of gingerroot, peeled and chopped

1 teaspoon pepper

1 garlic clove

2 tablespoons coconut oil

mung bean noodles, soaked and cooked according to package directions, or homemade

lemongrass, white part only, crushed with end of knife and chopped finely

2 lime leaves

Garnishes in Small Bowls

bean sprouts

4 shallots, peeled and finely sliced, fried in oil until crispy

fried shrimp crackers, called kroepoek

sambal or chili paste

limes, quartered

hard-boiled eggs, halved

Place the chicken in a pot of water and bring to a boil, skim the foam, lower the heat, and simmer for about 20 minutes. Remove the chicken, let cool, and then remove the meat. Shred the meat finely by hand and set aside. Add all the bones, giblets (except the liver), and skin back to the pot, and boil 1 hour or longer. Then pound all the fresh spices in a mortar or food processor. Fry these in coconut oil until fragrant but not browned. Set aside. Strain the broth into a pot and add the spice paste, lemongrass, and lime leaves. Soak the noodles or make them fresh (see any of the starch noodle recipes in chapter 6). Add the chicken back into the stock. To assemble place noodles in bowls, pour over the soup, and let diners garnish as they please. To make the sambal, mix fresh small hot chilies chopped, shrimp paste, minced garlic, dried ground galangal (laos powder), tamarind paste, and sugar; pound everything together, cook gently in peanut oil, and then cool.

NORTH DAKOTA: KNOEPFLE

This dish, pronounced *nefla*, was introduced to North Dakota by ethnic Germans living in Russia who were then exiled in the late nineteenth century to the U.S. prairie. It has relatives in Germany and Eastern Europe. The procedure is utterly simple. Start with chicken stock, into which you can add celery and onion, maybe dill. Mix 2 cups flour with 1 egg and add enough milk until you have a soft dough. Roll this into a long coil about 1 inch in diameter. Then use scissors to cut button shapes directly into the soup. You can add a splash of cream before serving, but *knoepfle* should be really plain.

9

RECONSTRUCTIONS

There is probably nothing more fun in the kitchen than taking a well-respected dish and thoroughly desecrating it, switching out ingredients or methods, or in this case totally deconstructing it and then reconstructing it as a noodle soup. Yes, sometimes it gets a little silly, but I promise you these all really do taste great or I wouldn't even think of trying to get you to make them.

Like many of you, long ago I tired of the scientific tricks with food that became so fashionable in high-end restaurants. It wasn't so much the way chefs sought to evoke rarefied emotions or frustrate your expectations or better yet—surprise you with familiar dishes reconfigured in some other form. As you'll see, I wholly applaud those efforts. It was simply that the manipulations grew so absurdly technical, requiring not only machines no ordinary person might own, but a large staff just to execute them. At one point I did own an alginate kit and made little caviar-size beads of cranberry juice. I was tempted to do it with soup, strewn about a bowl of noodles, sort of an inside-out soup dumpling. It might be fun, but how long does that frisson last? A minute or two. I then promised myself that if I was going to offer some strange reconstruction it would have to meet certain inviolable criteria. First, it would have to actually taste very good, if not better than the original dish it purported to reconfigure. Second, it would have to be something someone could do at home, perhaps with some serious time and effort, but a noodle soup that was worthy of a lot of fiddling. Last, the recipe resolutely could not call for a machine that I myself wouldn't want to purchase and own for some other purpose. So the centrifuge was out, likewise the 3-D printer.

Having said that, I did break the rule once, but that was only in creating out of clay the tiniest bowl that I could throw on a wheel, about the size of my pinky fingernail. I offer it because you can find suitable vessels in dollhouse supply shops, tiny Lilliputian bowls that are sometimes so well made that you should not worry about using them to serve your guests. The absurdity of the exercise is worth only a brief joke, but it's so much fun that I couldn't resist. I should mention that after this experiment I veered in the extreme opposite direction and made a single noodle the entire length of my dining room table. It barely fit in the pot and had to be served in a bucket. The logistics notwithstanding, I very nearly tried rolling out a giant noodle on the driveway and pouring boiling soup over it to cook.

ABSURDITIES

 **MICRON NOODLE SOUP**

First find the tiny bowls, or if you work in clay or know a potter, have some made for you. Next take 1 tablespoon flour and moisten it with about ½ tablespoon water. Knead as best you can until you have a tiny lump of dough that can be rolled out. Roll it as thin as you possibly can, adding flour to prevent sticking. With your best magnifying glasses, square off the dough and cut noodles so small that you can barely see them with the naked eye. Pour boiling water into a thimble or shot glass and add the noodles. They'll cook in just a few seconds. Then drain in a small sieve carefully, not letting them slip down the sink. Next take a single slice of carrot and cut into a *brunoise* exactly 1 micron squared. A single leaf of basil rolled up and sliced as thin as humanly possible comes next. To assemble, you need tweezers and an eye dropper. Add a few noodles to the bowl, arranging like a little nest. Drop bits of carrot on top and a few strands of basil chiffonade. With the eyedropper, put a few drops of broth in the bowl to moisten. If you are inclined, fashion chopsticks from the tips of wooden toothpicks. Serve to amazed guests and then pretend not to have a backup soup. Maybe these should be called soupçons.

 **REUBEN SOUP**

This might sound just silly, but trust me: if a Reuben is just about as delicious as a sandwich can get, its noodle soup reconstruction can be equally magnificent. The easy way to do this would be just to get premade ingredients that might go into a second- or third-rate Reuben and throw them together. But where's the fun in that? Everything here will be from scratch. A rye noodle, homemade pastrami, and even homemade sauerkraut. If you have the expertise and time, I'd even say make the Swiss cheese.

1 cup rye flour
1 egg
water

Above: The smallest possible noodle soup on earth, actually edible

Below: The flavors of the perfect Reuben sandwich in a noodle soup

¼ teaspoon mustard powder

1 teaspoon butter

---

1 raw brisket, about 2-3 pounds

salt

sugar

spices and herbs such as pepper, coriander, and crushed dried thyme

½ teaspoon Insta Cure (pink salt, which is sodium nitrite and salt)

---

1 head cabbage

---

1 slice good Swiss cheese

mayonnaise, ketchup, and chopped dill pickles

---

light beef broth

Start by liberally seasoning your brisket with about 1 teaspoon salt per pound. Then add a gentle sprinkling of unrefined sugar and the Insta Cure. If you prefer to use a celery powder cure, that's fine. It's all nitrates and, no, it won't kill you. It's necessary to get that lovely pink color and texture. You can leave it out, but it just won't be that good, like baked pork compared to ham. Finally, add crushed spices, the majority of which should be pepper, until you have a fairly thick coating. Put this into a sturdy plastic bag in the fridge for 2 weeks, turning every other day or so.

In the meantime, core and slice the cabbage very fine and put in a bowl with a handful of sea salt. Knead with both hands until it starts to exude water, about 10 minutes. Then stuff it and the resulting liquid into 1-quart glass Mason jar and screw down the lid. Place it in a cool dark place, but somewhere you can keep an eye on it. Wait one week and gently open the lid—it should bubble furiously. Put it in the fridge for another week. If you like it extra sour, you can let it ferment for the full 2 weeks.

After 2 weeks, smoke the brisket gently over sweet fruit wood for about 1½ hours. This is much easier than it sounds. I use a $30 smoker that looks like a red garbage can on little legs with a door on the bottom. I make a small fire inside with cherry, almond, or oak logs, or better yet, grapevine cuttings, and then close the door tightly. This puts out the fire, but there's enough air circulating beneath to keep the smoke going for a few hours. It will get a little hot, maybe 150°F to 200°F, which is fine for pastrami. You're not trying to cold-smoke it. Remove the pastrami and let it cool a little. Cut into very thin slices and set aside.

Mix rye flour with egg and mustard powder. Roll out a slightly thick dough and cut into medium-width noodles. A dark rye flour is wonderful for this. I have also added actual sourdough rye bread crumbs to this, which is not as uncommon in historic noodles as you might think. It makes a softer noodle, but one that tastes a little closer to an actual Reuben. Boil the noodles right in the beef broth. When the noodles are cooked through, place them in a pan with butter and sauté very gently until they become very slightly browned and toasty.

To assemble, place the noodles in the bottom of a heatproof bowl and layer some slices of pastrami on top. Then add sauerkraut on top of that and then the cheese. Pour over enough hot broth to make a soup, and broil until the cheese bubbles and the other ingredients are very hot.

Just before service, mix the mayo, ketchup, and pickle and put in a fine-tipped pastry bag and lash a few stripes of dressing on the top of your soup for decorative effect. This is as good as if not better than an actual Reuben sandwich.

GUMBO NOODLE SOUP

This soup replicates the flavors of a good gumbo as faithfully as possible but switches around a few things, most notably okra for a weird kind of noodle. There is no reason you couldn't use a vegetable stock and make a variation of the gumbo z'herbes, but I've used a simple beef stock.

If you like a slimy texture, okra provides it

1 pound small okra pods, sliced thin
½ cup flour
pinch salt
1 large egg
2 tablespoons oil, bacon grease, or marrow fat
2 tablespoons flour
1 rib celery
½ green bell pepper, chopped
½ onion, chopped
1 andouille sausage, sliced thin
3 cups beef broth
5 large raw shrimp, shelled
hot sauce to taste

Dehydrate the okra either in the sun, a low oven set at 150°F, or a dehydrator. Grind these into a fine powder. Place ½ cup of the powder in a small bowl, and reserve the rest for another batch or other use. Add flour and salt. Mix in egg and form a dough—you may need a little more water. Roll these out and cut into very thin noodles, either by hand or other device. Flour and set aside.

Next melt the fat and add the equal measure of flour. Cook on very low until dark brown, constantly stirring. It should be about the same color as your stock. Just be careful not to let it burn. This is your roux. Oil gives you the lightest flavor and marrow fat will yield the most intense. Add celery, onion, and bell pepper, and continue stirring until the vegetables begin to color, about 10 minutes. In the meantime, brown the sausage in a pot, add beef stock, and bring to a boil.

When you are ready to eat, put in the okra noodles and stir well, then add the roux and vegetable mixture. It should thicken up nicely and look very dark. At the last minute, add shrimp and cook until they are barely pink. Add a few good shots of hot sauce and serve up. You will find the noodles provide a perfectly delightful slimy texture for those who love that sort of thing, including me.

TUNA NOODLE CASSEROLE SOUP

Here's another mash-up of a favorite of mine. I have made it with fresh tuna, which is great, but honestly I think the taste of the can might add something to the final dish for those with nostalgic taste buds. I have of course avoided all other cans here. Although the original cream of mushroom soup was based on chicken, I've substituted fish stock for a better-aligned flavor profile.

about 20 brown mushrooms or shiitake, sliced

1 stalk celery, finely diced

1 tablespoon butter

1 teaspoon flour

½ cup milk

1 small can solid white albacore tuna (3 oz.) or 3 ounces fresh tuna

¼ pound egg noodles or fresh

½ cup bread crumbs mixed with 1 teaspoon butter

2 cups fish stock

a few sprigs of fresh dill, chopped

Sauté celery and mushrooms in butter on low heat just until they are softened, without browning. Stir in flour and cook another minute. Then add milk. This is a kind of improvised béchamel. Add the tuna, and if raw cut into small pieces and cook though for 1 minute. If canned, then add and break up the bits a little. Add the cooked noodles and stir through until it is thickened. Place this in a mound in a lightly buttered bowl. I like to pack it into a small ring mold and then unmold it into the bowl to get a perfect circle of the casserole. A tuna can itself with both ends removed might work. Cover with bread crumbs and butter mixture and bake at 350°F until the bread crumbs are toasty. To serve, pour your soup around the noodle mixture and top with dill.

Purple yam (*ube*) makes a beautiful noodle

If you look closely in a shop that sells Filipino ingredients, you may find a beautiful purple powder called *ube* (*Dioscorea alata*). If you cook this in water until thickened and then add enough rice flour to make a dough, it can be oiled slightly and rolled out between two sheets of plastic wrap. Remove one sheet and place the whole thing face down in a steamer, remove the second sheet, and put the steamer over a pan of boiling water, covered. In about 2 minutes remove to a plate and let cool. Then slice into noodles. Let these dry a little, and they curl, making beautifully strange Baroque noodles.

I served these in a kind of makeshift adobo soup. Take chicken thighs and marinate them overnight in soy sauce, palm or coconut vinegar, a lot of chopped garlic, pepper, and tomato sauce. The next day, simmer this whole mixture with enough water to cover for about half an hour. Then take out the chicken pieces, dry them as best you can, and fry in olive oil until brown. Then return them to the soup. Ladle the soup into bowls and top with the freshly steamed noodles. If you are using noodles that have dried thoroughly, just resteam them gently on a plate.

KUDZU NOODLES

Kudzu is considered an invasive weed in the United States, but in much of Asia they extract from the roots a starch that makes a really great noodle. You can buy this in a Japanese store or online as kuzuko.

1 cup kudzu starch
¾ cup boiling water
toasted sesame oil

Mix the starch and water with a spoon. When it's cool enough to handle, roll it into a smooth cylinder. Extrude this into well-salted boiling water for about 1 minute and then quickly plunge into ice water. The noodles suddenly turn translucent. Add a little sesame oil so they don't try out. The flavor isn't very pronounced, so use these in your favorite soup. I used it in lobster stock with broccoli rabe and octopus slices. This noodle is also very easy to roll out if you don't have an extruder.

MUSHROOM NOODLE TO THE 3RD POWER

1 pound mixed mushrooms (enoki, maitake, porcini, shiitake), all sliced thinly

1 tablespoon butter or olive oil

½ teaspoon salt

3 cups water

1 cup white wine

½ cup dried porcini powder

½ cup all-purpose flour

1 egg

3 slices portobello mushroom

1 teaspoon butter

½ cup milk

1 sprig dill

sour cream

Sauté mushrooms in butter or olive oil with salt. Let them brown. Put water and wine over, and simmer for 30 minutes. Strain the liquid into a pot and, with the mushroom solids in a sturdy cloth, squeeze out all the liquid into the pot. Discard solids. Combine porcini powder with flour and egg. Knead into a smooth ball and lightly oil. Roll out into a very thin sheet (without extra flour) and cut by hand into extra-thin noodles. Let these dry slightly on a wooden board. Sauté portobello mushrooms slices in butter, salting lightly. Heat mushroom stock and add milk and noodles. When cooked through, arrange in a bowl with mushroom slices, dill, and a dollop of sour cream.

Mushrooms as intense as they can get

 **CEVICHE NOODLE SOUP**

This isn't really cooking so much as assemblage of things you like best, so let me just describe it. Take the fish you prefer, such as snapper, shrimp, or scallops—actually, anything firm works. Salt it well and add 1 chopped shallot and 1 chopped serrano chili pepper, and cover with lime juice. Let it marinate in the acid for about an hour but not too long. To serve, fill a glass serving dish with translucent noodles (see Chilled Mung Bean Noodle, chapter 6) or Japanese *malony harusame*—which means spring rain. Pour over the ceviche and a splash of fish sauce if you like. Garnish with cilantro, avocado—in fact, anything green would be good. The "tiger's milk" or fishy lime juice should be drunk just like a soup.

 ONION NOODLE SOUP

You know how good real onion soup is. Now imagine instead of that soppy piece of wan bread, you get chewy noodles to fish out of the bowl with onion and stringy cheese all tangled together. Why no one has thought of this, I can't imagine. This recipe works only if you cook the onion on low heat in butter so long that it turns dark brown but is not burned. I prefer not to use stock, so you can taste the onion, wheat, and cheese without a lot of other distractions. But it's not exactly bad with beef stock, either.

2 small white onions, peeled and sliced thinly

2 tablespoons butter

1 teaspoon salt

¼ teaspoon thyme, or a little more fresh

3 cups water or stock, enough to come nearly to the top of your bowl

¼ pound thick wavy fresh egg noodles

1 thick slice Emmenthal, Gruyère, or other Swiss cheese, shredded

Brown the onions in butter with salt and thyme, as long as possible until they are thoroughly caramelized. Add water, stir well, and cook about 15 minutes. Put into a heatproof bowl and place the uncooked fresh noodles on top. Place the shredded cheese on top, so it just hangs over the edge of the bowl. Bake this in the oven at 300°F until the cheese melts and bubbles. Now, despite what I just said about the beauty of pure flavors, when you are in the mood for greater intensity, add some pinches of raw ground beef into the bowl or leftover steak. Barbecued tri-tip sliced thin is fabulous with a little sauerkraut and mustard—no longer onion soup, but stunning. Actually, while we're doing this, think seriously about "garbage soup"; brown the onions the same way, then add whatever leftovers you have in the fridge—any meat, any soup base, leftover cooked broccoli or cauliflower, coleslaw. Sometimes you are lazy or desperate. I understand this. With noodles and butter and melted cheese on top, do you really think anything could go wrong?

BLANCMANGER SOUP

You might not recognize this as a reconstruction because you probably have never tasted the original dish. It's about five centuries old and was originally made with cooked capon breast picked into fine threads and pounded with almond milk, sugar, and rose water until it resembled a smooth pudding. It tastes a lot better than it sounds. The name basically means white food, so I've retained that basic idea as well as the original flavor profile—more or less. Still, I think this variation is better than the original.

½ pound raw whole almonds with brown peel

3 cups boiling water, more or less

pinch of salt

4 ounces rice noodles (see any of the starch noodle recipes in chapter 6)

rose water (Middle Eastern, not concentrated rose flavoring for baking)

1 organic orange, zested

½ boneless chicken breast, poached in chicken stock, chilled, and shredded finely

¼ teaspoon white sugar

pomegranate seeds, optional

Blancmanger, a reconfiguration of a medieval favorite

Start by soaking almonds in water overnight. The next day, rub them until the brown peel comes off. You may have to use your fingernails, but the peel will come off. This is what blanching meant in the Middle Ages. They should be lily white. This will not work with toasted or precooked almonds. Next, pound the almonds in a mortar, gradually adding about the boiling water and salt. Or use your sturdy blender for this. Let sit for at least 15 minutes, then strain through a sieve into a bowl, pressing hard on the solids to extract all the liquid. This is real almond milk, not the flavored sweetened garbage you find in the store. I think it looks tastes and feels in the mouth almost exactly like cow's milk. Chill thoroughly.

Next, make basic fresh rice noodles or use medium-width dried rice noodles. Boil and rinse in cold water. To assemble, place your noodles at the bottom of the bowl. Add the chicken and then pour on top the cold almond milk and a drizzle of rose water. Place on top just a tiny bit of orange peel (or cut very fine threads without white pith). Sprinkle with sugar and serve cold. If you like, you can also garnish this with pomegranate seeds.

LASAGNA SOUP

This is more or less a standard lasagna, but messed with so thoroughly in terms of flavor that it rises far above what you might think of as just a slice of lasagna with soup poured over.

1 batch fresh noodle dough (see Basic Wheat Flour Noodles, chapter 6)

¼ cup olive oil

8 ripe roma tomatoes, roughly chopped with the sharpest knife possible so the liquid stays intact

1 clove garlic, chopped

1 sprig fresh oregano

½ cup red wine

salt, to taste

¼ cup ricotta

3 ounces mozzarella, or more if you like

grated Parmigiano-Reggiano

Roll out a standard egg noodle dough and cut into rounds about 6 inches in diameter. Boil these and set aside. Heat the oil in a pan. Just before it starts to smoke, toss in the tomatoes without stirring. Add garlic and oregano. Let it scorch just a bit. Toss the tomatoes, but don't break them up. You're trying to get a little color on them without boiling. Add the wine and then crush everything and cook until thickened and reduced. Pass this through a food mill to produce about a cup or so of thick sauce. Season with salt to taste.

Lay a little sauce in a baking dish, then a disk of pasta, followed by a bit more sauce, some ricotta, and a lump of mozzarella cheese, continuing until you've make a little tower, finishing with sauce and cheese on top. If you're making many servings make one per person. Heat these in a 300°F oven until the cheese is melted. Remove and cover with grated Parmigiano-Reggiano. Place the tower in a bowl and pour around it whatever stock you prefer. Vegetable stock is great, but so is chicken, and I've even used dashi stock. The real beauty of this is you can also garnish it however you like at this point. I've put in crumbled sausage, shredded sautéed yellow peppers, and sliced red onions. Capers are unbelievably good. A fork and knife are appropriate here. If you serve it really hot, the melted mozzarella creates long strings as you pull it from the soup—so messy and satisfying!

A hamburger reconfigured as noodle soup

HAMBURGER SAIMIN SOUP

You have probably seen something like this on TV, and there is even a real ramen dish in Japan with fried noodles standing in for the bun. But I've taken hamburger saimin very seriously as a proper noodle soup that replicates the flavors of a real hamburger. Geographically, I thought the aesthetic midpoint between East and West made the most sense, so I've chosen to use a Hawaiian saimin noodle, which is essentially a curly extruded thin Chinese noodle. The way it's used in Hawai'i suggested to me that a hamburger version would not be anything out of the ordinary there, since they do add Spam and the like. But again, hamburger ingredients tossed in soup just doesn't sound that good, so I had to seriously manipulate the technique itself.

⅓ pound beef chuck or your favorite mix, ground

1 teaspoon each of chopped pickles and chopped sun-dried tomatoes in oil

¼ pound dried saimin noodles

beef broth

a few leaves of Iceberg lettuce, shredded

1 green onion, chopped

garnishes, optional

You can buy ground beef, but this recipe has added textural interest if you actually chop the beef by hand. Mix in gently the pickles and sun-dried tomatoes. Press the raw noodles directly into the top and bottom of the beef patty in roughly the same shape so they look like a bun enclosing the meat, but leave the meat exposed on the sides. Place the patty in a pot just slightly bigger than the patty, and cover with beef broth. Add lettuce and green onions around the patty. Heat this gently on the stove top until the noodles are cooked through. Serve in a bowl and garnish with a dollop of blue cheese, a squirt of sriracha, crumbled bacon, or whatever floats your hamburger.

And on the side you must of course serve French Fry Noodle Soup (see next recipe).

FRENCH FRY NOODLE SOUP

This sounds gross, but it is not just some wet fries in ketchup soup but actually one of the most interesting soups I have made. Let me describe the process, because the detailed techniques appear elsewhere in this book. First, make a basic rolled starch noodle dough using only potato starch, a little oil and boiling water (see any of the starch noodle recipes in chapter 6). Roll the dough thick and cut into squares so they are roughly the same width as very thin fast-food French fries. Boil and set aside.

This soup tastes exactly like french fries in ketchup

Cook either fresh or canned tomatoes with ground cloves, a pinch of sugar, and a splash of vinegar. You don't want this so strong as to be ketchup, but rather to give the tomatoes just a hint of what signals that flavor profile. Then in a blender or using an immersion blender, puree the tomatoes to a thick but still soupy sauce. Pour that in a bowl and place your potato noodles on top. For those who like soggy fries, this is much more interesting as soup with a chewy noodle.

BREAKFAST BUTTERED-TOAST NOODLE SOUP

This is quite simply the exact same ingredients you would use for a perfect American breakfast, reconstructed into a soup that tastes almost exactly the same.

2 slices good white bread
1 teaspoon butter, melted
½ cup flour
3 cups chicken stock
1 raw egg, beaten
2 hard-boiled eggs, sliced thin
2 slices bacon, cooked and crumbled
chives, finely chopped

Toast the bread and whizz it in a blender to very fine crumbs. Add butter, flour, and just enough egg to moisten into a very soft dough. Place this in a pastry bag and squeeze out in strands into the gently simmering stock until just cooked through. To serve, put the noodles and soup in a bowl, and arrange the hard-boiled egg slices in a fan in the corner of your soup. Sprinkle bacon and chives on top. Alternately, you can add slivers of smoked salmon instead of the bacon, and chopped cooked spinach in another corner facing the eggs. You can also poach or fry the eggs instead of hard-boiling them. Actually, whatever you fancy for breakfast ought to go in this bowl. I can even imagine Britons making this with a round of black pudding, a spoonful of baked beans, a roasted tomato, and mushrooms. Now *that* sounds amazing.

PORTUGUESE SOUPISH CALDENE

This variation on the classic soup substitutes noodles for the potatoes. It's so good, I really wonder how the Portuguese themselves didn't come up with it. The directions are so simple that measurements aren't necessary. First, fry a sliced *chouriço* sausage. You can substitute another sausage, but don't use soft Mexican chorizo. Add 1 chopped onion, a good sprinkle of red pepper flakes, and a lot of chopped kale. Then add 3 cups beef broth, or whatever you have on hand, 1 bay leaf, and some dried thyme. Before serving, add thick penne or ziti—something with real gusto, and cook until pasta is almost tender. I like a dash of piri piri sauce or other hot chili sauce too.

NOODLE SOUP COCKTAILS

A completely unexplored genre hovering somewhere between bar snack and beverage awaits the addition of noodles to cocktails. I first thought of this when making a noodle out of ground black chia seeds, which I ended up putting in a soup made of blackberries cooked down with water and sugar, then strained. It was pretty boring until I added a little rum. Now this was delicious, especially served like a hipster concoction in a Mason jar, garnished with garden herbs. Any classic cocktail improves with the addition of noodles and a small pair of chopsticks to fish them out. Think of a martini with angel hair pasta, a manhattan with some cold thick udon to chew on, or—my favorite—a negroni with a wide rice noodle. The possibilities are endless. To start, I encourage you to try, when it's really hot out, a few slices of melon and berries in a chilled glass of Pinot Grigio and strands of cold mung-bean cellophane noodles. Luscious.

A cold boozy blueberry noodle soup

MIDDLE EASTERN NOODLE SOUPS

These next few soups were inspired by the flavors of the Middle East, a place where I contend that noodles arose independently many centuries ago and still exist in diverse forms today. The recipes that follow are not traditional but are instead reconstructions of other familiar dishes whose ingredients and flavor combinations are classic. I've just rearranged them here to become noodle soups.

Some people may protest this kind of experimentation as a violation of their cultural property, somehow even a theft of what belongs to them, an appropriation akin to colonialism since profit is involved. I understand well where such comments come from, and when a restaurant opens offering perhaps faux Mexican food at high prices while Mexicans themselves can only manage to operate inexpensive places, then yes, a kind of injustice seems to be involved. Likewise, when a recipe is such an integral part of a group's identity and then someone comes along and reconfigures it in a way that violates the spirit of the original, then I do recognize an injustice. The flat-bottomed fried taco shell that stands on its own that is being advertised on TV as I write may be a good example of this. In the commercial, supposedly authentic Mexicans wonder why they never thought of this. On the other hand, cuisines must evolve and they will do so whatever we think of the process. Historically, cooking traditions have fused with other influences in ways that have given rise to the greatest cuisines on earth. Filipino cuisine as we know it today would not exist without the influence of China, Spain, and the United States. Italian food would not exist in its current form without the influence of Mexico—I'm thinking of tomatoes, peppers, corn, chocolate, and so on. Ultimately, all cuisines are fusions. I mention this here because the recipes that follow are messed-up versions of my own culinary heritage, lest anyone complain of appropriation.

CHICKPEA NOODLE IN TAHINI SOUP

Chickpeas are tricky to get into noodle form since they have neither glutens nor the mucilaginous quality that holds together starch noodles. For that reason I mix 50 percent chickpea flour with 50 percent wheat, bound with an egg. The dough was rolled out by hand, but I prefer to cut it in the crank roller attachment. This soup tastes almost exactly like hummus.

Above: Chickpea noodles taste a lot like hummus

Below: Smoky eggplant in reconstructed baba ghanoush

½ cup chickpea flour
½ cup wheat flour
1 egg
3 tablespoons tahini paste and hot water to thin
1 dollop thick Greek yogurt
¼ teaspoon za'atar (spice mixture with wild thyme, sumac, and sesame seeds)
vegetable garnishes, like tomatoes, cucumber, crushed almonds

Mix flours and egg until a firm dough forms. Roll out and cut using a knife or a cutter attachment on a hand-cranked machine. Mix the tahini paste with hot water to a soupy consistency. Boil the noodles and then transfer into a bowl with the tahini soup. Garnish with a sprinkle of the za'atar and raw vegetables you have on hand.

BABA GHANOUSH NOODLE

This recipe is similar in spirit to the previous one but takes a serious twist with the overall flavors. It is among my favorites and well worth the effort. Eggplant is one of those strange vegetables that has little flavor or nutritional value on its own, but it can be coaxed into one of the most delicious things on Earth. Nonetheless, in the past people thought it was poisonous, no doubt because it's in the same *Solanacea* family as the deadly nightshade. However, so too are tomatoes, so there you go. In Italy they claimed (falsely) that the word *melanzane* comes etymologically from *meli insani*, or insane apple, because they might drive you insane. The author of the first printed cookbook in the fifteenth century, Platina, borrowed an eggplant recipe from his friend Martino of Como but then pointed out at the end that it's so bad you should feed it to your enemies. I beg to differ.

1 large eggplant
1 cup wheat flour
water or 1 egg
1 tablespoon tahini paste
3 cups fish stock
10 smoked scallops
additional tahini paste as garnish, optional
za'atar and black sesame seeds or other herb

Place your eggplant directly over the gas flame of your stove or over the open flame of your backyard grill. If you have neither, make a fire somewhere safe and position the eggplant over the flames, because this simply does not work unless you can actually char the entire outside surface of the eggplant. It will take about 10 minutes, so keep turning the eggplant. When it's completely blackened, place it in a large paper shopping bag and roll down the top to enclose it. This process steams the skin. Let it sit for at least 15 minutes. Remove the eggplant and carefully peel off the charred skin. Don't rinse in water. The same process works for bell peppers, incidentally. What you will have is a wet gloppy mass of cooked smoky eggplant that's normally mashed with tahini to make baba ghanoush, into which you dip flatbread. Instead, mash the eggplant and spread it on a plastic mat, then dehydrate it or place on a parchment-lined baking sheet in a low oven until completely brittle and dry. Crush this or grind it in a spice grinder. In the end, you will have about 1 tablespoon of fine powder, utterly concentrated eggplant essence.

Mix the eggplant powder and flour and add enough water or egg to make a noodle. Roll out and cut or extrude, however you prefer. Boil until cooked through but still chewy. To serve, place the noodles in a rich fish stock in which you have gently simmered smoked scallops. The flavors blend beautifully. Then decorate with a little tahini thinned with stock and sprinkle on za'atar and black sesame seeds, or just powdered sumac works very nicely too. Or if you don't have these, any fresh green herb is nice, even mint.

Powdered Gaziantep pepper goes right into the noodle

GAZIANTEP PEPPER NOODLE SOUP

I was invited with a group of food writers to celebrate the election of the city of Gaziantep, Turkey, to the status of UNESCO World Heritage Site for its cuisine. The food was amazing, but among everything else what sticks out in my mind was a coarsely ground red pepper, both sweet, with a little heat and a hauntingly alluring flavor that I have tasted in no other pepper. Isn't it incredible that this little New World plant should somehow get to places as far-flung as Thailand, Hungary, West Africa, and India, all in a few decades, where the flavor of each type of pepper evolved on its own and became completely unique and almost indispensable to the local cuisine? The Gaziantep pepper did just that. If you can't find these, I would recommend air drying a few red bell peppers and one small spicy red chili pod, then grinding them coarsely. You don't want a fine paprika-like powder, but something with tiny flecks. Or if you like, a pleasant variation on this would be using smoked Spanish *pimentón de la Vera*.

¾ cup wheat flour

¼ cup Gaziantep chili or other powdered sweet chili

1 egg

3 cups lamb stock

4 ounces shoulder lamb chop, raw, thinly sliced

salt, pepper, ground cumin, dried oregano

cornstarch or other starch

½ bunch cilantro, stemmed

¼ cup olive oil

½ cup yogurt

cracked pepper, to taste

Mix flour, chili, and egg into a dough, roll out, and cut. Be sure not to use spicy chili powder or chili flakes, which will make the noodles inedible. If you are using powdered sweet bell peppers, feel free to use them in equal proportion to your flour (50:50). In either case, you want as much chili flavor without scorching your mouth. Next, slice the lamb, removing from the bone all traces of gristle, and fat too, if you prefer. Season the slices well with salt, pepper, a dash of cumin, and oregano. Then dust the lamb lightly with cornstarch and set aside. Put the cilantro leaves in a mortar and pound fine, adding a little oil at a time to make something between a thick pesto and a smooth oil. When you are ready to serve, boil the noodles directly in the stock. Remove from the heat, stir in the yogurt, and then transfer immediately to your bowl. Drizzle cilantro oil on top and add a ton of cracked black pepper if you like. I do. You definitely need to serve this in a bright Turkish ceramic bowl.

MORE RECONFIGURATIONS

 **CHOCOLATE NOODLE SOUP**

I tested many different combinations of flavor to go with chocolate noodles, even dashi stock, which—trust me—does not work. A Southeast Asian peanut curry with turmeric and coconut was close, as was an Italian ragù, but my instinct was right—chilies and a kind of molé-flavored soup. Thanks to all the friends who steered me from disaster on this one.

Chocolate works surprisingly well in a noodle

¼ pound pork shoulder cut into cubes, or ribs chopped into sections

salt, pepper, and ground cumin, or seasoning to taste

1 tablespoon olive oil

1 onion, chopped

1 garlic clove, crushed

2 dried pasilla chilies, soaked, stem and seeds removed, then blended in 3 cups water

1 cinnamon stick

1 bay leaf, crushed

¼ cup blanched almonds, crushed coarsely

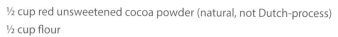

½ cup red unsweetened cocoa powder (natural, not Dutch-process)

½ cup flour

1 egg

1 pot water, heavily sweetened

1 tablespoon strained yogurt

fresh herbs like oregano, cilantro, or other, optional

Start with cubes of boneless pork shoulder, dusted with salt, pepper, and cumin. Brown these in a small pot with oil, add onion and garlic, and continue frying. Then add pasillas, cinnamon stick, bay leaf, and almonds. Let this simmer for 1½ hours, adding more water if necessary.

Make the noodles by combining cocoa powder, flour, and egg. Roll out and cut into noodles. Let them dry thoroughly for several hours. Don't be tempted to taste test these in plain water—they're very bitter at this stage.

Remove the meat from the broth and set aside in the refrigerator. Strain the broth, discarding solids. Chill in the refrigerator, then remove the solid fat on top.

Heat the broth and add the meat. Cook the noodles in the sweetened water and drain. Assemble in a bowl with meat around the noodles and a dollop of yogurt on top. Garnish with fresh herbs if you like.

SAFFRON ANGEL HAIR

Why this pasta makes me think of Botticelli, I don't know, but it uses an odd technique reminiscent of the Renaissance. Like noodles of that era, it uses only egg yolk and an Italian superfine Tipo "00" flour. You can use all-purpose too.

2 egg yolks
1 pinch whole saffron stamens, crushed
1 cup 00 flour
olive oil
shellfish broth
2 raw scallops, sliced horizontally
laurel leaves and pink carnations, as garnish

Mix egg yolks with saffron and let sit a few minutes. Mix this with flour, adding a few drops of water if necessary to make a stiff dough. Knead a few minutes, wrap in plastic, and let it sit for 1 hour. Then lightly oil the dough and roll out as carefully as you can to make one extraordinarily thin sheet. Cut this into the most minute strips you can and pile up like a bird's nest. I think these would be delightful with a few strips of chicken and quail eggs, but keeping with the Botticelli theme, cook the pasta in a very delicate shellfish broth, serve in a large shell on a plate, and garnish with raw scallop slices. Adorn the plate with a few laurel leaves (bay leaves) and pink carnations, and those who love the painter and Simonetta Vespucci will understand the obscure construction.

NOT YOUR MAC 'N' CHEESE SOUP

The idea for this recipe came to me after my son prepared a box of Kraft Instant Mac 'n' Cheese. He left half of it in the pot and I thought, I can just add stock to that, no? Don't worry—I'm not going to suggest you do this. But I will give you yet one more spin on the traditional mac 'n' cheese, which I think is so superior to the versions with bacon or lobster or foie gras, or the fried balls or even the latest trend: mac 'n' cheese bars where you can garnish a cocktail glassful with all sorts of yummy bits. Moreover, the lurid orangey-yellow color achieved in this noodle soup resolutely does not come from a box.

1 kabocha squash
½ cup wheat flour
1 egg
1 tablespoon butter
1 tablespoon flour
1 cup ale

An extruded squash macaroni adds vibrant color

4 ounces cheddar cheese, grated

2 cups chicken broth

2 slices bacon, cooked and crumbled, or bits of lobster, foie gras, etc. (optional)

Using a sturdy cleaver or heavy knife, chop the squash into wedges following the indentations in the outer skin. This makes it easier to peel the skin. You can use another squash, but kabocha is just about as good as this vegetable gets, and it has the best color for this dish. Remove all the skin and seeds, and chop the flesh into the thinnest slices you can. Dehydrate these outside, in the oven, or in your dehydrator, then grind into a powder. It will be bright orange. Combine ½ cup of this flour with ½ cup flour, or whatever quantities you are using in the proportion of 50:50, and bind into a dough with egg. For this dish you need an extruded macaroni shape, so use whatever hand-powered machine you have to make noodles as close as you can get to those that come in a box. Set aside to dry a little so they don't collapse or stick together.

Next combine butter and flour in a pot and stir on low heat for a few minutes but not allowing them to take on any color. Slowly add the beer, which will probably foam up. For this dish you really don't want a beer with a lot of hops, which makes the dish way too bitter, or anything too dark, which muddies the color in the end. But you also don't want a flaccid lager. I used Sierra Nevada. To this mixture add the cheese and gently simmering chicken stock in small increments so the cheese melts gradually. For the cheese I would use something really sharp and well aged. A local Fiscalini bandage-wrapped cheddar worked perfectly for me, but if you can get your hands on something great from Vermont or, better yet, a real English cheddar, go ahead. In a separate pot of boiling water, cook the squash macaroni and then add it to the thick cheesy soup. You can garnish however you like, with chopped chives or bacon or even more extravagant ingredients.

SALMOREJO CORDOBÉS

This cold tomato soup is a close relative of gazpacho from Córdoba, Spain. It's essentially a tomato, olive oil, garlic, and salt puree thickened with bread. There's no water. What if you just replaced the bread with tiny noodles so every spoonful offered something toothsome? The recipe is simple, but don't bother unless you have remarkably ripe luscious summer tomatoes. Throw these in a blender, add a sliver of garlic, or more if you're fond of it, then a pinch of salt and a drizzle of olive oil. Measuring this seems entirely against the spirit of the soup. Whiz until smooth. Dole into bowls, then drop in a spoonful of cold tiny alphabet noodles, ditalini, macaroni—anything diminutive. That's it. Don't chill it, either, or you'll mute the flavor of the tomatoes. If you really want to garnish with a chiffonade of basil, that's OK (roll up a few leaves and cut across, making thin strips). In Córdoba they add a thin slice of cured ham; a chiffonade of that on top would be great.

$$\textbf{(10)}$$
INVENTIONS

I cannot begin to tell you how much fun the following experiments were. Some are for alternative ways to make noodles, a few of which I think I ought to patent. But this chapter opens with complete noodle soups that I proffer to you simply because they worked well. In the two years of research for this book, I made a different noodle soup nearly every morning I was home, and some weekends I tested a half dozen or so. That adds up to about 700 noodle soups, so what I'm offering is only a small cross-section of the entire oeuvre. I hope you'll use some of these ideas as a springboard for your own inventions.

 **SPRING FAVA BEAN NOODLE SOUP**

When fava beans first arrive in the spring, they have a marvelously fresh green flavor. They taste nothing like the mature bean or bean flour, which gets a bit acrid and starchy, as with commercial bean pasta. The appeal of fresh favas may be that there's so much labor involved that by the end of shelling and skinning them you feel they *have* to be worth it. I think they are.

Fava beans are the essence of spring

2 pounds fresh young fava beans shelled, skinned, and split
½ cup wheat flour
1 egg (for dough)
⅛ teaspoon salt
3 cups chicken broth
1 egg, poached
drizzle of olive oil
a few leaves of parsley, chopped

Dry the fava beans in the sun for a few days, in an oven set at 120°F, or in a dehydrator. The latter will take about 6 hours. Then grind them in a coffee grinder into a fine powder. You should have about ½ cup. Add flour, 1 egg, and salt, and work into a dough, adding a few drops of water if necessary. Roll out on a well-floured board as thin as possible and cut into noodles. Set these aside. Boil the broth and add the noodles, cooking for about a minute or two until just cooked through. Pour into a bowl and top with the poached egg, olive oil, and parsley.

COUNTY FAIRGROUND SOUP

I love when serendipity, season, and whim dictate the contents of a recipe. A cooking demo for a farm-to-table event and whatever happened to be available at the vegetable stands one hot day in July prompted this combination, which I don't believe I would ever have come up with myself. The ingredients cost 25 dollars and made a very large stockpot full of soup. The quantities are of course entirely variable, and you should, given the spirit of the recipe, use whatever you happen to find in an unusual farmer's market. The dump-and-boil method here works.

2 cups flour
2 eggs
water to half fill a stockpot
7 cloves garlic, crushed
5 red onions, thinly sliced
1 large bunch kale, ribs removed and chopped
1 bunch cilantro, chopped with stems
10 limes, juiced
2 oranges, juiced
7 jalapeños, chopped
1 fresh coconut, grated, with its water
10 tamarind pods, flesh removed from pods, soaked, broken up in hot water, and strained
10 tomatoes, coarsely chopped
1 pound fresh scarlet runner beans, removed from pods
salt

Make a small soup pasta by hand with the flour and eggs—gnochetti are perfect, formed with two little ridged paddles. Just cover the beans with water and then boil until tender, about 20 to 30 minutes. Add the rest of the water. Dump in all the other ingredients. Boil until you stop. Serve. It's really spicy and sour and although it seems to suggest Italy in the pasta and Mexico in the ingredients, the final soup could really come from Africa, Southeast Asia, or just about anywhere else in the world.

ŞALGAM SUYU

There's a wonderful drink they serve on the street in Istanbul called şalgam suyu, of which I am inordinately fond. It's made of black carrots, which are now available in the United States. It's served with the carrot and other vegetables, but it's also incredible as a cold soup with noodles and finely diced pickles. It takes about a week to ten days to make. Start with a 1-quart Mason jar. Cut lengths of black carrots, turnips, and a few green chilies to fill the jar vertically. Cabbage works too. Then take a square of doubled cheesecloth and place inside a few raw dried chickpeas, bulgur wheat, and a lump of stale sourdough bread. Tie it up tightly and place on top of the vegetables. Cover everything with water, add 1 tablespoon salt and a pinch of raw sugar. Put the lid on and wait. When you open it, be careful—it will bubble up violently. Put the lid back on and chill it thoroughly. To serve, place cold cellophane noodles in a bowl, cover with the chopped vegetables, and pour over some of the liquid. This is not something any self-respecting Turk would ever do, but maybe someday they will.

EAT YOUR WORDS

My love of rare books is one of the reasons I became a historian. I love the feel of old vellum, the look of chain lines in archaic paper as you hold pages up to the light, the way old type strikes the paper, leaving an impression. Every now and then you'll even find a strand of hair embedded in paper made 500 years ago. The trails left by bookworms can be charming. But above all else, it is the aroma of old books that is so tantalizing. Very old books were made with paper composed mostly of rags with low acid content, so they tend not to age or develop much aroma. Caxton's printing of Chaucer in the late fifteenth century is still as crisp and new as when it came off the press. Sixteenth-century books have their own distinct subtle aroma, traces of sheep in the binding, and even a faint wooliness in the paper, which becomes slightly brown. But if you want to see really dramatic effects of aging, get a nineteenth-century book made with cheap, high-acid paper. The vanillin of aged wood pulp exudes a kind of cigar box aroma with hints of coffee. It's discernably sweet on the nose. I have one old French dictionary, a single whiff of which is like expensive perfume. In fact, some books can only be described as delectable, as in worthy of being eaten. Didn't St. John eat books—in his mouth as sweet as honey? Why not cook with books?

For a brief moment I entertained the notion of actually putting torn-out words from old books directly into noodle soups. The text could match the period and style of the book. So a swordfish chowder might have a few words of Hemingway thrown in. James Fennimore Cooper would need a venison bisque. I can imagine an eighteenth-century vermicelli in fine turtle soup from Hannah Glasse liberally seasoned with the heavy verbiage of Boswell's *Life of Johnson*. But then who wants the bellyache that St. John got? So how about making printed and inscribed noodles? That's really only one aesthetic level beyond alphabet soup.

The difficulty of an inscribed noodle is that the words will run when cooked. They do make markers with edible ink for decorating cookies, but I wanted an actual ink that could go into a quill pen or on a brush. What worked reasonably well in the end is a mixture of powdered *Alkanet tinctoria* and olive oil. The perfectly edible alkanet was once used in medieval cuisine to color food, providing the extra frisson of delight because it behaves like litmus paper, changing color with acid or base. See below for magical color-changing noodles. The only difficulty with the oil base is that it won't really dry completely in plain air, so you have to steam the noodle gently, and the oil seeps into the noodle itself and doesn't run too much. What is great about it is that you can in fact pull off some lovely gothic hands with this ink, and it works equally well on the end of a Chinese paintbrush. And more strangely, the dried noodle rather resembles vellum. I drew up some passages from a Latin Mass, and the pen floated over the noodle better than on any paper.

Another idea completely is to impress the noodle. Using rubber stamps with letters, I randomly spelled out words and then cut out long sentences on the noodle. I love the idea of eating soup and finding a secret message stamped into your noodle. The long noodles reminded me of the ticker-tape pronouncements you often see issuing from the mouths of angels in medieval illuminated manuscripts.

Calligraphic techniques with edible ink

 **BOOZLES**

On a whim I started adding various liquids to hydrate flour and make noodles. Acids don't work too well because they prevent the noodle from cooking properly. Carbonated water is interesting and has a slightly leavening effect, as might be expected. Actually there's an *e-fu* (also *Yi-fu* or *yi meni*) noodle from China that uses carbonation and then is fried dry so it puffs up nicely. It's then cooked in soup to become really chewy. The same effect happens with alcohol, which evaporates as the noodle is boiled, making the texture slightly aerated. Moreover, you can flavor the noodles by the adding various kinds of booze. Ouzo makes a delicious noodle that works well in a fish broth with octopus and tomato. The juniper flavor of gin matches well with game and a rich broth. You can't really taste alcohol, but the aromatic herbs do come through.

PINE NOODLE SOUP

The aroma and flavor of pine is among the most exhilarating on Earth. Think of showering with pine tar soap, the aroma of pine oil in a sauna, or drinking good Lapsang souchong, which is smoked over pine needles. I even adore chewing spruce gum. I collected some delicious sap while hiking around Banff with a friend, but there's also a good tree in the parking lot near my office. Just make sure the pine tar is very hard (it won't work with soft sap), to clean out the debris, melt it, and filter it through a mesh sieve. If you find clean "tears" dripping from a tree, scrape this off and use as is. You know, this might just be a good use for your leftover Christmas tree.

Above: If you like pine aroma, pine noodles present an interesting spin

Below: Corzetti or croxetti are a stamped noodle from Liguria

4 or 5 small grains of sap from white pine or spruce, crushed, to yield ½ teaspoon
½ teaspoon granulated sugar
1 cup flour
water
½ tablespoon green matcha tea or vegetable powder
3 cups chicken stock, heated
½ cup pine nuts, toasted
spruce tips, for garnish

Crush the sap grains in a mortar with the sugar or process in a spice grinder. Add this to the flour and mix in just enough water to make a dough. If you like you can color this green with matcha tea or vegetable powder. Roll out and cut into very thin noodles that resemble pine needles. In a blender, combine the hot stock with the toasted pine nuts until you get a smooth creamy white soup. Serve in a wooden bowl, preferably of pine, with the noodles and garnish with spruce tips or a sprig of pine needles for decoration only. The noodles will be strangely chewy, something like the Greek spoon sweets that are made with mastic—*vaníllia*.

STAMPED AND ROLLED NOODLES

Pressing patterns into noodles with individual stamps is nothing new. For example, the traditional Ligurian corzetti, or croxetti, are a stamped noodle. More effective than actual stamping, however is the little roulette wheel mounted on a handle, something like the cylinder seals ancient Sumerians used to sign their names. These modern versions of these are also made for working clay and

other craft uses, but rolling a pattern into the noodles makes them stunning. Among the most beautiful noodles I've ever made were achieved with a dark green noodle base on top of which was a plain white sheet of noodle. When you roll over this with a Sculpey roulette, the green shows through giving you an exquisite pattern, in this case leaves on a vine. It was perfectly fitting because the base was made with dandelions from the yard. The Sculpey tool comes with a handful of different patterns, but there is no reason you can't make some yourself out of clay or a wooden dowel carved with a pattern. I have even gotten beautiful textures in noodles by rolling them over tree bark, window screens, and other unexpected surfaces. Why there aren't industrial noodles with beautiful surface textures like these, I can't imagine—they are delightful to eat.

Above: Simple tools like this Sculpey roulette make interesting patterns in dough

Below: Instant noodles put up in jars

INSTANT SOUP

For years I've been enthralled by the idea of a product that was popular in the eighteenth century called pocket soup. I always picture some starch wigged dandy pulling a brown lump out of his waistcoat to the surprise of the savants gathered in a salon, dropping it in a bowl of hot water and exclaiming, "My Dear Sirs, Observe Carefully: Pocket Soup." Everyone politely claps, expels some oohs and aah, and a few bars of Haydn magically sound through the hall.

Pocket soup was of course just the precursor to the bouillon cube, perhaps a bit more gelatinous. If you have a dehydrator, you can actually make a whole soup, a really good soup, instant.

The easy way is to cook the noodles in a very rich stock and then dry them, though I've never seen anyone else do it this way. The harder way, and it does indeed work, is to make a batch of noodles, cook, drain, and set them on a dehydrator rack. Cook down a totally lean and tasty stock to a thick syrup, spread that on a dehydrator mat, adding thinly sliced carrots, celery, greens, anything you like, on another rack. Dehydrate everything—you can also do this in a low oven. When everything is absolutely and utterly dry, break up the sheet of stock and put it at the bottom of a 1-quart glass Mason jar. Layer the noodles on top—you'll probably have to break them a little—then the vegetables, which will have become microscopic. This is just beautiful and makes a fabulous gift: homemade soup you can mail. An even better trick is if you had rubber-lined pockets, you could keep a serving of this instant soup in your pants at all times, just pour in some hot water and voilà—pocket soup!

 MAGIC LITMUS NOODLES

Years ago with my older son for a school project, we designed an experiment to test the pH of various common foods. It was great fun. You basically just cook red cabbage in water, soak paper in that water, and let it dry. Then you place droplets of things like acidic lemon juice and alkaline baking soda onto the paper—the colors will change dramatically, giving you greens and pinks. Years later I had an aha moment and thought, why not psychedelic acid test noodles? Just rolling out an ordinary flour and water wheat noodle and cooking it in red cabbage water works OK, but no vibrant colors will result. For this you really need to dehydrate the cabbage, grind it, and mix it with an equal

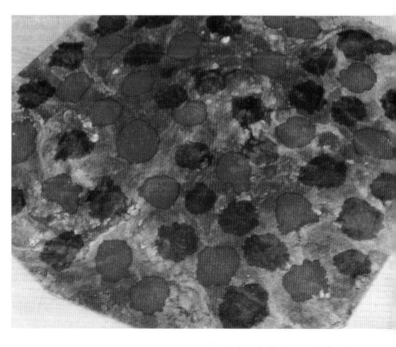

Acids and alkalis react differently to a litmus noodle

amount of wheat flour. This produces a deep purple noodle. Then drop the acid on the noodle or brush it on in swirling patterns. Baking-soda water will give you a vibrant contrast. While doing this I suggest listening to something really "out there," maybe Atom Heart Mother or other early Pink Floyd. Let the noodles dry and then steam them to cook so the colors should "not fade away."

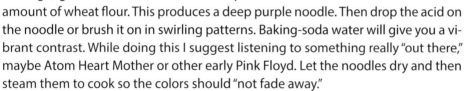 MARBLEIZED NOODLES

This experiment suggested to me not only a magnificently colorful noodle looking like nineteenth-century decorated endpaper, but actually a whole new way to make noodles. Marbleization is normally done with colored inks floating on water or a more viscous solution, ox gall, oils, gums, and other odd ingredients and can be stunningly beautiful. There might be a way to transfer a pattern from a tray onto a sheet of a noodle as a monoprint, but not with edible dyes as far as I can tell. My solution, which literally came to me in a vision, was to make the noodle itself a viscous surface onto which other colored batters could be applied. Any

Marbleizing wet batter, as is done with ink on paper

deeply colored noodle batter should work; to get distinctly Victorian colors I chose gaudy tomato and olive drab, dried, ground, and then mixed into a thin slurry with wheat and water. First, take a thick wheat-based batter and pour it onto a plastic mat. It should not run off. Then put the colored batters into piping bags and express swirling lines, circles, droplets, whatever you like, on top. The more colors you use, the more interesting the final noodle. With a toothpick, feather through the colors, alternating directions to produce beautiful patterns. Then simply let the whole thing dry. When it is leather hard, cut it into noodle shapes or decorative squares. You can also let it dry completely and then break it into pieces. The colors remain distinct as long as you don't use something like beets. These noodles floating in clear soup are breathtaking. Wear an ascot tie and rose-colored glasses while consuming it.

BOILED SOUP À LA CHINESE SCIENTIST

I spent one summer doing research in the charming town of Wolfenbüttel, Germany, where I shared a kitchen in an apartment with a Chinese scientist. He spoke no English and I spoke no Chinese, so we communicated as best as we could in our broken German. When our paths crossed in the kitchen, I tried to pay attention to him, hoping to pick up some interesting techniques. I noticed a precise pattern to his daily cooking: boil a pot of water, chuck everything in. That would mean vegetables, marinated spare ribs or chicken, noodles or rice, soy sauce, packets of ketchup. He ate it right out of the pot. I thought this was crazy, and obviously he knew nothing about cooking. Only years later did I learn there is a revered tradition in Chinese cuisine based on a definite logic. Not only is it very easy, but it's the best way to make a filling meal with very little money and very few utensils. It reminds me of a soup my dad described from the Great Depression—if you had no money, you could ask for a cup of hot water, add a few free ketchup packets and soup crackers if they were on the condiment tray, and have a meal for nothing.

With the spirit of my Chinese flatmate, this soup is easy and inexpensive. The most costly ingredient would be the ribs, but this soup still won't cost more than about 2 or 3 dollars per serving, or less than a Styrofoam bowl of instant soup. This makes 3 or 4 servings. For a single serving, freeze the remaining ribs in small plastic bags for later use.

½ rack pork ribs, about 2 pounds
1 onion, finely diced
1 clove garlic, finely chopped

4 tablespoons soy sauce
2 tablespoons rice wine vinegar
1 small knob gingerroot, peeled and grated
8 packets ketchup or ¼ cup, ideally homemade
1 pound dried spaghetti or thin Chinese noodle

Have your butcher saw through the ribs crossways several times so you have small cross sections rather than long ribs. Or do this yourself with a heavy cleaver. Separate the ribs, then chop through each bone into four squares per rib. The half rack is 6 ribs, each chopped into 4 pieces, which gives you 24 pieces in total, 6 pieces per serving for 4 people, or 8 pieces for 3 servings. Cutting them up maximizes the surface area, helps everything cook quicker, and will make the pork easier to eat in a soup. Marinate the meat for at least 1 hour in all the other ingredients except the noodles. You can also substitute chicken thighs with bones and skin for the pork ribs, if you like. Boil a small pot of water and throw everything in, including all the marinade. Simmer gently for 1½ hours or until the meat is tender. Before you're ready to eat, add the spaghetti, cook until still slightly chewy, about 7 minutes. Eat out of the pot.

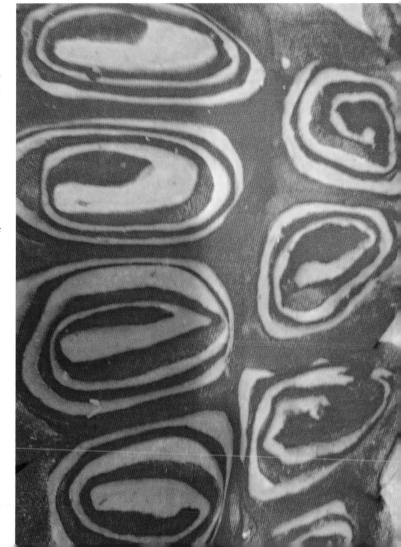

Cut and rolled *neriage* noodles use a clay technique

NERIAGE NOODLES

Pottery techniques sometimes work surprisingly well in the kitchen. That's not always the case in reverse. I've wanted to throw dough on the potter's wheel so badly, but it simply doesn't behave the same way as clay. But this technique works wonderfully. Take various colored doughs, wet enough so they stick together. Roll into sheets and then lay these on top of each other, cut into broad strips, and then again stack these on top of each other. Roll out so they stick together. Then cut into thin noodles. The cross section is striped. Now take those same strips and roll them up and cut diagonally through them. Colored concentric ovals emerge. Fold the dough in a zigzag or twist it to get a different pattern. The possibilities here are endless. With a little practice you can get black and white zebra patterns, leopard or giraffe patterns, or totally funky random-colored noodles. Since you lose a bit of the overall design if you cut into thin noodles, wide

noodles makes more sense, or better yet, take the ball of colorful twisted doughs and shave it into thin slices on a mandolin. Then the overall shape will be equally as funky as the color pattern. This is actually much easier than trying to lay out a colorful regular pattern in dough.

HARLEQUIN NOODLES

If you have the patience, this technique yields the coolest-looking noodles I've ever made. Roll out two sheets of dough, one white, the other red. I used a black carrot dehydrated and powdered, but you can use any colorful vegetable. Cut the sheets into precisely measured strips of equal width. Use a ruler—these can't be eyeballed. They can be ½ inch or up to 1 inch, but the narrower they are, the more work there is for you. Now weave all the noodles together, in a lattice pattern as you would for a pie crust, over and under, alternating colors until you have a perfect checkerboard pattern with no spaces between the strips. Roll this over with your pin to adhere the strips into a solid sheet. Now turn the entire sheet diagonally so you have diamonds instead of squares facing you. With your ruler, carefully cut straight lines down the edges of the colored diamond shape to make noodles with a harlequin pattern. This is really the only way to effectively get a pattern on both sides of a noodle. It's a lot of work, but you and others will marvel at your artistry as you fish them out of the bowl.

If you like, you can try other patterns without this meticulous weaving. You simply lay shapes of colored dough over each other, roll them, and cut into noodles. Regular cookie cutters are usually too big for this use, but if you find small ones, or even strips of tin that you can fashion into interesting stars or other shapes, place these on the dough to make decorated noodles. The edge of a shot glass works very well to cut out crescent shapes, which can be overlapped or laid out in patterns. You can also use pinking shears or other decorative scissors to cut out colored shapes, or just cut them out with a knife. The only thing to beware of is that you are increasing the thickness of the noodle every time you lay

Above: Patterned noodles can be made to look like quilts

Below: Overlapping various colored dough made with dehydrated vegetables

down another shape, so be sure to work quickly before the dough dries, and roll out everything you do to get a thin noodle in the end. There's nothing worse than a beautiful noodle that's thick and clunky to eat. And remember the golden rule, which I still find myself breaking on occasion: however gorgeous the noodle, it's not worth a thing if it doesn't taste good.

SNOWFLAKE NOODLES

I broke the rule stated just above once—with these noodles. So you know how to make snow-flakes out of paper. You fold over a few times and then cut out sections and when you unfold it you get a lovely see through snowflake. It works perfect-ly fine with a sheet of dough, too. The only problem is that if the sheet is fairly big, how do you serve it? I considered cooking it and laying it on top of the bowl of soup, so you could see through to the con-tents. It looked nice, but you really needed a knife and fork to eat it—just a little awkward. Or why not just make them really small so you have a lot of snowflakes floating in a winter-themed soup, some-thing a little thick so the noodles will stay on top? It's very time consuming and difficult to make them that small; you need tiny scissors and deft fingers.

Although it's fun to cut snowflakes, they're difficult to eat

Instead, I suggest cutting out shapes with various cookie cutters, perhaps a circle with a lot of little holes cut out, or a small star with an even smaller one inside. You don't get quite the drama as with a cut snowflake, but it's still a lot of fun.

Where I violated the rule above was in coloring the snowflake. I cut a big one that looked like a tribal mask and used edible markers to color it in cool patterns. It was so ingenious that I hung it from the ceiling in my kitchen and never ate it. If you want art, noodles are an excellent medium, but I think they should be eaten.

THE MICROWAVED NOODLE

When I was young I was convinced that the microwave was the work of the devil. The house I now own came with one, so I started using it to cook whole po-tatoes, sliced eggplant or zucchini, and of course to defrost stock quickly. I respect it and usually keep my distance. What a surprise then that the contraption actually inspired what may be one of the most significant discoveries to emerge from this book: you can make noodles in the microwave. I don't mean heat them or cook noodles you've already made. I mean actually use the microwave to form the noo-dle. It's very simple.

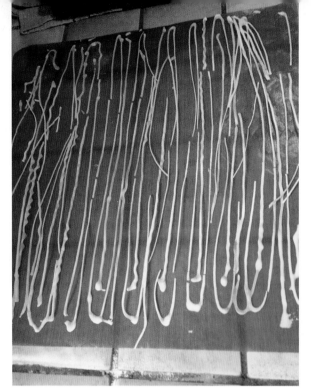

Microwaved noodles: "The discovery of a new dish confers more happiness on humanity than the discovery of a new star."—Jean Anthelme Brillat-Savarin

Take equal parts rice flour and sweet potato flour, and add water to form a slightly thick batter—a little thicker than you would use for a pancake. I use ½ cup of each for a single serving. Put this in a piping bag and on a plastic microwaveproof sheet extrude thin straight lines. A very fine tip produces very thin noodles; a thicker tip yields wide ones. Don't worry if they're not perfectly straight, either, once they cook, no one will notice. Microwave the sheet for exactly 1 minute and 15 seconds. Let this cool and then scrape up the noodles, plunge into boiling water for 1 minute or until cooked through but still chewy, then rinse under cold water. If you have a lot of plastic sheets you can do this very quickly and make a lot of noodles for a big crowd. Once it goes into soup, they are virtually indistinguishable from any starch-based noodle you might purchase or make with another method.

In order to expedite this process even further, I thought of other ways to lay lines of batter on the mats. A paintbrush doesn't work, though dribbling batter with it was a lot of fun and the results were edible. A water pistol was also a lot of fun, but the nozzle is too narrow. A plastic squirty ketchup bottle works OK, as does a water bottle with a nozzle for a thick noodle. Let your imagination run wild here. If you're really adventuresome, try making a colored batter piped into a complex pattern, microwaved, and then cooked very gently in a large skillet so it keeps its shape. If you're dexterous enough to transfer that into a wide bowl, it sure is fun to eat. With this procedure you can also add vegetable powders and make colorful worm-shaped noodles for kids who like to be grossed out—and get vegetables into them at the same time!

 **FROG KATSU**

I love frogs. Like many of you, I grew up with Kermit. The flavor is light but with just a hint of something fishy. Not like chicken at all. My pal Paul once gigged a few wild ones, and I put them into a Provençal stew with tomatoes and onions. But I would rather taste the pure unfettered frog flavor without distraction. I think this recipe nails it. If you can find whole frogs, by all means use them. Usually the legs are easier to find.

5 pairs frogs legs
salt and pepper to taste
water
1 shallot, chopped
1 carrot, diced

1 stalk celery, diced
2 lime leaves
pinch saffron
1 cup Pinot Grigio
red dulse
bread crumbs
2 tablespoons butter

A whole frog or just pairs of legs
can be used in this lovely soup

First remove the upper thigh from each leg, cut it lengthwise, and carefully re-move the bone so you have a small cutlet from each thigh. Salt and pepper these and set these aside. Place the bones and lower leg sections in a pot of water with all the soup ingredients and the Pinot Grigio. If you are using whole frogs, remove the skin and innards and place with everything else in the pot. Gently simmer this stock for about an hour. The saffron will make it bright yellow.

Then dip your frog cutlets into egg and then into bread crumbs. Fry them light-ly in butter and set aside.

In the meantime, finely pound or grind your red dulse and mix it with flour and egg. Equal parts dulse and flour is a little too strongly flavored, so try 25 percent dulse and 75 percent flour. To my surprise, it isn't really salty as you might expect. Roll the dough out and cut into noodles. Strain the stock and cook the noodles right in it.

To serve, arrange your noodles in a nice nest in a suitable amphibiously themed bowl. Pour over the stock and then place the cutlets overlapped on one side of the bowl, just as you might find in a Japanese soup. A sprig of parsley or some other green—nori, for example—is all the garnish you need. In the end you'll find the cutlets are so sweet and delicate, the soup so rich, that you will wonder why we don't eat frog more often.

RABBIT NOODLE SOUP

Rabbit is another meat that I adore and wish were more widely consumed and regularly available. It is very low in fat, so low in fact that if it is the principal source of protein, malnutrition results. Despite my love of Bugs Bunny, I have taken the opportunity to eat rabbit as often as I can. It occurs to me that all Warner Brothers cartoons were essentially about one creature trying to eat another, whether rabbit, duck, pig, or chicken. So why didn't kids raised on these cartoons want to eat them too? In any case, do not treat rabbit like chicken. Breading and frying it is passable but doesn't bring out the depth of flavor. For that you really must slow-braise it.

1 whole rabbit
2 onions, diced
½ cup raisins
1 cup Marsala, sweet sherry, port, or other sweet wine
water as needed to cover
salt and pepper to taste
¼ cup dough made from flour and water
4 ounces wide egg noodles with flouncy edges, homemade or dried

Cut the rabbit into small pieces and place in a pot with the onions, raisins, and Marsala. Add water so the rabbit is just barely covered. Add a little salt and pepper. Put the lid on the pot and seal with a strip of dough all the way around. Place the pot in an oven set at 250°F and forget about it for about 3 or 4 hours. The longer and slower it cooks, the better. Remove the lid and let cool slightly. Remove all the meat to a platter and remove all the bones. Return the meat to the pot and add enough water to make a thick soup. Serve poured over the already cooked noodles. This is lovely just as is, but you can also add fresh peas or other green vegetable if you want to lighten the overall texture and taste of the dish.

CANDY NOODLE SOUP

If you really want to go wild, here is a noodle to unleash your imagination. The noodles are simply made of marzipan rolled thin and cut into strips. They look almost exactly like a wheat noodle. Of course you don't cook them, and be very careful so they don't break. Just arrange them carefully in bowls curled up the way noodles fall. Then garnish them with candy such as broken peppermint sticks, nonpareils, colored sprinkles, or little slices of candy bars arranged in a fan so they look like pork. The soup is the really fun part. I melted chocolate in a double boiler, then added cream and a shot of bourbon, which is of course only for grown-ups. The way to get it under the well-arranged noodles is to use a turkey baster to squirt it into the bottom of the bowl so you don't sully the candy. You can use any other thick liquid as the base, even Irish cream or some other sweet liqueur that goes well with candy. If you're making it for children, replace the alcohol with thick chocolate milk or something similar.

Candy is indeed dandy, even as noodle soup

HAM SPAETZLE SOUP

The dehydrator works not only on vegetables but even on meat, which can then be put directly into a noodle. Keep in mind that you usually want to be starting with raw meat and that some ingredients just don't make a very palatable noodle. Beef jerky is a good example. Dried fish in a noodle is classic in Asia, especially shrimp powder directly in a noodle. There are even some that use fried pork skin in the noodle. This one was a reconstructed dish so it belongs in this chapter, but there are other examples of meat or fish elsewhere in this book. This recipe worked so nicely that it had to be included.

¼ head red cabbage, cored and sliced thinly

1 tablespoon butter

½ cup raisins

sweet red wine

2 tablespoons vinegar

salt, to taste

3 thin slices home-cured ham or store-bought, dehydrated and ground

1 cup wheat flour

1 egg

⅓ cup milk

mixed stock

prepared mustard, optional

If you want to cure the ham yourself, here's a really simple way to do it. Get a shoulder cut weighing about ½ pound or a larger piece if you want to do more. These are often sold as country ribs but are actually shoulder, as is a butt or picnic ham (whoever named these parts must have wanted to confuse us). For every 1 pound of meat, add 1 tablespoon salt, 1 tablespoon sugar, and ⅛ teaspoon Insta Cure (sodium nitrite and salt). A few leaves of sage are perfect. Maple sugar works really nicely too. Put in a zippered plastic bag and store in the fridge for at least a week, turning every so often. This is now cured but unsmoked. If you want to smoke it, do so at a very low temperature so you don't overcook the meat. This same home-cured ham is fantastic sliced thinly raw and added to boiling soup at the last minute. For this soup, cut the cured ham in very thin slices and cook very gently in a pan with fat for just 1 minute per side. Then dehydrate for a day or so and grind up into a fine powder. Mix ½ cup ham powder with flour, eggs, and milk. Let sit to let the flavors meld.

In the meantime, soak raisins in the wine. Gently fry the cabbage in butter. Then add the raisins and vinegar and continue to cook. Add salt to taste.

Either with a spaetzle maker or with a board and offset spatula, make the noodles right in a pot of boiling stock—a mixed stock with chicken and pork bones is perfect. To serve, spoon the spaetzle into a bowl and add a dollop of the cooked red cabbage in the center. You can also offer mustard to stir right into the soup. The fun of this soup is that no one really realizes where the ham flavor is coming from.

 **TEA-SMOKED DUCK STOCK AND RICE NOODLES**

Duck is as good as food gets, but it is uninteresting if dried out and overcooked. This is a way to intensify the flavor without losing its unctuousness. This serves about 4 people. If making for 1, freeze ¾ of the stock and meat.

1 whole duck
¼ cup tea, cinnamon stick, cloves, and other spices
½ cup uncooked rice
aromatic vegetables: mixed carrots, celery, parsnip, onion
1 handful shiitake mushrooms, sliced
1 bunch kale, ribs removed and sliced finely
1 pound dry wide rice noodles
1 teaspoon soy or more to taste
1 teaspoon black vinegar

Break down the duck into thighs, legs, breasts, wings, back, and so on. Mix the spices and put them in several layers of tin foil with a small opening at the top. Make a small fire at the bottom of your smoker and put the package of tea, spices, and rice atop the fire. Place the duck parts and all the giblets except the liver on a rack high in the smoker and smoke for about 1½ to 2 hours. (Save the liver, sautéed in butter, for yourself.) Next, place all these parts in a stockpot covered with water and simmer gently for 1 hour with aromatic vegetables. Remove the meat and shred, discarding bones and skin. Return meat to the pot and add mushrooms, kale, and rice noodles. Boil until the noodles are cooked through. Add soy and vinegar to season.

Another really interesting thing to do with duck is to cook a confit leg in a pan slowly. Shred it finely, remove the bones, and keep cooking the meat until it makes crispy threads. Garnish a soup like this with it. Actually, it's a wonderful topping for any noodle soup.

PEANUT NOODLE SOUP

Peanut butter just doesn't work in a noodle. It's too thick and rich and oily. But peanuts themselves raw are more leguminous and make a fine noodle. Shell, skin, and grind raw peanuts. Add the same volume of wheat flour and 1 egg to bind. Wrap the dough in plastic and chill to firm up. Using your palm, push the dough through a grater with large holes, making small dough curls. Let these dry at room temperature.

Peanut noodles go especially nicely in Southeast Asian soups. Try a fish stock based soup like mohinga, adding coconut milk, galangal root, lime leaves, chilies, and shrimp paste or even ground pork. It comes together with just enough peanut flavor so as not to overpower everything else. Or think West African. The noodles act something like a fufu. Cook them in a broth of tomatoes, grated gingerroot, onion, chili, melegueta pepper, and vegetable stock.

RHUBARB NOODLE SOUP

Not all noodle soups need to be so very savory as above—some of the most interesting can be made with fruit, or even this weird sour vegetable stalk once thought to be highly medicinal. This recipe is simple and just a suggestion for which you can substitute just about any dehydrated fruit. Thin slices of rhubarb are dehydrated and ground and mixed with wheat flour and egg. Very thin extruded noodles work much better than cut ones because you want the flavor and mouth-feel to be light and refreshing. If you are using a crank roller, just roll out very thin and use the finest angel hair attachment to cut the noodles.

Cook these in water and then serve in a cold broth made of very lightly sweet-ened water, with other fruits such as strawberries. Even watermelon juice is won-derful. You can also add rosé or white wine and serve it in a glass. Garnish with small pieces of fruit. Think of this as a cross between a cold noodle soup and a fruity sangria. It is refreshing on a hot day, and the noodles provide the snack that you might have had along with your drink.

POSTSCRIPT

N oodle soups have become amazingly popular globally. I have tasted decent versions recently in as far-flung places as a backstreet in Dublin, in the Naschmarkt in Vienna, in a trendy spot in downtown Kyoto—no surprise— the Lower East Side of Manhattan, a winding hilly street in Istanbul, a busy corner in Heidelberg, and downtown Rio de Janeiro. If I were into making predictions, I would say that, just like hot dogs and pizza before it, noodle soup will become standard U.S. fare, and indeed great ramen will be found in restaurants around the world thanks to chefs like David Chang and Ivan Orkin. Other noodle soups will follow suit, as the recent craze for phở suggests. The home-cooking scene will plod along slowly behind it, but I hope this book will have nudged it along a little further.

I'm not sure what to make of all the exotic instant noodle soups hitting the market nowadays, not just in cups and instant packets, but some serious little kits for relatively unknown noodles. Often they call for fresh ingredients to be added as well. They seem to be following the trend catering for people who don't like to shop and don't have time to cook but who still want interesting meals at home that are not junk. I have no doubt many of the ingredient boxes and home-delivery services will send you all the ingredients for a noodle soup.

The more interesting phenomenon, which emerged while I was writing this book, is the proliferation of non-wheat-based noodles. This can only be a good thing, obviously for helping those with allergies, intolerance, or disease that prevents them from eating wheat, but it has also expanded exponentially the range of noodles in the average store. Many of them are quite good. I have no idea how they're made industrially, and naturally I'd prefer to make them myself, but from a purely gastronomic vantage point, the new noodles on the market now are really

A carefully designed bowl delights the eye

fascinating and count among the few truly novel foods that will probably last long after we've forgotten pomegranate juice and cronuts.

In the end, I would not have put the effort into this book if I had no faith that there will always be people out there who like to cook, enjoy sharing food, and who care seriously what they eat in terms of health, environment, and gastronomic pleasure. For those of you who made it to these final words and have made some good noodle soup, I salute you.

ACKNOWLEDGMENTS

So much of the information in this book was crowd sourced simply because dozens of friends offered their help. People not only gave me valuable feedback on crazy ideas but often brought to my attention new dishes from around the world after seeing a noodle soup I'd posted online.

To all my colleagues and fellow food scholars, hoodies, food writers, former students, old high school and camp friends and those many Facebook friends whom I have yet to meet in person, all of you helped me immensely, at conferences like the ASFS, Oxford Symposium, IACP, in Turkey, China, Spain, Germany, and other fabulous places, in person, online, on planes, and elsewhere, I am truly blessed to have friends like you. And seriously, you all really did help me in one way or another.

In no particular order: Rachel Thoo for so much help with Asian recipes, Brian Duboff for inspiring me to think vegan, Tonia Deetz Rock for commenting on every soup I ever posted, Harold McGee for chemistry, Katherine McIver, Bob del Grosso for bone broth yo, Linda Civitello, Raylene McCalman, Judith Klinger, Marlena Spieler, Pamela Lange Levins, Aylin Oney Tan for everything Turkish, Kelly Donati, Mike Anastasio for cool machines, Fabio Parasecoli, Erica Peters for phở history, Thy Tran, Charlene Elliott, the Mounts: TantaMount, ParaMount, CataMount, Janet Chrzan, Christine Schupbach, Linda Miller Nicholson for stunning noodles, Domenica Marchetti, Laura Kelley for the Silk Road, my oldest pal Andrew Martin and Damon Kirsche, Lucey Bowen, Lisa Deutsch for L.A. noodles, Faye Levi, Sandra Guttierez, Jinx Staniec, Peter Hertzmann, Sylwia Qualls for all things Polish, Nathan Crook for buckeyes, Carrie Tillie for thinking small, Samantha Martinez for cooking with me, Dallas Holsten, Mercy Newmark, Laura Grogan-O'Mara, May Fridel, Denise Amon, Emily Moore, Catherine Lambrecht, Madeleine Kemeny, Davis Porterfield, Maggie Zhu, Andrew McGowan, Jonathan Deutsch, Andrea Nguyen, Stacy Sims, Renee Marton, Michael McFadden, Lauren Sevrin, Katrine Klinken for all things Danish.

I would also like to thank Emily Contois, Kathleen Collins, Krishnendu Ray, Nancy Baggett, Heather Arndt Anderson, Elaine Corn, Kristin Davis, Aglaia Kremezi for all things Greek, Kelila Jaffe, Julia Sforza, Martha Esersky Lorden, Volcher Bach for the sixteenth-century German recipe, Tammy Lee, Birdiee Fré, Helen Saberi for all things Afghan, Abby Wilkerson, Joanna Tahar, Deana Sidney, Chrissy Braun Giglio, Faith Kramer, Jennifer Sanborn, Leo Pang for goose heads, Amy Halloran for pancakes, Greg de St. Maurice for katsuobushi, Cathy Barrow, Irina Dumitrescu, Wendy Neufeld, Noel Gieleghem for watti, Karen Peters, Lisa Cooperman, Noel Buttigeig, Pascal Baudar, Joyce Gillingwater, Rosa Mariotti, Julie Gracie, Barbara Meyer Zu Altenschildesche, Hamidatun Karapetian, Caroline Rowe, Anneke Geyzen for all things Belgian, Scotty Harris, Judy Witts Francini for all things Italian, Kristina Nies, Konstantina Johnson, Mia Wasilevich, Saralynn Pablo for all things Filipino, Melody Elliot Koontz, Julia Skinner, Maya Parson, Eve Jochnowitz, Suzanne St. Clair, Urtatim al-Qurtubiyya, Leena Trivedi-Grenier for an okra day, Nadine Crispeen LeBean, Charlene Trist, Lacey Harrison, Camille Trentacoste, Lissa Rosenthal-Joffe, Amanda Johnson, Pauline Cashman, Emy Mercy, Nicolette Hahn Niman, Lucy Norris, Claudia Morain for great PR, Priya Vadi, Geneviève Reyes, Leigh Bush, Annette Cottrell, Merry White, Nanna Rögnvaldardóttir, Cathy Erway, Francine Segan, Dianne Jacob, Jeff Albucher, Charles Perry, Monica Bhide, Diane Kochilas, Robyn Grace Jennings, JoAnn Olwen Turner, Riki Saltzman, Kim DeBoer, Jennifer Burns Bright, Jim Hetrick, Shaun Chavis, Amy Sherman, Megan Brown, Elisabeth Luard, Gene Anderson, Wendi Schnaufer, Dan Strehl, Amber O'Connor, Ove Fosså, Jessica Ebbers the best Jewish mom, Amanda Mayo, Cindy Messina, Karin Vaneker, Laura Martin Bacon and Zebot, Janet Clarkson, Sandra Mian.

And let's not forget Joanna Pruess, Ann Mazzaferro, Jeremy Fletcher, Nina Quirk, Kyle Turner, Steve Sando, Jonell Galloway, Emilie Sibbeson, Michael Twitty, Kristine Eagle, Anne Mendelson, Christina Potters, Alice McLean, Linn Steward, Karen Kensinger, Susan Fox, Eden Rain, Ruth Mossok Johnston, Brian Yarvin, Aldea Mulhern, Vivian Savares, Alison Pearlman, Mark Dornfeld, Richard Wilk who made me a gorgeous wooden bowl, Johanna Bakmas for marketing, Nicolas Vincelette, Betty Fussell, Jeremy Cuevas, Kim Golding, Cristie Spackman, Simona Carini for beautifully formed noodles, Patrick Giblin for the Wiki, Hannah Hoffman, Glenn Gorsuch, Rebekah Burr-Siegel, Cara de Silva, Carrie Schroeder, Awanthi Vardaraj, Nancy Harmon Jenkins, Kelly Evans, Paul Ustach, Anne McBride, Linda Speight, Willa Zhen for everything Chinese, Gary Allen, Jenn Louis, Sean Timberlake, Elatia Harris, Margot Finn, Dari Sylvester Tran, Jeffrey Miller, Anita Stewart, Andy Smith and Chris Larson who saw this entire project unfold from beginning to end. I am sure I've forgotten someone, sorry, but thanks!

By a quirk of fate I was also fortunate to have met a few of my culinary heroes while working on this project. Jacques Pépin, who thought this was a good idea. Martin Yan, from whom I not only learned how to chop, but also to count. He was tasting a small bowl of noodle soup next to me at a CIA conference. I asked what he thought, and he said "nice chewy homemade noodle." He had no idea it was my recipe. Nathalie Dupree was another TV star from whom I learned so much about cooking while in college. I met her at an IACP conference and later became friends on Facebook. She gave me so much valuable advice for this project. And thanks to Claudia Roden for great advice. You have always been and always will be an inspiration.

Thanks to Marika and all the great people at the University of Illinois Press who "got" what I was doing with this project, especially the anonymous reviewers. And, finally, Deborah Oliver for one amazing copyediting job.

NOTES

3. Noodle Soup History

1. Lu Houyuan et al., "Millet Noodles in Late Neolithic China," *Nature* 43, (2005): 967-68; Francoise Sabban, "A Scientific Controversy in China over the Origin of Noodles," *Carnets du Centre Chine*, October 15, 2012, http://cecmc.hypotheses .org/?p=7663; H. Lu et al., "Component and Simulation of the 4,000-Year Old Noodles Excavated from the Archaeological Site of Lajia in Qinghai, China," *Chinese Science Bulletin* 59 (2014): 5136-52.

2. Wei Ge et al., "Can Noodles Be Made from Millet?," *Archaeometry* 53, no. 1 (2011): 194-204.

3. See Sarah R. Graff and Enrique Rodríguez-Alegría, *The Menial Art of Cooking: Archaeological Studies of Cooking and Food Preparation* (Boulder: University of Colorado Press, 2012).

4. Silvano Serventi and Francoise Sabban, *Pasta: The Story of a Universal Food* (New York: Columbia University Press, 2002), 272-75.

5. Quoted in ibid., 288.

6. Donald Harper, "The Cookbook in Ancient and Medieval China," paper presented at "Discourses and Practices of Everyday Life in Imperial China," Columbia University, 2002, www.ihp.sinica.edu.tw/~wensi/active/download/active03/ Harper.doc.

7. Hsiang Ju Lin, *Slippery Noodles: A Culinary History of China* (London: Prospect Books, 2015), 37-38.

8. Serventi and Sabban, *Pasta*, 309.

9. Ibid., 317.

10. Teresa Wang and E. N. Anderson, "Ni Tsan and His Cloud Forest Hall Collection of Rules for Drinking and Eating," *Petits Propos Culinaires 60: Essays and Notes on Food, Cookery and Cookery Books* 60 (1998).

11. Paul D. Buell and Gene N. Anderson, *A Soup for the Qan: Introduction, Translation, Commentary, and Chinese Text* (Abingdon, UK: Routledge, 2000), Kindle version 4660-64.

12. B. L. Ullman, "Horace Serm 1.6.116 and the History of the Word Laganum," *Classical Philology* 7, no. 4 (1912): 442-49.

13. Muḥammad ibn al-Ḥasan Ibn al-Karīm, *A Baghdad Cookery Book: A Book of Dishes (Kitab al-Tabikh)*, transl. Charles Perry (Totnes, UK: Prospect Books, 2005), 48.

14. Benedictus de Nursia, *Opus ad sanitatis conservationem* (Bologna: Domenico de Lapis, 1477), O5.

15. Marianne Mulon, "Deux traités inédits d'art culinaire médiéval," in *Les problèmes de l'alimentation*, vol. 1 of *Bulletin philologique et historique (jusqu'à 1610) du Comité des Travaux historiques et scientifiques. Année 1968: Actes du 93e Congrès national des Sociétés savantes tenu à Tours* (Paris 1971), 369-435, www.staff.uni -giessen.de/gloning/tx/mul2-lib.htm. My translation.

16. Ibid.

17. Ludovico Frati, ed., *Libro di Cucina del Secolo XIV* (Bologna: Arnaldo Forni, 1986), 35-36.

18. Maestro Martino, *The Art of Cooking: The First Modern Cookbook*, transl. Jeremy Parzen (Berkeley: University of California Press, 2005), 67.

19. For the Latin text I have used *Platina, On Right Pleasure and Good Health: A Critical Edition and Translation of "De honesta voluptate et valetudine,"* transl. Mary Ella Milham (Tempe, AZ: Medieval and Renaissance Texts and Studies, 1998), 328-29. Milham mistranslates this passage completely, misunderstanding the wrapping of the dough around the stick.

20. Doris Aichholzer, *Wildu machen ain guet essen: Drei mittelhochdeutsche Kochbücher: Erstedition, Übersetzung, Kommentar,* (Bern, Germany: P. Lang, 1999). Translation by Volker Bach.

21. Rupert of Nola, *Libro de guisados* (Toledo: 1525), fol. xxviii. My translation.

22. Bartolomeo Scappi, *Opera* (Venice: Tramezzino, 1570), 78. My translation.

23. Angelo Constantini, *La Vie de Scaramouche* (Paris: Hôtel de Bourgogne et Claude Barbin, 1695), 106.

24. Vincent La Chapelle, a contemporary, explains that it is made with 8 or 10 pounds buttock or leg of beef, carrot, onions, turnips, celery, a fowl and knuckle of veal, not boiled too much. Vincent La Chapelle, *The Modern Cook* (London: Nicholas Prevost, 1733), 1:1.

25. Francois Massialot, *Le cuisinier Royal et Bourgeois* (Paris: Saugrain Fils, 1750), 306-8. My translation.

26. Hannah Glasse, *The Art of Cookery Made Plain and Easy*, reprint of 1805 ed. (Bedford, MA: Applewood Books, 1997), 215-16.

27. T. Williams, *The Accomplished Housekeeper and Universal Cook* (London: J. Scatcherd, 1797), 125.

28. The recently retired president Thomas Jefferson wrote to purveyors on December 30, 1809: "I have mentioned the article of Maccaroni, not knowing if they are to be had in Richmond. I have formerly been supplied from Sartori's works at Trenton, who makes them well, and would be glad to supply you should the Richmond demand make it worth your while to keep them. I paid him 16 cents the pound." Jefferson to Gordon, Trokes & Co., in J. Jefferson Looney, ed., *The Papers of Thomas Jefferson, Retirement Series*, 13 vols. (Princeton, NJ: Princeton University Press, 2004–), 2:109, accessed at www.monticello.org/site/research-and-collections/macaroni# ref-5.

29. Mary Randolph, *The Virginia Housewife: or, Methodical Cook* (Baltimore, MD: Plaskitt and Fite, 1838), 95.
30. *Alexis Soyer Shilling Cookbook for the People* (London: Routlege, 1860), 10.
31. Conversion is per "Computing 'Real Value' Over Time with a Conversion Between U.K. Pounds and U.S. Dollars, 1774 to Present," www.measuringworth.com.

5. Stocks

1. Hieremias Drexelius, *Aloe Amari, sed salubris succi Ieiunium* (Munich: Cornelius Leysserius, 1637), 137. "Exempli gratiâ, qui sabbato cenam omittit, ei Dominico die cibus incredibiliter sapit: si pridie lautiùs cenasset, voluptas illa neutiquam tam sauvis accideret. Suave cibi condimentum est ieiunium." My translation: "For example, if you skip supper on Saturday, food will taste incredible on Sunday. If you eat lavishly the night before, it will be not so pleasurable. Fasting is the condiment for tasty food."
2. Bartolomeo Scappi, *Opera* (Venice: Tramezzino, 1570), 396v. My translation.

6. Noodles

1. Hugh Plat, *Certain Philosophical Preparations of Foode and Beverage for Sea-Men* (N.p.: [broadside], 1607).
2. Harold McGee, "For Old-Fashioned Flavor, Bake the Baking Soda," the Curious Cook, *New York Times*, September 14, 2010, www.nytimes.com.

8. Global Classics

1. Alum can be found where pickling supplies are sold or online, and in Asian groceries it's sold in big clear crystal rocks that can be pounded down before using. Some countries have reservations about using alum, and apparently there are substitutes like chitosan. A discussion on how to use it appears in Paul Adams, "Recipe Quest: Shear-Thickening Starch Noodles," *Cooking Issues: The International Culinary Center's Tech 'n Stuff Blog*, www.cookingissues.com/index .html%3Fp=5950.html. Alginate apparently also works, and many packaged dry "glass" sweet potato noodles include it in the ingredient list with ascorbic acid.

SUGGESTED READINGS

Anderson, E. N. *Food and Environment in Early and Medieval China.* Philadelphia: University of Pennsylvania Press, 2014.

Anderson, E. N. *The Food of China.* New Haven, CT: Yale University Press, 1988.

Chang, K. C. *Food in Chinese Culture: Anthropological and Historical Perspectives.* New Haven, CT: Yale University Press, 1977.

Cwiertka, Katarzyna. *Modern Japanese Cuisine.* London: Reaktion, 2006.

Dalby, Andrew. *Siren Feasts: A History of Food and Gastronomy in Greece.* London: Routledge, 1996.

Helstosky, Carol. *Garlic and Oil: Politics and Food in Italy.* Oxford: Berg, 2004.

Hildebrand, Caz, and Jacob Kenedy. *The Geometry of Pasta.* London: Boxtree, 2010.

Ishige, Naomichi. *The History and Culture of Japanese Food.* New York: Kegan Paul, 2001.

Kiple, Kenneth. *A Moveable Feast: Ten Millennia of Food Globalization.* Cambridge: Cambridge University Press, 2007.

Kushner, Barak. *Slurp! A Social History of Ramen—Japan's Favorite Noodle Soup.* Leiden, Germany: Global Oriental, 2014.

Lin, Hisang Ju. *Slippery Noodles: A Culinary History of China.* London: Prospect, 2015.

Lin-Liu, Jen. *On the Noodle Road: From Beijing to Rome with Love and Pasta.* New York: Riverhead, 2013.

Parasecoli, Fabio, and Peter Scholliers, general eds. *A Cultural History of Food.* 6 vols. London: Berg, 2012.

Rath, Eric. *Food and Fantasy in Early Modern Japan.* Berkeley: University of California Press, 2010.

——, and Stephanie Assmann, eds. *Japanese Foodways, Past and Present.* Urbana: University of Illinois Press, 2010.

Schafer, Edward H. *The Golden Peaches of Samarkand: A Study of T'ang Exotics.* Berkeley: University of California Press, 1985.

Serventi, Slivano, and Françoise Sabban. *Pasta: The Story of a Universal Food.* New York: Columbia University Press, 2002.

Simoons, Frederick J. *Food in China: A Cultural and Historical Inquiry.* Boca Raton, FL: CRC Press, 1991.

Solt, George. *The Untold History of Ramen.* Berkeley: University of California Press, 2013.

Visser, Margaret. *Much Depends on Dinner: The Extraordinary History and Mythology, Allure and Obsession, Perils and Taboos, of an Ordinary Meal.* New York: Grove, 1986.

Wang, Q. Edward. *Chopsticks: A Cultural and Culinary History.* Cambridge: Cambridge University Press, 2015.

Yarvin, Brian. *A World of Noodles.* Woodstock, VT: Countryman Press, 2014.

Yue, Isaac, and Siufu Tang. *Scribes of Gastronomy: Representations of Food and Drink in Imperial Chinese Literature.* Hong Kong: University Press, 2013.

Zanini de Vita, Oretta. *Encyclopedia of Pasta.* Berkeley: University of California Press, 2009.

Zubaida, Sami, and Richard Tapper. *A Taste of Thyme: Culinary Cultures of the Middle East.* London: Taurus Parke, 2000.

INDEX

tofu, 105; skin, 5, 110
tomato, 54–56, 83, 88, 102–4, 111, 113–14, 120, 127, 140–41, 144–45, 152, 154, 162; and food globalization, 100, 144; paste, 88–89, 92; powder, 75–77, 158; roasted, 142; sauce, 39, 111, 136; soup, 88, 126, 149, 167; sun-dried, 141; water, 52
torchio ad bigoli, 39
tortellini, 5, 49
trahanas, 116
troccolaturo, 28, 37
trout, 95
tsukemen, 70
tsuyu, 99, 110
tuna, 51–52, 126, 135; Tuna Noodle Casserole Soup, 135
turkey, 93; carcass, 50; ground, 82, 94; necks, 50; stock, 82
Turkey, 21, 116, 171; Gaziantep, 146; Istanbul, 152
turmeric, 55, 89, 98–99, 104, 111, 113, 121, 128, 147
tweezers, 41

ube (purple yam), 136
udon, 22, 61–62, 85, 143
umami, 51–52, 92
Uyghur laghman, 119–20

veal, 47, 49
vegetables, 86–91; Salad Noodle Soup, 77, 78; stocks, 57–58. *See also specific vegetables*
vegetarian and vegan, 55, 57–58, 105, 112–13
velveting, 94
verjuice, 49
vermicelli, 22, 25, 29, 60, 100–103, 110–11, 118, 153; soup, 31–32
Vienna, 26–7

Vietnam, 53–54, 60
vinegar, 22, 57, 77, 88, 91, 110, 141, 165–66; apple cider, 115–16; black, 102–3, 166; coconut, 136; rice wine, 159

wabi sabi, 10
wakame, 81
Wedgewood Pottery, 10
wheat: ancient relatives of, 64–65; and buckwheat, 99, 107–8; bulgur, 116, 153; charred, 64; durum semolina, 32, 59, 63, 72–73, 116, 127; flavor, 63, 64, 138; gluten in, 20, 60, 62, 66, 72; grass, 64; history, 20–23, 60, 100; noodles, 61–62, 107, 138, 140, 151–52; noodles, dried, 115; noodles, with other ingredients, 76–77, 79, 83, 144–46, 148, 157–58, 167; orzo, 122; spaetzle, 165–66; starch, 21, 66; varieties of, 61–63; whole, 63, 116
William, T., 31
wine, 17, 73, 91, 94, 167; for deglazing, 47, 48; malvasia, 49; red, 48, 140; rice, 47, 91; shiraz, 117; sweet, 91, 164–66; white, 55, 56, 57, 137
wonton, 5, 33

Yaka-Mein, 121
yam, purple, 136
Yanagi, Soetsu, 10
Yankee Doodle, 29
Yiddish, 104
yi-fu/yi mein noodles, 154
yogurt, 95, 103, 113–14, 116, 144, 146–47

za'atar, 89, 144
Zheng He, 22
ziti, 20
Zotatz Gmues (Shaggy Spoon Dish), 27
zucchini, 55, 87, 161; spiralized, 5
Zupa Owocowa, 110

KEN ALBALA is a professor of history and food studies at the University of the Pacific. He has authored or edited twenty-four books on food, including *Eating Right in the Renaissance, Food in Early Modern Europe, Cooking in Europe, 1250–1650, The Banquet, Beans: A History, Pancake: A Global History, Grow Food, Cook Food, Share Food*, and *Nuts: A Global History*. He was co-editor of the journal *Food, Culture, and Society* and has also co-edited *The Business of Food, Human Cuisine*, and *Food and Faith* and edited *A Cultural History of Food: The Renaissance* and *The Routledge International Handbook of Food Studies*. Albala was editor of the Food Cultures Around the World series, the four-volume *Food Cultures of the World Encyclopedia*, and the three-volume *Sage Encyclopedia of Food Issues*. He is also series editor of Rowman & Littlefield Studies in Food and Gastronomy, for which wrote *Three World Cuisines*. He has co-authored two cookbooks: *The Lost Art of Real Cooking* and *The Lost Arts of Hearth and Home*. His latest works are *The Food History Reader*, a translation of the sixteenth-century *Livre fort excellent de cuysine*, and *At the Table: Food and Family Around the World*. His course *Food: A Cultural Culinary History* is available on DVD from the Great Courses.

The University of Illinois Press
is a founding member of the
Association of American University Presses.

Text designed by Dustin J. Hubbart
Composed in Myriad Pro 10.5/13.5
with Cyclone Layers Inline display
by Dustin J. Hubbart
at the University of Illinois Press
Cover designed by Dustin J. Hubbart
Cover illustration: Handmade wheat noodles, short ribs, and vegetables in beef broth.
Photo by Ken Albala with assistance from Lauren Sevrin.
Manufactured by Versa Press, Inc.

University of Illinois Press
1325 South Oak Street
Champaign, IL 61820-6903
www.press.uillinois.edu